D1718393

FROM THE DELTA

From the Delta
English Fiction from Bangladesh

Edited by
Niaz Zaman

Ⓤ The University Press Limited

The University Press Limited
Red Crescent House
61 Motijheel C/A
P. O. Box 2611
Dhaka 1000
Bangladesh

Fax : (88 02) 9565443
E-mail: upl@bangla.net
Website: www.uplbooks.com

Second impression 2010
First published 2005

Cover etching by Kalidas Karmakar
Cover design by Ashraful Hassan Arif

ISBN 978 984 506 004 2

Published by Mohiuddin Ahmed, The University Press Limited, Red Crescent House, Dhaka 1000, computer design by Ashim K. Biswas, produced by AMS Enterprise, printed at Akota Offset Press, 119, Fakirapool, Dhaka, Bangladesh.

Contents

Preface

This collection of short fiction begins with a story published in 1905 and ends with one published in 2005, covering a hundred years. Roquiah Sakhawat Hossein's *Sultana's Dream*, first published in English and then translated by the writer herself into Bangla, reveals that the English language for a variety of reasons was not just a lingua franca or the language of education or administration but was also the language of creative communication. Sakhawat Hossein's reason for writing *Sultana's Dream* was not to entertain but to critique the prevailing injustices of a male-dominated society. In creating Ladyland, where women take part in public life while men remain secluded in the *murdana* — a parody of the *zenana*, the woman's space, where women were forced to remain indoors, behind the veil —Sakhawat Hossein was not just being fanciful but using her imagination to satirize the social inequities she saw around her. Most of Roquiah Sakhawat Hossein's writing is, however, in Bangla as she tried to persuade her community to leave behind the old world for a modern one where women were free to study and work. In the school that she founded in her husband's name — and for which she is known for enabling a whole generation of girls to go to school and later take up her mantle — girls were expected to learn women's skills like sewing and embroidery but were also encouraged to take part in sports and games along with their studies.

There is a gap of several years between Sakhawat Hossein and Syed Waliullah who, like Sakhawat Hossein is better known for his Bangla writing but who also wrote in English, several short stories as well as one novel. Syed Waliullah also perhaps himself translated his most famous novel, *Lal Salu*, into English as *Tree Without Roots* —though the English version, a transcreation rather than an exact translation, lists four translators, not including himself. There are at least three short stories that Syed Waliullah wrote in English: "The Escape," "Cargo," and "No Enemy" — which was translated by Syed Shamsul Haq and then later by Waliullah himself and included in *Dui Teer*.

While Waliullah was doing his creative writing in Bangla in the mid-forties, he was also working for the *Statesman*, perhaps at the time the leading English daily in India. After Partition — which forms the focus of his Bangla story, "Ekti Tulsi Gaccher Kahini" as well as "The Escape," written in English — Waliullah moved to Pakistan. He was transferred to West Pakistan after a short stint in East Pakistan. It was perhaps in order to reach an audience which did not read Bangla that Waliullah wrote his short stories in English while also translating a number of his Bangla stories into English. Waliullah's stories appeared in Pakistani anthologies, magazines and journals such as the PEN *Miscellany, Under the Green Canopy* and *Pakistan Quarterly*. From Karachi, Waliullah was posted to a number of Pakistan missions abroad and finally to UNESCO, Paris. While continuing to write in Bangla, he occasionally took up the pen in English, writing "The Ugly Asian" — which has not yet been published, though a Bangla translation was printed in the *Prothom Alo* Eid Special in 2004, as well as "How Does One Cook Beans." "No Enemy" —included in this anthology — was written in Karachi and has perhaps not been published earlier.

Most writers in East Bengal/East Pakistan, however, wrote in Bangla and occasionally in Urdu — not just the "Biharis" but also writers such as Rahat Ara of Chittagong who chose to write in Urdu. There was some English fiction published in newspapers such as the *Pakistan Observer* and the *Morning News* and magazines such as *Young Pakistan*. However, there was no reading public in East Pakistan for creative writing in English, though in the more affluent West Pakistan, where English continued to be the language of education in schools such as Aitchison, Burnhall, Lawrence College, Jesus and Mary, Karachi Grammar School, to name a few, there was a small English reading public which helped generate fiction for magazines such as *Mirror, She, Herald*, etc. and helped in the creation of a number of some writers, though unlike India, it took Pakistan much longer to gain recognition in the international arena as a producer of English-language fiction.

By contrast, in Bangladesh, English, which had a tenuous hold at best in pre-Liberation days, was deliberately rejected after Liberation. The monolingual policy of Bangladesh meant that the medium of instruction became Bangla, with English being relegated to a foreign-language status. At the universities as well, English was discarded for Bangla. A few English newspapers continued to be published, but the *Bangladesh Times*, which succeeded the *Pakistan Times*, soon went out of business and the many internal problems of the *Bangladesh Observer* meant that no attempts were made to upgrade the quality of the paper or improve the get-up. The publication of the *Daily Star*, however, changed the face of the English newspaper in Bangladesh. With its pages for young people and its Friday magazine, it encouraged creative writing in English, as did the later *Independent*. Both the *Daily Star* and the *Independent* publish original stories in English, apart from English translations — with the *Independent* also having a regular poetry page.

In June 2003, *New Age* started publication. Like the *Daily Star*, it has a Literature page which occasionally publishes stories in English or in English translation. Its festival specials also publish stories. A number of the stories in this anthology have been taken from these three newspapers. Farhana Haque Rahman's story as well as Niaz Zaman's story were originally published in a *New Age* Eid Special. The stories by Aali A. Rehman, Shabnam Nadiya, Rubaiyat Khan and Farah Ghuznavi were originally published in the *Daily Star*; Mohammad Badrul Ahsan's story appeared in the *Independent* and Towheed Feroze's story was originally published in the *Independent* Weekend Magazine.

In 2001 an English reading public welcomed the publication of *Six Seasons Review*, a literary magazine inspired by the *London Magazine*. *Six Seasons Review* published photographs, poems, book reviews and short stories, both in English and English translation. Khademul Islam's. "An Ilish Story" appeared in its second issue. However, after the first year, the magazine became irregular. A change in management is in the offing, and it is expected that it will start publication again.

Two internationally known writers from Bangladesh — Monica Ali and Adib Khan — are conspicuous by their absence from this anthology. The omission is deliberate. Most of the contemporary writers included here, despite an occasional publication, are less well known and I believe deserve to be known better.

The inclusion of Kazi Anis Ahmed's story like Razia Sultana Khan's reflects a new trend: the growth of the "professional writer." Dr Ahmed, who completed his doctoral studies in creative writing in the States, and Razia Sultana Khan, who is doing her graduate studies in creative writing, are among the new generation of Bangladeshis who are opting to be writers. If others follow suit – there are to my knowledge at least three other Bangladeshis who are studying creative writing in the US and the UK — and with the growth of English medium education and private universities, some of which have their own English literary magazines as well as arrange competitions of creative writing, there will be a growing number of writers in English. Adib Khan and Monica Ali will be joined by others as well. Perhaps a hundred years after Roquiah Sakhawat Hossein published *Sultana's Dream*, it is time to reclaim our English heritage. Hence this volume of short stories from the Bengal Delta.

There are many people without whose help and contribution this book would not have been possible. First of all, I would like to honour the memory of Roquiah Sakhawat Hossein who showed that a language learned through one's own efforts, a language not learned so to speak at the mother's knee, could be used to express one's thoughts and feelings. To the other writers in this volume, I owe an immense debt of gratitude. Without their stories there would not have been a volume of stories in English from the Delta. To Mohiuddin Ahmed, who has been my friend for more than thirty years and my publisher for over a decade, I express my heartfelt thanks. To both the Babuls, at the Department of English, University of Dhaka, and The University Press Limited, who helped prepare this material for the press — often deciphering my undecipherable corrections — my deepest thanks are due.

Sultana's Dream *

Roquiah Sakhawat Hossein

One evening I was lounging in an easy chair in my bedroom and thinking lazily of the condition of Indian womanhood. I am not sure whether I dozed off or not. But, as far as I remember, I was wide awake. I saw the moonlit sky sparkling with thousands of diamondlike stars, very distinctly.

All on a sudden a lady stood before me; how she came in, I do not know. I took her for my friend, Sister Sara.

"Good morning," said Sister Sara. I smiled inwardly as I knew it was not morning, but starry night. However, I replied to her, saying, "How do you do?"

"I am all right, thank you. Will you please come out and have a look at our garden?"

I looked again at the moon through the open window, and thought there was no harm in going out at that time. The men-servants outside were fast asleep just then, and I could have a pleasant walk with Sister Sara.

I used to have my walks with Sister Sara, when we were at Darjeeling. Many a time did we walk hand in hand and talk light-heartedly in the Botanical Gardens there. I fancied, Sister Sara had probably come to take me to some such garden and I readily accepted her offer and went out with her.

When walking I found to my surprise that it was a fine morning. The town was fully awake and the streets alive with bustling crowds. I was feeling very shy, thinking I was walking in the street in broad daylight, but there was not a single man visible.

* This story was first printed in *Ladies Magazine* in 1905. It was later published in book form. Roquiah Sakhawat Hossein also translated the story into Bangla as *Sultanar Swapna*. This version was taken from *Rokeya Rachanabali* ed. Abdul Kadir et al., second edition (Dhaka: Bangla Academy, 1999). Some spelling and punctuation have been modernised and obvious errors corrected.

Some of the passersby made jokes at me. Though I could not understand their language, yet I felt sure they were joking. I asked my friend, "What do they say?"

"The women say that you look very mannish."

"Mannish?" said I. "What do they mean by that?"

"They mean that you are shy and timid like men."

"Shy and timid like men?" It was really a joke. I became very nervous, when I found that my companion was not Sister Sara, but a stranger. Oh, what a fool had I been to mistake this lady for my dear old friend, Sister Sara.

She felt my fingers tremble in her hand, as we were walking hand in hand.

"What is the matter, dear?" she said affectionately.

"I feel somewhat awkward," I said in a rather apologising tone, "as being a *purdahnishin* woman I am not accustomed to walking about unveiled."

"You need not be afraid of coming across a man here. This is Ladyland, free from sin and harm. Virtue herself reigns here."

By and by I was enjoying the scenery. Really it was very grand. I mistook a patch of green grass for a velvet cushion. Feeling as if I was walking on a soft carpet, I looked down and found the path covered with moss and flowers.

"How nice it is," said I.

"Do you like it?" asked Sister Sara. (I continued calling her "Sister Sara," and she kept calling me by my name).

"Yes, very much; but I do not like to tread on the tender and sweet flowers."

"Never mind, dear Sultana. Your treading will not harm them; they are street flowers.

"The whole place looks like a garden," said I admiringly.

"You have arranged every plant so skillfully."

"Your Calcutta could become a nicer garden than this if only your countrymen wanted to make it so."

"They would think it useless to give so much attention to horticulture, while they have so many other things to do."

"They could not find a better excuse," said she with smile.

I became very curious to know where the men were. I met more than a hundred women while walking there, but not a single man.

"Where are the men?" I asked her.

"In their proper places, where they ought to be."

"Pray let me know what you mean by 'their proper places.'"

"O, I see my mistake, you cannot know our customs, as you were never here before. We shut our men indoors."

"Just as we are kept in the *zenana*?"

"Exactly so."

"How funny," I burst into a laugh. Sister Sara laughed too.

"But, dear Sultana, how unfair it is to shut in the harmless women and let loose the men."

"Why? It is not safe for us to come out of the *zenana*, as we are naturally weak."

"Yes, it is not safe so long as there are men about the streets, nor is it so when a wild animal enters a marketplace."

"Of course not."

"Suppose, some lunatics escape from the asylum and begin to do all sorts of mischief to men, horses and other creatures, in that case what will your countrymen do?"

"They will try to capture them and put them back into their asylum."

"Thank you! And you do not think it wise to keep sane people inside an asylum and let loose the insane?"

"Of course not!" said I laughing lightly.

"As a matter of fact, in your country this very thing is done! Men, who do or at least are capable of doing no end of mischief, are let loose and the innocent women shut up in the *zenana*! How can you trust those untrained men out of doors?"

"We have no hand or voice in the management of our social affairs. In India man is lord and master. He has taken to himself all powers and privileges and shut up the women in the *zenana*."

"Why do you allow yourselves to be shut up?"

"Because it cannot be helped as they are stronger than women."

"A lion is stronger than a man, but it does not enable him to dominate the human race. You have neglected the duty you owe to yourselves and you have lost your natural rights by shutting your eyes to your own interests."

"But my dear Sister Sara, if we do everything by ourselves, what will the men do then?"

"They should not do anything, excuse me; they are fit for nothing. Only catch them and put them into the *zenana*."

"But would it be very easy to catch and put them inside the four walls?" said I. "And even if this were done, would all their business–political and commercial — also go with them into the *zenana*!"

Sister Sara made no reply. She only smiled sweetly. Perhaps she thought it useless to argue with one who was no better than a frog in a well.

By this time we reached Sister Sara's house. It was situated in a beautiful heart-shaped garden. It was a bungalow with a corrugated iron roof. It was cooler and nicer than any of our rich buildings. I cannot describe how neat and how nicely furnished and how tastefully decorated it was.

We sat side by side. She brought out of the parlour a piece of embroidery work and began putting on a fresh design.

"Do you know knitting and needlework?"

"Yes: we have nothing else to do in our *zenana*."

"But we do not trust our *zenana* members with embroidery!" she said laughing, "as a man has not patience enough to pass thread through a needlehole even!"

"Have you done all this work yourself?" I asked her, pointing to the various pieces of embroidered teapoy cloths.

"Yes.

"How can you find time to do all these? You have to do the office work as well? Have you not?"

"Yes. I do not stick to the laboratory all day long. I finish my work in two hours."

"In two hours! how do you manage? In our land the officers, magistrates, for instance — work seven hours daily."

"I have seen some of them doing their work. Do you think they work all the seven hours?"

"Certainly they do!"

"No, dear Sultana, they do not. They dawdle away their time in smoking. Some smoke two or three cheroots during the office time. They talk much about their work, but do little. Suppose one cheroot takes half an hour to burn off, and a man smokes twelve cheroots daily; then you see, he wastes six hours every day in sheer smoking."

We talked on various subjects; and I learned that they were not subject to any kind of epidemic disease — nor did they suffer from mosquito bites as we do. I was very much astonished to hear that in Ladyland no one died in youth except by rare accident.

"Will you care to see our kitchen?" she asked me.

"With pleasure," said I, and we went to see it. Of course the men had been asked to clear off when I was going there. The kitchen was situated in a beautiful vegetable garden. Every creeper, every tomato plant was itself an ornament. I found no smoke, nor any chimney either in the kitchen — it was clean and bright; the windows were decorated with flower garlands. There was no sign of coal or fire.

"How do you cook?" I asked.

"With solar heat," she said, at the same time showing me the pipe, through which passed the concentrated sunlight and heat. And she cooked something then and there to show me the process.

"How did you manage to gather and store up the sun heat?" I asked her in amazement.

"Let me tell you a little of our past history then. Thirty years ago, when our present Queen was thirteen years old, she inherited the throne. She was Queen in name only, the Prime Minister really ruling the country.

"Our good Queen liked science very much. She circulated an order that all the women in her country should be educated. Accordingly, a number of girls' schools were founded and supported by the Government. Education was spread far and wide among women. And early marriage also was stopped. No woman was to be allowed to marry before she was twenty-one. I must tell you that, before this change, we had been kept in strict-purdah."

"How the tables are turned," I interposed with a laugh.

"But the seclusion is the same," she said. "In a few years we had separate universities, where no men were admitted."

"In the capital, where our Queen lives, there are two universities. One of these invented a wonderful balloon, to which they attached a number of pipes. By means of this captive balloon which they managed to keep afloat above the cloud-land, they could draw as much water from the atmosphere as they pleased. As the water was incessantly being drawn by the university people no cloud gathered and the ingenious Lady Principal stopped rain and storms thereby."

"Really! Now I understand why there is no mud here!" said I. But I could not understand how it was possible to accumulate water in the pipes. She explained to me how it was done; but I was unable to understand her, as my scientific knowledge was very limited.

However, she went on, "When the other university came to know of this, they became exceedingly jealous and tried to do something more extraordinary still. They invented an instrument by which they could collect as much sun-heat as they wanted. And they kept the heat stored up to be distributed among others as required.

"While the women were engaged in scientific researches, the men of this country were busy increasing their military power. When they came to know that the female universities were able to draw water from the atmosphere and collect heat from the sun, they only laughed at the members of the universities and called the whole thing 'a sentimental nightmare'!"

"Your achievements are very wonderful indeed! But tell me how you managed to put the men of your country into the *zenana*. Did you entrap them first?"

"No."

"It is not likely that they would surrender their free and open air life of their own accord and confine themselves within the four walls of the *zenana*! They must have been overpowered."

"Yes, they have been!"

"By whom? By some lady warriors, I suppose?"

"No, not by arms."

"Yes, it cannot be so. Men's arms are stronger than women's. Then?"

"By brain."

"Even their brains are bigger and heavier than women's, are they not?"

"Yes, but what of that? An elephant also has got a bigger and heavier brain than a man has. Yet men can enchain elephants and employ them, according to their own wishes."

"Well said, but tell me please, how it all actually happened. I am dying to know it!"

"Women's brains are somewhat quicker than men's. Ten years ago, when the military officers called our scientific discoveries 'a sentimental nightmare,' some of the young ladies wanted to say something in reply to those remarks. But both the Lady Principals restrained them and said, they should reply, not by word, but by deed, if ever they got the opportunity. And they had not long to wait for that opportunity."

"How marvellous!" I heartily clapped my hands.

"And now the proud gentlemen are dreaming sentimental dreams themselves. Soon afterwards certain persons came from a neighbouring country and took shelter in ours. They were in trouble having committed some political offence. The king who cared more for power than for good government asked our kind-hearted Queen to hand them over to his officers. She refused, as it was against her principle to turn out refugees. For this refusal the king declared war against our country.

"Our military officers sprang to their feet at once and marched out to meet the enemy. The enemy, however, was too strong for them. Our soldiers fought bravely, no doubt. But in spite of all their bravery, the foreign army advanced step by step to invade our country.

"Nearly all the men had gone out to fight; even a boy of sixteen was not left home. Most of our warriors were killed, the rest driven back and the enemy came within twenty-five miles of the capital.

"A meeting of a number of wise ladies was held at the Queen's palace to advise as to what should be done to save the land.

"Some proposed to fight like soldiers; others objected and said that women were not trained to fight with swords and guns; nor were they accustomed to fighting with any weapons. A third party regretfully remarked that they were hopelessly weak of body.

"If you cannot save your country for lack of physical strength, said the Queen, try to do so by brain power. There was a dead silence for a few minutes. Her Royal Highness said again, 'I must commit suicide if the land and my honour are lost.'

"Then the Lady Principal of the second university (which had collected sun-heat), who had been silently thinking during the consultation, remarked that they were all but lost; and there was little hope left for them. There was, however, one plan which she would like to try, and this would be her first and last efforts; if she failed in this, there would be nothing left but to commit suicide. All present solemnly vowed that they would never allow themselves to be enslaved, no matter what happened.

"The Queen thanked them heartily, and asked the Lady Principal to try her plan.

"The Lady Principal rose again and said, 'Before we go out the men must enter the *zenanas*. I make this prayer for the sake of purdah.' 'Yes, of course,' replied Her Royal Highness.

"On the following day the Queen called upon all men to retire into *zenanas* for the sake of honour and liberty.

"Wounded and tired as they were, they took that order rather for a boon! They bowed low and entered the *zenanas* without uttering a single word of protest. They were sure that there was no hope for this country at all.

"Then the Lady Principal with her two thousand students marched to the battlefield, and arriving there directed all the rays of the concentrated sunlight and heat towards the enemy.

"The heat and light were too much for them to bear. They all ran away panic-stricken, not knowing in their bewilderment how to counteract that scorching heat. When they fled away, leaving their guns and other ammunitions of war, they were burnt down by means of the same sun-heat.

"Since then no one has tried to invade our country any more."

"And since then your countrymen never tried to come out of the *zenana?*"

"Yes, they wanted to be free. Some of the Police Commissioners and District Magistrates sent word to the Queen to the effect that the military officers certainly deserved to be imprisoned for their failure; but they never neglected their duty and therefore they should not be punished and they prayed to be restored to their respective offices.

"Her Royal Highness sent them a circular letter intimating to them that if their services should ever be needed they would be sent for and that in the meanwhile they should remain where they were.

"Now that they are accustomed to the purdah system and have ceased to grumble at their seclusion, we call the system *murdana* instead of *zenana*."

"But how do you manage," I asked Sister Sara," to do without the police or magistrates in case of theft or murder?"

"Since the *murdana* system has been established, there has been no more crime or sin; therefore we do not require a policeman to find out a culprit, nor do we want a magistrate to try a criminal case."

"That is very good, indeed. I suppose if there were any dishonest person, you could very easily chastise her. As you gained a decisive victory without shedding a single drop of blood, you could drive off crime and criminals too without much difficulty!"

"Now, dear Sultana, will you sit here or come to my parlour?" she asked me.

"Your kitchen is not inferior to a queen's boudoir!" I replied with a pleasant smile, "but we must leave it now; for the gentlemen may be cursing me for keeping them away from their duties in the kitchen so long." We both laughed heartily.

"How my friends at home will be amused and amazed, when I go back and tell them that in the far-off Ladyland, ladies rule over the country and control all social matters, while gentlemen are kept in the *murdanas* to mind babies, to cook and to do all sorts of domestic work; and that cooking is so easy a thing that it is simply a pleasure to cook!"

"Yes, tell them about all that you see here."

"Please let me know, how you carry on land cultivation and how you plough the land and do other hard manual work."

"Our fields are tilled by means of electricity, which supplies motive power for other hard work as well and we employ it for our aerial conveyances too. We have no railroad nor any paved streets here."

"Therefore neither street nor railway accidents occur here," said I. "Do not you ever suffer from want of rainwater?" I asked.

"Never since the 'water balloon' has been set up. You see the big balloon and pipes attached there to. By their aid we can draw as much rainwater as we require. Nor do we ever suffer from flood or thunderstorms. We are all very busy making nature yield as much as she can. We do not find time to quarrel with one another, as we never sit idle. Our noble Queen is exceedingly fond of botany; it is her ambition to convert the whole country into one grand garden."

"The idea is excellent. What is your chief food?"

"Fruits."

"How do you keep your country cool in hot weather? We regard the rainfall in summer as a blessing from heaven."

"When the heat becomes unbearable, we sprinkle the ground with plentiful showers drawn from the artificial fountains. And in cold weather we keep our room warm with sun-heat."

She showed me her bathroom, the roof of which was removable. She could enjoy a shower bath whenever she liked, by simply removing the roof (which was like the lid of a box) and turning on the tap of the shower pipe.

"You are a lucky people!" ejaculated I. "You know no want. What is your religion, may I ask?"

"Our religion is based on love and truth. It is our religious duty to love one another and to be absolutely truthful. If any person lies, she or he is — ."

"Punished with death?"

"No, not with death. We do not take pleasure in killing a creature of God — specially a human being. The liar is asked to leave this land for good and never to come to it again."

"Is an offender never forgiven?"

"Yes, if that person repents sincerely."

"Are you not allowed to see any man, except your own relations?"

"No one except sacred relations."

"Our circle of sacred relations is very limited; even first cousins are not sacred."

"But ours is very large; a distant cousin is as sacred as a brother."

"That is very good. I see purity itself reigns over your land. I should like to see the good Queen, who is so sagacious and farsighted and who has made all these rules."

"All right," said Sister Sara.

Then she screwed a couple of seats on to a square piece of plank. To this plank she attached two smooth and well-polished balls. When I asked her what the balls were for, she said, they were hydrogen balls and they were used to overcome the force of gravity. The balls were of different capacities to be used according to the different weights desired to be overcome. She then fastened to the air-car two wing-like blades, which, she said, were worked by electricity. After we were comfortably seated, she touched a knob and the blades began to whirl, moving faster and faster every moment. At first we were raised to the height of about six or seven feet and then off we flew. And before I could realise that we had commenced moving we reached the Garden of the Queen.

My friend lowered the air-car by reversing the action of the machine, and, when the car touched the ground, the machine was stopped and we got out.

I had seen from the air-car the Queen walking on a garden path with her little daughter (who was four years old) and her maids of honour.

"Hallo! you here!" cried the Queen addressing Sister Sara. I was introduced to Her Royal Highness and was received by her cordially without any ceremony.

I was very much delighted to make her acquaintance. In course of the conversation I had with her, the Queen told me that she had no objection to permitting her subjects to trade with other countries. "But," she continued, "no trade was possible with countries where the women were kept in the *zenanas* and so unable to come and trade with us. Men, we find, are rather of lower morals and so we do not like dealing with them. We do not covet other people's land, we do not fight for a piece of diamond though it may be a thousandfold brighter than the Koh-i-Noor, nor do we grudge a ruler his Peacock Throne. We dive deep into the ocean of knowledge and try to find out the precious gems, which Nature has kept in store for us. We enjoy Nature's gifts as much as we can."

After taking leave of the Queen, I visited the famous universities, and was shown over some of their manufactories, laboratories and observatories.

After visiting the above places of interest, we got again into the air-car, but, as soon as it began moving, I somehow slipped down and the fall startled me out of my dream. And, on opening my eyes, I found myself in my own bedroom still lounging in the easy chair!!

No Enemy*
Syed Waliullah

An uneasy, hushed silence fell on the small town. The coloured and fancy kites soaring against the white-cloud-patched blue, breezy sky, were quickly brought down. The townfolks left their work and gathered here and there, near the street corners, near the doors of their shops and homes, women half-hiding behind the barred windows and mat-curtained side doors, even small children standing with their big round bellies pushed out, all waiting in awkward silence for the old, dying man to come their way.

Sun shining on his high armenoid nose, eyes sunk in the shadows of the deep sockets, the gaunt old man walked through the narrow streets, looking for friends and enemies. What did he want of them? Nothing. Nothing except their forgiveness.

It was a strange mission for a dying man who should have been in bed waiting to die peacefully, with his dear and near ones around him, they praying and crying, and he thinking of God. But then that was how he thought he should spend his last hour, seeking forgiveness, for he felt his eternal journey would be lighter with the burden of his sins lightened, and where from did a man's sins come but from his association with other fellow beings whom he was going to leave forever. So he had set out, in his dying hour, to ask them to forgive him.

Majestically alone, grim in his determination to carry out his last mission, the old man had been walking doggedly for some time. He brandished the cane he held in his right hand with unexpected firmness when his people, especially his now wild-haired, sobbing and frantic daughter, came near him to persuade him to return home. He also shook his cane when the children, who had gathered behind him, tried to close up on him. His face straight, eyes staring ahead, he maintained a strange but steady pace, his knees and legs alternately jutting out with a queer but regular suddenness like two wooden legs

---

*Syed Waliullah wrote this story in Karachi, dating the completed typescript "2.2.1959." He later translated this story himself into Bangla and included it in *Dui Teer* as "*Nishphal Jiban Nishphal Yatra.*"

moved by machine. His back was as straight as his gaze and as his cane.

And perhaps because of the sun that shone so brightly on his high nose which looked sharp and hard like steel and which made his face look devoid of any sense of humiliation or perhaps because this sense in a dying man is more within than outside, he appeared to demand rather than solicit forgiveness. And he did not beg less forgiveness of those who were his friends. Today, there was no small sin and big sin, and all men were equal.

His daughter wailed incessantly behind him. Come back, Father, she would cry out in deep anguish now and then, come back, come back home.

He paid no attention to her entreaties. When she failed to get any reply, she sobbed violently.

Now and then the dying man would stop before a man whom he thought he had harmed or hurt in some way at some time or other in his life and, solemnly, in a voice rigid yet quivering, he would beg him for his forgiveness. Some forgave him readily, some did not know what to say, and some did not understand what it was that the dying man wanted of them. However, if anyone got stuck for words, his daughter came running from behind and pleaded, He only seeks your forgiveness. Forgive him, forgive him.

Now everyone knew what he was seeking, for the news had spread. The dying man had now only to stand silently before a friend or an enemy and he would be forgiven. He would then resume his steady, strange march.

Father, his daughter would cry now and then, everyone loves you. Everyone forgives you. Come back home, come back.

From behind, the daughter, now panic-stricken, came up running and moaned, Come back, Father, come back. Or they will hate you. I tell you they will hate you. They will place a curse upon your head. O Father, come back.

The gaunt old man brandished his cane at his daughter.

The old man knew where he was heading. Although he had followed a zigzag path, taking this road and that, turning here and going straight there, he had as his last destination the house of the man he wanted to meet most of all. This man was no friend. As a matter of fact, this man was his enemy. He had hated him all his life, and this hatred was there even when as a small boy he had played with him while evening shadows had deepened across the fields and while the smell of mustard had come from the neighbouring farmland and he had kicked him, knocked him down and in return had been beaten mercilessly — a vicious boy who was now a bald man with a tired, sagging mouth and eyes cushioned in red-veined pouches. These eyes were still filled with hatred for him.

The old man muttered to himself a wordless vow, I must reach him. I must not die before I have seen him. I must ask for his forgiveness.

By now he had left behind the town and, as he approached his last destination, he grew tense. As he walked, he did not hear any more his own footsteps pounding on the street. He kept his face straight. Within him there was a deep, hollow and dark well, the well of his life where like dead leaves bits of his life had fallen. From the well now came voices, sounds. Every time his feet would jerk forward and drop on the street, he would step on some reminiscences that flashed out in clear brightness. He heard human voices, their cry and laughter. He saw the mustard field, bright yellow and sprawling low on which the spring breeze created soft, silent waves, heard more voices, known and unknown, even the long forgotten voice of a sad looking man who had driven the bullock cart through the shafts of light and shade of the tall, big-leafed *segun* forest, a sad face seen from behind once and never seen again.

He saw his life, but saw it in fragments and then saw again the same mustard field and the silent but cruel and vicious fight between him and the boy whom he had hit again and again, again and again, and every time harder and harder, so much so that suddenly the boy had turned away, crouched on the ground and burst into tears. Then came that moment. He stopped fighting and stared at the crying boy in amazement, in great amazement, because at that moment the boy only cried, he only cried: he had no resentment, no anger, no hatred. He just cried, looking lonely, utterly lonely. Suddenly the world around — and time — seemed to have become deeply silent, like the silent stars, silent past, silent tears. He ceased to hear the boy's crying, for he had been engulfed in the void of not knowing and of nothingness.

That evening he had walked away without a word, leaving the boy all alone in the growing darkness, not speaking to him, not even looking back once. In that moment of great loneliness he could not think of anybody. No one mattered to him, not even the small crying boy, badly hurt.

I will ask you to forgive me for that moment, the dying man said in unuttered words, at least for that moment when you had cried not out of anger, not out of hatred, but as every man must cry in his loneliness that is utter, that is absolute.

Perhaps he was mixing up things and that did not matter either.

Round the next corner a large group of men were standing near a white-domed mosque, at the head of which stood a venerable religious man in long grey robe and flowing beard. They kept their eyes fixed on the approaching, gaunt old man who stared straight ahead. As he came nearer, the vulnerable man invoked in a loud, pulpit voice, God's blessings and muttered a brief prayer.

Then he said, Have you asked God's forgiveness?

The old man did not slow down but continued to walk at his steady pace. He stared ahead of him, his eyes fixed and unmoving as usual. He neither saw nor heard the venerable man.

As he passed by, the religious man, looking extremely surprised, asked again in his loud voice, Have you, tell me, my dear man, asked God's forgiveness?

The old man walked on, his face looking grimmer in the deep shadows cast by the strong sun. Soon behind him there was a howl of indignation from the group, the voice of the venerable man being heard the loudest. The daughter, fearing the wrath of the religious man on her father, ran to him, held his hand and began to beg his mercy, her whole body shaking with uncontrollable fear. The dying man, unaware of all the commotion behind him, walked on, his head held high, his nose unfalteringly and unwaveringly pointing to his ultimate destination. He only twitched his nose as if a fly had sat on it.

Soon the old man saw the house which would bring him to the end of his last mission on earth. Now a little timid like a shy boy, he stared at the house which he had hated as much as he had hated its owner, at its green door, the small bower over the bamboo-fenced gate, the white bars of the windows shining brightly in the sun. Then he saw the form of a man standing under the bower, a short man, his bald head glistening, waiting for him. His enemy was waiting for him.

Suddenly the dying man heard a groan rise up from the extreme depth of the well within him, the groan every human being must hear some time or other in his life, the groan of a man seeking companionship, warmth and love in the emptiness of the desert, seeking a straw in the endless, waveless ocean, seeking meaning in nothingness, and then his despair turning into love deeper than the love a man can have for another man.

As the old man walked forward he heard his own footfall resounding in the well, the closed well of his life, and knew that every step was carrying him to a place where one found some meaning in life even when it was a desert, even when it was nothing but an empty space and where life began.

But then, curiously enough, he was no longer thinking of the lonely boy crying in the field or of the loneliness that had come over him, of his leaving him without a word, or of the question whether it was a sin.

As a matter of fact, he could have laughed at himself for his silliness for going to this bald old man with heavy eyes. But he did not. One went to God before dying. One must go to someone, somewhere. He was going to this man so that his life, a life as meaningless and as void as that moment near the mustard field, ended significantly.

The Return
Razia Khan

My grandchild is strumming over my broken piano — half of its reeds froze during the long journey and the other quarter were ruined by a man who, in the name of repairing it, shook it so violently that only about ten reeds remained functional. But the basic sound was good. On this untuned and ruined thing my own fingers have picked up some sort of music too. I had never imagined   I would come back to the old house, abandoned on the advice of people who did not realise how heart-breaking — or, for that matter, back-breaking — the whole thing would be.

The first day in the new flat spelled disaster. A heavy faucet fell on my foot. The next day the neon light in another bathroom smashed on the floor. Centipedes crawled in the bedrooms. Rain water gushing through the chink under the door ruined carpets.

No one bothered about the spell of depression which paralysed me. Having got me out of my roots seemed a triumph. My manuscripts, collection of books, bric-a-brac remained behind as the new place was too small to hold the collections, made over decades. The house cat whined and moaned, sorely missing us. There was a deafening noise on the floor above. Either they were grinding spices half-a-dozen of times or polishing the mosaic. When there was load-shedding, the generators of three adjoining apartment-buildings along with ours howled like deranged monsters. Security was only nominal. Starting from fishmongers down to mendicant mullahs, anyone could reach my door and ring the bell.

When I pulled out of the apartment to return to my own place, a bevy of sparrows and a sweet-singing golden bird greeted me unreservedly. The wild growth of trees, though unkempt, swayed in the breeze like lithe dancers. All around me faces were cross. Champions of modernity, these apartment-lovers constantly complained of the strain of climbing up and down the staircase which incidentally shone in its marble refulgence, unlike the dirty mosaic of the apartment stairs. I took up the mop and scrubbed the stairs lovingly. The moss on the window-sills was an enticing shade of green, and a constant shower of fragrant *bakul* flowers on them took my breath away. I missed the poinsettias and red lilies, the white rose-creeper — all of which had been destroyed by the poison used by the fumigators. Only the lonely *champak* flaunted its light golden glory.

The door-bell rings. In comes Selina, bursting with joy. My face falls as I spot the gross printing mistakes in the foreword of the book she has brought. Discovering them after she has left, I swallow the displeasure. Opening my appointment-book, I realise most of the do's I had been invited to had nullified my role as a writer. I cross them out one by one. For years I have not been able to publish anything of my own. Nor have I ever found a critic who cared to discuss my work with the concentration that I used in judging others. "Ah well," I sigh in indifference. The phone rings. I pick it up. Another request to be a Chief Guest in a poetry reading session! I have to listen for hours to ·thirteen poets and then express my appreciation of their blessed pieces. No thanks! Experience has taught me wisdom. Back in my house I am going to spend time on my own work.

Again the door-bell. It is Jamil — my student — with a periodical in his hand. His face is grave.

"Yes, Jamil? What makes you so despondent? Is it anything I have written?"

"No, Madam, it is this critique by Bishu Ghoshal which dismisses your work as 'aimless!'"

"Aimless? What does he want? Didactic literature? Marxist engagé propagandist, I will not be. Please don't show me that piece of trash. Have some tea."

"When I have improved my style I will write something on you."

"You don't have to do anything of the kind. You do what is good for you. I don't need any accolades. I know what I am worth."

I stroke his dishevelled hair and cut him a piece of the cake I baked that morning.

Revived by the caress, he smiles. "This house is just the right place for writing and thinking!"

"Yes it is! Its not meant for the kind of gregarious waste of time which goes on in other places. I use every minute creatively."

"Really? How?"

"I jump from poems to short stories — from critiques to novels."

The youth suddenly blushes. "I want you to write about me. I'm in love! You know her."

"I do? How wonderful! How does it feel? Describe it. I mean the feeling — not her."

"It's magic. It's like a rainbow. Spring blossoms! April showers! Morning dew."

"That's sheer poetry. Now can I go back to my work? More tea?"

"No thanks, Madam. Parul is waiting for me at the TSC."

"Have you ever seen these flowers? I mean *parul* blossoms? The Bengali dictionary describes them as rust-pink. I would love to see some!"

"I'll bring them along if I spot them anywhere."

I am glad to see him in this happier mood. He has a baby face but his eyes are intelligent. He is one of the very few young people who take time to read good books.

As he leaves, my granddaughter walks in with a lollypop in her fingers. She demands a story. Warding off her sticky touch, I resist this additional encroachment on my time. But she is persistent.

"Well, there was a witch who learnt magic. She wrote books. Each one was good because of this magic. Other wizards who wrote books got jealous."

"Wizards?"

"Male witches."

"You mean like the Wizard of Oz?"

"Yes, darling — something like that."

"Now what did they do?"

"They destroyed the witch's books. No, they hid them under bushes so that no one could see them."

"How mean! Nanu, I don't like this story — it's so boring!"

The child runs outside to chase butterflies, the house cat following her. The two of them, with the grasshoppers and butterflies flitting around the gardenia bush, make an idyllic picture. On the whole — not a bad day — I conclude. At least, no upsetting visitors who have nothing to say — nor any urge to listen to me. They sit with bland faces, with furtive eyes — always avoiding looking me straight in the face. I have no idea why they are so afraid of eye contact. They follow current fashion like slaves. Quarter-sleeve blouses, dark-brown lipstick, Afro hair. They go to beauty parlours to turn ugly. A minute with them is for me sheer agony. They seem live personifications of

Hazari's "Some Bureaucrat's Wives." These women have their male counterparts also. They are doyens of brinkmanship and expediency. They could have done doctorates on sitting-on-the-fence. Somewhere along the way they have thrown away their souls. Their only weapons are a half smile, noncommittal statements and a sort of frozen tact which is aimed at self-preservation, rather than sparing other people's feelings.

With dusk falling, my grandchild settles down to her homework — which is a lot. Why infants are tortured with loads of homework is something I have never understood. School for the child is a torture chamber. From time to time she declares: "I hate school."

I peep into her room and am horrified by the twisted lessons on religions — which can only create barriers and prejudices. Such stuff is hardly the material to be imposed on seven-year-olds. As she spells the difficult word "synagogue" again and again, I cannot help thinking that our educators of bygone days were far more sensible. I rescue the child in tears and total confusion — reading to her the squirrel-poem by poet Nazrul Islam. From a deep dolorous mood, she turns to jubilant laughter.

The clouds are cleared — we walk hand in hand on the gravel pathway which divides the garden, refreshed by the scent of opening tube roses.

As she is about to pick some of them, I prevent her: "Don't. This is their time to sleep. You see they are actually tiny fairies in the shape of flowers."

Her eyes grow mellow with a sudden spark of comprehension. She nods in agreement.

All around construction and development have turned the area into a concrete prison. Only my wild garden provides shelter to birds and insects. Very soon I shall also yield to the pressure of the vogue for intense property development, making the birds cry in their hapless state of homelessness. Concrete upon concrete. I feel it in my bones that my oasis is soon to disappear — the house to be torn down. And this child of the future will beget progeny who will have seen no greenery around them. Parks will be more and more unsafe even for adults — leave alone children — because of hijackers and attackers.

The soft flesh of the child's palm inside mine trembles as if reacting to my dark vision of the future. A night owl hoots. Perched on the *bakul* branches, her eyes glisten ominously.

Mariam and the Miser*

Niaz Zaman

There were many stories Mother told us, my brother and me, stories that she had heard from her mother and her mother before her, stories from English books that she translated as she narrated them, and stories that she must have made up herself, because, when I was older and able to read books for myself, I did not come across many of these stories. I wish I had asked her from where she had got these other stories. But it is too late now, for she has been gone these twelve years.

There were many stories that Riaz and I shared — my brother was two years younger than me and my boon companion in mischief — but there were some stories that he did not know so I realised afterwards that there were some stories that she hadn't told him, but only me. One of these special stories — women's stories, I would call them today — was about the woman who married a miser.

Mother's stories didn't always have titles, so I have had to make one up for this story. Nor did the characters in her stories always have names. I have named the woman in the story Mariam, but I don't think the woman in Mother's story had a name.

Mother wasn't a feminist. She went to college and worked for a year, but, after getting married, she gave up her job. Later, when all of us were grown up and busy with lives of our own, she took up volunteer work, but she was never one — vocally, that is — for women's rights. Nor did she much practise women's rights at home. Between my father and my brothers — there were three after Riaz — she and I were generally left with the bones. I became so used to eating bones, that, to this day, I am unable to eat the good pieces of chicken — drumsticks and breasts. I will generally take the neck or the wings or the ribs. Perhaps there was an advantage to eating so many bones while I was growing up — my need for calcium was met.

---

* *Mariam and the Miser* was earlier published in the *New Age Eid* Special 2003.

But though chicken drumsticks and breasts and thighs were reserved for the "men," when we ate mutton, there was one special piece reserved for me: an ear-like piece of cartilage. It was one piece that my brothers did not get. That was because, my mother said, the male passage was too small to allow them to excrete bone or cartilage. Perhaps that is not quite scientific. By the time bones — and meat — have gone through the digestive tract both men and women excrete the remainder from holes of the same size. Anyway, the advantage of being a girl was that I always got the *kurmuria haddi*. True, there wasn't much meat attached to the *kurmuria haddi*, but the thought that here was something reserved for me that my brothers could not have gave me a sense of triumph in what I saw as a mainly unfair world.

There were other disadvantages to being a girl. Eggs, though not forbidden, were restricted and only offered in the shape of a sliver of omelet, a couple of slices of French toast, and the occasional egg curry when one had a whole egg to oneself.

With all these restrictions on food, it is surprising that my mother should have told me the story of the woman who married a miser — a story that was all about food.

"There was once a miser," my mother said, cutting the onions fine so that they would turn a crisp golden brown in the ghee — in those days we cooked with pure ghee when we were not cooking with mustard oil — "who wanted to get married. Like most bridegrooms he too wanted a tall and pretty girl who was clean and well-mannered."

With tears streaming down my cheeks, I listened to my mother, wondering why there were no tears in her eyes.

"But," Mother went on, "he was so miserly that he also wanted a bride who would cost him nothing to feed. 'I don't want a woman,' he said, 'who will eat me out of house and home and who will eat so much that every year I will have to buy her ten yards of cloth to clothe her. The woman I marry must be a small eater. For her one grain of millet, ground seven times and sieved seven times, should be enough for a meal.'"

I had never seen a grain of millet. I didn't even know what it was. So Mother explained to me what it was and how small it was and how only poor people ate it.

"Everyone laughed. They said, 'Not to speak of a woman, even a bird could not survive on such a diet.'

"But the miser was rich, and there were no end of matchmakers, both professional and amateur, to help him find a bride. Old women, who were seeking a place in heaven and had not finished the required seven to assure a heavenly place for themselves, hunted for a suitable bride for free. Professional matchmakers, who make their living by arranging marriages, had a long list of unwed girls whom their fathers would be too happy to marry off to suitable or unsuitable bridegrooms. Marriage was important, compatibility [Mother, of course, didn't use the word but she meant it] was not.

"Now most bridegrooms want fair, tall, pretty, clean and well-mannered brides, so matchmakers had long lists of brides who were suitable. But one condition of the miser's was difficult to meet. The miser didn't mind a bride who was less than fair if fair was not available, nor did he mind a short bride if tall was not available, nor did he mind a less than pretty bride if pretty was not available — as long as she was not downright ugly. The problem was that no girl — or her mother or father who spoke for her — was willing to accept the food ration the miser had specified for his wife.

"If any condition was impossible this was it. Parents of marriageable daughters — as well as unmarriageable daughters who were above the age of marriage — shook their heads when they heard the condition.

"Failing to find a bride in his own village, a persevering matchmaker went to the neighbouring village where there dwelt a man who had seven daughters, all of them of marriageable age. The man was poor and seven daughters is a lot of daughters to marry, especially if the father is poor and the girls are not all too pretty. Mariam was the eldest. Unless she got married, the other sisters could not get married. Now Mariam was no beauty: her complexion was olive, she was of middling height and, though she was not downright ugly, she was not pretty — except as all girls of a certain age are pretty.

"When Mariam's parents heard the condition, they shook their heads. Even though they had seven daughters, no parents in their right minds could allow their daughter to marry a miser who refused her food. But Mariam, who overheard what the matchmaker said, boldly stepped out from behind the curtain — after modestly covering her head.

"'I would be happy to marry the miser,' she said.

"'What are you saying, daughter? Do you know how small a grain of millet is? You'd starve to death.'

"Mariam retorted — but politely, as she had been properly brought up, 'Yes, I know how small a grain of millet is. And, no, I will not starve to death.'

"Mariam's mother wept, but Mariam was adamant. She would get married to the miser whether her parents approved of her action or no.

"The day of the wedding arrived. True to his nature, the miser brought only one red silk sari and a few small ornaments. Wearing her new sari and jewellery, Mariam was married and set off for her bridegroom's home.

"The miser showed Mariam where the oils and the spices, the rice and wheat flour were kept. He told her that in the morning she was to make six *chapatis* for him; three *chapatis* he would have for breakfast with a cup of tea, and the remaining three she was to tie up with a fresh onion in a piece of cloth for his lunch. When he returned home he would expect four *chapatis* with either *dal* or vegetable for dinner. The days he did not go to work, he would have rice for lunch. He showed Mariam the grindstone with which she would have to prepare wheat flour out of wheat when the wheat flour was finished. She was to use the same grindstone to prepare flour for her bread. Every morning before leaving he would give her three grains of millet for her meals. The days he had rice for lunch, she too could have rice as a treat. There must be no wastage. And he did not like or want guests. If guests came, all she could give them was a glass of water.

"Early next morning Mariam lit the fire and made six *chapatis* for her husband; three *chapatis* she tied up with a fresh onion in a piece of cloth for his lunch. She then made a cup of hot tea, sweetening it with *gur*, and served that to her husband for breakfast with the remaining three.

"Had she eaten, the miser asked. No, she said, she would eat after she had swept and cleaned the house and washed his clothes. Then she handed him his lunch and saw him off.

"After the miser left, Mariam sat down in the kitchen and ate the two *chapatis* she had kept away for herself, twisted in a fold at her waist. Breakfast done, she swept and cleaned the place, bathed and dressed, knowing that people were bound to visit to see how she was faring.

"Sure enough, no sooner was she ready than the neighbours started pouring in. Curious, they asked her whether she had eaten. She showed the grindstone with its powdery remnants of grain.

"The neighbours were surprised.

"Mariam excused herself for not offering the neighbours any food. The miser had very little food in the house, she told the neighbours.

"Mariam, however, seemed happy, and the neighbours left puzzled, wondering how a live human being could survive on what was insufficient even for a tiny sparrow.

"Days passed. Every morning the miser would measure out the wheat flour and count out three grains of millet. Mariam would make her *chapatis*, tie up three with a fresh onion in a piece of cloth for his lunch and give him three with a hot, sweet cup of tea. Four she would tuck up tight in the fold of cloth at her waist to eat for breakfast and lunch. Mariam's only problem was dinner which she had to eat before she expected her husband to return.

"The miser was happy. His wife not only made soft *chapatis* and tasty *dal* or vegetable, she had also started looking fairly pretty. One afternoon when work was slight, the miser decided to go home early. Mariam had made the small hut so cheerful and bright with colourfully embroidered bedcovers and pillowcases that he counted himself fortunate to have a wife who not only was a small eater but had an aesthetic sense in the bargain. In front of the hut where there had been long grasses and weeds, she had planted rose bushes and flowering creepers. Yes, the miser said to himself, he was indeed a fortunate man.

"Mariam would be pleasantly surprised, he thought, to see him so early in the day. As he neared the hut, he wondered how she occupied herself at this time of day. He himself had earlier eaten the neatly packed three *chapatis* and onion. Perhaps he thought, after finishing her *zohr* prayers, she might have sat down with her embroidery.

"He quietly stepped up to the threshold and knocked on the door.

"'Who is it?' Mariam called from inside.

"Wanting to give her a surprise, he made his voice sound like an old woman's. 'It is only me, an old beggar woman, begging for alms.'

"'Go away,' Mariam called from inside. 'We don't give alms in this house.'

"To the miser, Mariam's voice seemed strangely muffled. If he hadn't known better, he'd have sworn that her mouth was full of food. But he knew that a grain of millet could not fill anyone's mouth.

"Again he called out, mimicking an old woman's voice. 'Give me a few pice, *beti*, or an old dress of yours.'

"This time Mariam peered through the bars in the window on the side of the door. Her head was bare, and, yes, she did have something in her mouth.

"Seeing her husband, she quickly withdrew and, covering her head, she opened the door. She seemed to have swallowed something hurriedly, and her right hand showed unmistakable evidence of food.

"The miser stormed into the kitchen. There, in front of him, was a plate with a half-eaten onion and one and a half *chapatis*. He looked from the plate to Mariam and back to the plate.

"But Mariam, instead of looking ashamed or embarrassed, laughed. 'So you've found me out at last. Did you really think that any woman could survive on one grain of millet ground seven times and sieved seven times for a meal? I may need less food than you, but I too must eat.'"

My mother's story ended at that point. But happy endings are important when you are small, so I wanted to know whether the two of them lived happily ever after as fairy tales tell us. But Mother asked me what I thought happened.

Well, I said, thoughtfully, the miser must have been silent thinking that he had truly been a fool. But he must also have been angry that Mariam had lied and cheated. But he also knew that if she hadn't lied and cheated, he wouldn't have married her. But she had made his home so pleasant that he couldn't think of life without her.

And Mariam, my mother asked.

Mariam too must have grown to love the miser. He was foolish indeed to have thought that any woman could live on air. But she *had* lied and cheated so perhaps he would be right to send her away.

But then I thought the miser must have asked for Mariam's forgiveness for the conditions he had placed on her, and she too must have asked for his forgiveness for deceiving him.

But Mother's story was not about love, so her story ended there, on that fateful afternoon when the miser returned home early and Mariam showed up the miser for a fool. What Mother was telling me through the story — before I knew the words "feminism" or "gynocriticism" or "feminist theory" — was that women had to learn to manage situations they found themselves in. I also realised that she was telling me through this folktale that women must look after themselves, eat enough to stay well and strong.

But today I would have put other questions to my mother. I would not have asked for an ending. I would have asked why Mariam had had to marry the miser. Wouldn't she have been better off without marrying him? A miser and a fool? Of course, I know that even a few years ago marriage was important — it still is in many cultures. Even in the most advanced societies people worry about the falling marriage rate and the falling birth rate.

But I would also think about the impossibility of a story like Mariam's ever happening. Mariam would have moved into her in-laws' house and, if her husband had laid a condition on Mariam, her mother-in-law would have seen to it that Mariam didn't steal food. But then I realise that daughters-in-law of strict mothers-in-law also resort to other tricks — unless they are unfortunate enough to have married truly wrong men who torture them till they die "accidental" deaths.

I wonder whether other mothers also teach their daughters deception? Other daughters when speaking about their mothers describe how their mothers taught them to live for others, to be ideal daughters-in-law and wives and mothers. Why did my mother, a woman who was honest and who sacrificed herself for her family and who lived for others, teach me long before there was any thought of marriage to look after myself? How well have I kept the lesson she taught me in the kitchen weeping over onions?

The Debt

Raza Ali

I had hardly known Majeed when we were classmates at University. He always sat at the front of the room, and, as was the norm for students attending university lectures in those days, rarely spoke up in class. My own seat was at the back, where I could freely daydream, doodle, or exchange notes with Kareem.

Outside the classroom, I had my own set of friends and, apart from Kareem, saw little of any of my fellow students. There were few social events involving the class, though there is a photo of our group at a rare picnic organised the year we graduated. The girls are in their sarees, posing demurely in the front of the picture. Kareem and I are predictably at the back, the contrast between us quite striking, he being as round and short as I was then skinny and tall. Majeed is in the middle row, off to one side. He is dressed in a white open-collared shirt and white pants, looking as though he is just about to go on to the cricket field. He has a slight smile on his broad and handsome face. At the time, Majeed could have been no more than nineteen or twenty, but there is just the suggestion of a receding hairline.

There is another photograph, a faded one of Majeed and me in a dramatised play reading that had been organised by the department. We are dressed in ridiculous costumes and are both sporting absurdly large and stylish moustaches. The one-act play, based on some imaginary episode in the career of Tipu Sultan, had been penned by one of the younger teachers in the department. All I remember now is a great deal of posturing and long-winded speeches. Majeed and I, however, had no more than one or two lines each.

All in all, there was little in common between us, and only once can I recall a moment in which it might be said there was a point of real connection. I was representing Salimullah Hall in some race, and, as I rounded the track, struggling to stay abreast with another runner, I caught a glimpse of him off to one side. He came over to me at the end of the race, and I knew that as I had fought my way toward the finish line, he too had been struggling with me, willing me to pass the other runner with every ounce of his being.

After I graduated, I did not see Majeed for some years. I spent some time studying accounting and entered the family business. Over a period of time, I acquired a new circle of friends, and even Kareem I hardly saw at all. When Majeed showed up at my office one day it was a surprise. He had not changed much though his hair was thinner than I remembered it. He came to the point right away. His sister was to be married, and his family was having some difficulty meeting the expenses. In addition, the bridegroom's family had increased their dowry expectations. Majeed wondered if it would be possible for me to lend him five thousand rupees. He would pay me back as soon as he was able. At that time five thousand rupees amounted to about three months of my income. On the principle that one should be only willing to loan an amount that one could really afford to lose, I offered Majeed a loan of half the amount, and in the end Majeed gratefully accepted my cheque for twenty-five hundred. As he left he assured me that he would be paying me back as soon as things settled after the wedding.

A year or so passed, and I had not heard from Majeed. I had no idea where he lived, but found out his address from a common acquaintance. When I called on him, he apologised profusely for not having been in touch. It turned out that the wedding expenses were a lot more than they had expected. Also, things had not been going well for him in his business, and he was not at the moment in a position to return the loan. As soon as things improved he would pay me back. He wanted me to know how grateful he was and how his whole family was beholden to me. I had saved them all from certain disgrace, and he didn't know how they could ever really repay me.

More time elapsed, and there was no word from him. Once I ran into him at the little shop by the Stadium where I would frequently stop for a coke and a *paan*. He was dressed in white, but it was not the spotless immaculate white that is commemorate in the picnic photograph. He was smoking a cigarette in what I remember was a characteristic way of his. He held his cigarette in his closed fist at the base of his fingers and puffed away at it noisily and deeply through the opening between his curled first finger and thumb. We talked briefly, but he did not mention the money that he owed me, and for some reason I could not bring myself to say anything about it.

I went to see him once before I left Dhaka to look after the family's business interests in London. He was no longer at the address where

I had called on him previously. The people who lived there mentioned that he had gone back to live in his village. I put the whole business out of my head and decided that it was no longer worth pursuing. Money, it is said, is like the dirt on one's palm: you collected it, it washed off, it came back.

When I returned from England three years later, I don't know why I brought up the subject of the unpaid loan when I met Kareem for coffee at the Intercon.

"Well, it is now a certainty," said Kareem, "that the loan will remain unpaid."

"What do you mean?"

"Majeed is dead," he replied.

It had happened two years ago. The bridegroom's financial demands had continued after the marriage. Majeed's sister had been subjected to verbal and physical maltreatment. Majeed had gone to his brother-in-law's village and attempted to take her away with him. The bridegroom's men had caught up with him at the river bank. There had been a struggle involving supporters on both sides. In the confusion someone had drawn a knife and stabbed Majeed.

I thought back to that afternoon that he had come to see me in my office. How could he have known that he was setting in motion a series of events that would one day end with him bleeding his life out on the bottom of a boat?

Penance of Love*

Mohammad Badrul Ahsan

Love came on a rainy day as he ran for shelter and she followed him. They stood under the canopy of a shop with raindrops pattering on the ground, splashing dirty water on their shoes. Love shone in their eyes as they looked at another and thought they were made for each other.

The confession, however, came much later on a dry sunny day, when she told him in a hospital bed how much she would regret it if she had to die before her dream came true. He came home and prayed in earnest that if the time had come for her to go, then he should go with her as well. He walked around the hospital in the middle of the night, unable to visit her in the cabin because her mother was staying with her.

In the frenzy of love that looked as if it would end before it started, he vowed to himself again that if only death spared her from its clutches, he would never let go of her from his bosom. The memory of the rainy day revolved in his mind, and he was convinced it was destiny that love should cast its spell on both at once. After she got well and went home, he distributed sweets in the neighbourhood mosque and told his friends that he was fortunate amongst men, because God had answered his prayers.

She said to him that if anything had brought her back from the gorge of death, it was the power of love. She promised to love him for the rest of her life and asked him to promise that he would do the same in return. He caught a butterfly for her and described the colours on its wings. She wept on his shoulder like a child because it reminded her of the colours in her own life since she fell in love with him. She told him between tears that dreams were wings for human beings, and she wished to spread her wings in the sky of love.

One night the police picked him up from the house as a suspect in the killing of a student leader. He pleaded his innocence, but the court

*Published in *The Independent*, August 22, 2003.

slammed detention on him for fifteen days. She visited him in jail, taking food, books, and cigarettes. She told him that her father was one of the best lawyers in town, and he would fight his case in court. Then she placed his hand on her head and asked him to swear on their love that he would quit politics as soon as he got out of jail.

After his release, he discussed politics with her. He argued that students should be concerned about the future and prepare themselves to take the responsibility of their country. She disagreed with him and called politics poison for young minds. The young men hardly knew the difference between good and evil, and politics only made them tools in the hands of wicked politicians.

He reasoned that it was his duty to love his country. She reasoned that love could never be a duty so much as honesty could never be a policy. She claimed that a mother didn't love her child because it was her duty, but because it was her nature. Politicians must adopt politics based on character, not on charisma. He wanted to know what was the difference. She explained that character thrived on principles, whereas charisma thrived on prejudice. Character led to the truth and charisma led to a target.

He asked what if politics could make truth its target. She said it couldn't because politics required compromise, which condemned truth. Politics was based on mobile truth, she added, which was why politicians shifted their strategy to avoid sacrifice and suffering, which were needed to establish the absolute truth. He retorted that she was talking about prophets, not politicians. She replied that politicians were the secular prophets, the inspired teachers and leaders for the common masses, but only if they were sincere and honest.

During a student unrest in the university, he went into hiding. She told him that she was disappointed in him, failing to understand why he had to make her unhappy when it wasn't necessary. He regretted his mistake and promised to give up politics, once that particular trouble was resolved. He claimed that he was innocent, and politics was nothing but a dirty game where people used and blamed others.

Her father talked to his friends and used their influence to have all charges dropped against him. When he came out of his hiding, the families got together and decided that they ought to put the yoke of marriage on his shoulder in order to ensure that he stayed out of harm's way. He took her to a Chinese restaurant to celebrate the decision and bought her a diamond engagement ring. She reminded him that it was the power of love that carried them through hurdles and hardships. He promised to love her forever because she was the best thing that had ever happened to him.

Two months later he called in the middle of the night and told her that the police were after him again. When her father called the police station, the officer-in-charge told him that his would-be son-in-law was involved in a plot to assassinate a political figure. When he called again in the morning, she told him that he had betrayed her by getting involved in politics again. He said he knew nothing of any plot against anybody and he had not met anyone in the political circle since he got engaged to her.

For the first time since she met him, her mind wavered. Her father warned her that the young man she loved had streaks of a politician in him, and he couldn't be trusted. She felt humiliated by him, embarrassed before her own family. She failed to understand how a man could love her deeply if his promises were so flimsy. She refused to take his calls and told her parents that she would call off the engagement.

He sent her flowers on her twenty-second birthday, wishing to see her for a moment. She refused to take the flowers and told the deliveryman that she no longer had anything to do with the sender. He called her house throughout the day, but she refused to come to the phone. Her parents asked him not to call again.

Next day he died in a police encounter outside a student hostel. There were conflicting accounts of how he died: some said he was killed elsewhere and then brought to the hostel; some said he was hiding in the hostel and he was killed during a police raid. She fainted when she heard the news of his death and only regained her senses two days later. She told everyone who came to know how she was that she had taken a dive into death with the man she loved and come out on the other side of his grave.

Love, she concluded, was no different from politics. One has to lose for another to win. She would need the rest of her life to sort out who had won and who had lost. Meanwhile, she wished to die for him every day, because the love that had come on a rainy day now burned in her heart like a blazing sun.

Grandmother's Wardrobe*

Aali A. Rehman

I

Mr. Osman, back from the mosque after prayers, was slowly preparing for bed when his daughter Marufa came in on her usual brief nightly visit to his room. Her eyes flicked around, from force of habit, to see what needed cleaning or arranging in the room.

"Baba," she said, after she had tightened a cord on his mosquito net and retrieved a tea cup from the bedside table, "do you have a lot of your things in Grandmother's wardrobe? I was wondering — if there's room to spare in it — could I use it too for some of my clothes?" Apologetically, she added: "With the children growing up, the two closets and the steel trunks that we have upstairs aren't really enough. I've been tucking things away here and there so much that my room is looking really untidy. I thought if I could store some of our winter clothes in Grandmother's wardrobe I could make space in my trunks for other things."

Mr. Osman looked speculatively at the wardrobe that stood against the western wall of his room. It was actually an old-fashioned, solid-looking teak *almirah*, a large closet, partitioned into halves with shelves and drawers on the right side and wardrobe space on the left where a brass rail at the top accommodated hangers. Traditionally referred to in the family as "Grandmother's wardrobe," it had originally belonged to his mother, having been a present from her husband, who had had it brought over for her from Calcutta in an uncharacteristic fit of extravagance.

In Mr. Osman's boyhood home it had been by far the most expensive and most handsome piece of furniture. Upon his mother's death, soon after that of his father, neither of his two elder brothers or their wives had cared to keep it on, considering it an old relic that needed to be sold and replaced with something modern. Mr. Osman, on the other hand, had a deep attachment to the so-called relic and he had let it be

---

*Serialised in the *Daily Star* (Dhaka) Literature Page in four weekly installments from July 11, 1998 to August 1, 1998.

known that if no one else wanted the thing he would gladly take it off their hands at the appropriate time. After his marriage, he had offered it hesitantly to his wife and, to his great pleasure, she had accepted it almost as if it was a family inheritance and had continued to call it just as he did from force of habit, "Mother's wardrobe." And she had used it exactly as his mother had done: it became the repository of the family's valuables, jewellery and important papers, and of their best, rarely used clothes. The wardrobe had moved with them several times when they changed houses but had come to rest in this room some twenty years ago when he had finally built his own home. For twelve years, ever since his wife's death, it had stood where it was now, though its contents were not what they once were. His wife's clothes-for-occasions, including the saris she had received at her wedding, his own clothes, the *sherwanis* and *achkans* that he had once worn, the well-washed, starched and carefully folded bed-linen that was meant for guests and festival occasions, had long ago been either given away or used up and never replaced.

The wardrobe now contained the few winter clothes that he had, and the drawers were mostly filled with papers, documents acquired over the years, useless really, but which he had not been able to bring himself to throw away, among them his father's diaries. The only important items that it contained were the deeds and records of taxes paid on property that he still owned: the house and a small amount of land just outside the city. During all the years that the wardrobe had stood in the room it had never been used by anyone else, and it was well known in the family as the one possession that he still valued. It was this that accounted for Marufa's hesitant and apologetic tone, as if she was asking for the loan of a personal belonging or of intruding upon her father's privacy.

Mr. Osman's gaze wandered over the wardrobe. "No," he said, "I don't have too many things in there. Yes, of course you can use whatever space there is. In fact I think I could make more space for you. I'll go through the drawers tomorrow and see if I can't get rid of some of the papers and files I have in them."

"Oh no, Baba," Marufa said quickly. "That won't be necessary. I wouldn't want you to exert yourself. You don't have to get rid of anything. I only want the space you're not using."

"I won't exert myself," said Mr. Osman mildly, to put her at ease. "I'll look through the drawers at my leisure, maybe take the whole day tomorrow to do it, and you can start putting your things in the day after. The inside of the wardrobe does need cleaning up, you know. There must be dust and even cobwebs in there. The last time it was cleaned up was when your mother did it." And I don't want to remember how many years ago that was, he told himself

Marufa looked at him doubtfully. "All right. But if there's any cleaning to be done, I'll do it. Don't you go and start dusting and brushing. After you've been through the papers, call me and I'll do the cleaning."

"I will," said Mr. Osman shortly and she left the room, teacup in hand. Marufa usually treated him as if he were too old for any kind of work and he had expected protests of the kind that she had just uttered. Nevertheless, he did not intend to call her when he started cleaning up the wardrobe the next day.

II

After his usual late breakfast the next morning, he found himself actually looking forward to the task of going through the drawers of the wardrobe. These days he had so little to do in the house that the prospect of a few hours activity, even a mundane one, gave him a feeling of pleasurable anticipation. For many years after his retirement from government service, and especially after his wife's death, it had been he who had really run his household. He had always, early every morning, done the grocery shopping for the day's meals, often decided what each meal would consist of, had looked after the small kitchen garden in the backyard, seen to the little repairs around the house, even to the daily sweeping and cleaning and general tidying up. It had kept him busy, and after decades of keeping busy, he had never imagined any other kind of life. But during the last few years he had gradually surrendered almost all household duties to Marufa and her husband and resigned himself to the position that, it seemed to him, his daughter and son-in-law wanted him to occupy, the position of the elderly parent who needed to be looked after.

He had receded into the background not only within the family but in his community as well. Few people bothered now to look in his direction as he sat on the front porch in the afternoons, or took his "constitutional," as he still called it, on this street that had been so quiet and backwaterish when he built his house here twenty years ago but which had become so noisy and crowded and bazaar-like in recent years — filled with small shops, large shops, workshops, auto and motorcycle repair-shops, garment factories, even a cinema hall. Twenty years ago he was an acknowledged figure on the street; he was an elder of the neighbourhood, residents brought their problems to him, asked favours of him, he sat in judgement in quarrels and disputes; he was invited to every wedding, attended every funeral — funerals that had become more frequent as, one by one, and sometimes within weeks of each other, old residents of the street, his peers, had died off.

Marufa and her husband Jalal had lived with him for eighteen years, from the beginning of their marriage. Jalal was the proprietor of a book and stationery shop in the central city market where he spent the greater part of each day. He was moderately successful in his business but had never really prospered, which had been the original reason why, after Marufa had insisted upon marrying him when she was only seventeen, that Jalal had taken up residence with his father-in-law. When Mr. Osman's other two children, his eldest daughter and only son, had settled abroad, it had been understood that Marufa and Jalal would continue to live with him and inherit the house after his death.

But Marufa now had little time to give him from the beginning of one day to its end, though she saw to his needs dutifully and conscientiously. She cooked dishes occasionally that she knew he liked, put meals on the table at the times he preferred, had his clothes washed, his room on the ground floor cleaned and tidied, and sent his tea to him in the mornings and afternoons. His grandchildren, the sixteen-year-old Amer and his eleven-year-old sister Amena, had once provided diversion and pleasure but when they had ceased to be little children, they had begun to live their own lives and have their own diversions which he could not share. Miraculously, he had been spared the usual illnesses of old age. Beyond the arthritis that had been his companion from a relatively early age, he had no medical complaints and he had often thought that it was partly his excellent health that had relegated him, in his home, to the status of a well-worn piece of furniture, so familiar that it was little regarded — like the wardrobe that stood in his room with the unmistakable patina of age upon it.

In the years since his wife's death, he had learnt to come to terms with his loneliness. Throughout his marriage, like most husbands, he had never thought that his wife would die before him. But she did die before him, and he had striven to cope with that fact and with his grief. The edge of the pain had dulled by now, though it remained as an ache within him, coming to the surface sometimes on sleepless nights or when random moments and random sights reminded him of her and shook free a thought or touched a memory.

When he opened the doors of the wardrobe that midmorning, more than one memory floated free as the mustiness of the interior washed over him in a cloud. The wardrobe smelt of damp and aging paper but he could detect in it distinctly the odour that was, as far back as he could remember, peculiar to it: a mixed redolence of the amber *attar* favoured by his parents, of mothballs, old brocade, starched clothes washed in locally-made soap, and the dried *neem* leaves that had lain on the bottoms of drawers for years in the belief that they kept white ants and termites away. It had smelt like that when his mother had used the wardrobe and it had continued to do so ever after. There were no vials of amber *attar* in it any more, or brocade *sherwanis* or Benarasi saris, but the suggestion of these things had definitely remained trapped in it, apparently forever. Cupboards and closets didn't exude odours like that any more, he thought; it was a smell that belonged to an age that had passed away.

Mr. Osman stood for a while, breathing in the vestiges of it while little memories flashed through his mind; of himself as a boy, rushing into his parents' room after prayers on the mornings of I'd-ul-Fitr, in company with his brothers, to receive from his mother shiny one-rupee coins taken from the middle drawer of the wardrobe; of his wife, standing placidly before these open doors, taking out clothes to air on the first cool and sunny day after the rainy season; of how the ancient smell of the wardrobe used to fill the room, even in the most humid weather, when his wife opened it for some reason.

He stood for a while, looking blankly into the interior of the wardrobe but then, shaking his head with a small sigh and telling himself silently to get on with the job, pulled open the first drawer. There were more mementos there, for among the papers in it were several envelopes filled with faded black-and-white snapshots and several more of old letters, tied up with thick white cotton string Mr. Osman knew very well what they contained; he had himself put away each photograph and each letter there years ago, but he resolutely resisted the urge to look at them now. He took out everything from the drawer in bundles and piled it all up on his bed. Pulling up a stool, he sat down beside the bed and began to sort through the bundles.

III

By noon, when Marufa entered the room with a cup of tea and a plate of biscuits, he had been through most of the papers and documents in two of the drawers.

"Finished, Baba?" she asked brightly.

"Well, not quite," he said. "There's still a lot to look at. But I *have* managed to make some extra space for you." He pointed to a pile of paper that he had torn up on the floor beside his bed.

Marufa looked at the shredded sheets and folders. "You're not throwing anything away that you wanted to keep, are you? On my account?" she asked anxiously.

"No, not really," he said, softening at the concern in her voice. "These are all odds and ends that I suppose I shouldn't have put away in the first place. They're of interest to no one except me. And I've decided there's no need to keep them any more. I'm going to preserve only the really important documents — and perhaps some of these." He indicated the old letters and snapshots. "You might want to keep them on too."

Marufa shook some of the snaps out on the bed. "Oh, those! Yes, I was wondering where all these old pictures were. I haven't seen them for years. Yes, I *would* like to keep them, they're family history, after all, aren't they? Here's one of me as a baby. I certainly was a funny-looking baby! What a strong resemblance I had to Amer at the same age."

"You mean," said Mr. Osman, peering at the small snap, "what a strong resemblance Amer has to his uncle. That's not you, that's your brother."

"Really?" she laughed. "That picture is so much like the one I have in my album. I suppose all of us children must have looked alike." She sat down on the bed and began to look at the faded and yellowed snapshots one by one.

When Mr. Osman finished his tea, Marufa sprang up and said: "I want to look at all of them before you pack them away, but I've got to get back to the kitchen or lunch will be delayed. I'll come back after lunch to clean the wardrobe. Shall I send Milly now to take away that pile of paper?" Milly was the servant girl who usually cleaned the room.

"Umm — no, don't send her right now, let me do the other drawers and then when I'm done she could clean up everything at the same time. And as for you cleaning the wardrobe, well, I think I won't have it ready for you until tomorrow."

"That's all right, Baba. Whenever you've finished."

When Marufa left, Mr. Osman took everything out of the drawers and then slid the empty drawers out too and put them on top of each other on the floor There was a certain amount of dust and cobwebs at the back of the wardrobe which the drawers had hidden, but not much considering how long it had been since it had been cleaned. He took out the clothes that were hanging in the other half of the wardrobe as well as the blankets and a few bed sheets that were reposing on the bottom shelf. For some reason, more dust lay on these shelves than elsewhere.

Getting a damp rag from the clothesline in the verandah, he proceeded to rub the bottom shelf on the hanging half of the wardrobe. As he did so, something small caromed against the sides. It was a little T-shaped block of wood, about half the length of his thumb in size, loosened perhaps by his vigorous stroking of the dry and unvarnished shelf. He peered into the interior, wondering where it had come from, and found a space of the same shape cut into the shelf against the outer side of the wardrobe. When he put the block into the space, it fitted so perfectly that he could hardly distinguish the lines of the joints.

Mr. Osman sat back on his stool for a moment and contemplated the spot where he had replaced the little block of wood. Strange. Why should there be a little piece cut out of what appeared to be a single solid board that made up the bottom shelf of the wardrobe? Perhaps there had been a flaw there originally that had been cut out and the little block put in to replace it. Carpenters sometimes did that, he knew. If that was the reason here, he thought, then what painstaking work the construction of this wardrobe must have been. Furnishers today would hardly bother about a small flaw like that, especially as it could not be easily noticed since it was on the inside, and right at the bottom too. The makers of this piece of furniture, he mused, must have been really good at their trade. He looked up at the tiny brass plate, tarnished now, that was affixed to the inside top of the right-hand shutter of the wardrobe. What was the name that was inscribed there? He had forgotten. Getting his reading glasses from the bedside table, he stood on the stool to read the words. The brass plate simply said:

> *Hoosein and Hoosein*
> *Cabinet Makers*
> *Calcutta and Bombay.*

Must have been some high-priced furnishers considering that they had branches in two cities so far apart from each other, catering probably to the aristocracy of those days.

And yet .... Something about the little block intrigued him. He
passed his hand all along the sides of the bottom shelf, rubbing them
with the damp rag and then his finger. Nothing there except the block
that he had replaced. The shelf seemed to be made of a single plank of
wood and it passed underneath the partition that divided the wardrobe
into two sections. He peered into the space at the other end of the
wardrobe from where he had taken out the bottom drawer. It was a
little dark there but he passed his rag along the sides and felt them
with the edge of his hand as well as the tips of his fingers. He was
about to give up and return to his task of sorting through the papers
when he found it. There, right in the middle, against the right edge of
the shelf, he could feel, though barely see, a T-shaped joint exactly like
the one on the opposite side. As he rubbed the place hard with the rag,
the outline became clearer.

He withdrew his hand and sat back on his stool again, staring at
the outlined joint he had uncovered. Interesting, he thought. Why does
the bottom shelf have these two little pieces cut out of it? There could
hardly be little flaws in the wood on both sides of the shelf of exactly
the same size. He took the rag and rubbed hard at the outline he could
see, trying to make it come loose as the first one had. When it didn't,
he knelt down and tried to pry it free with his fingernail. But the block
was wedged so tightly in place that it seemed as if nothing short of a
chisel would make it come out. Mr. Osman turned his attention to the
other one, the first one, which had apparently so easily come free from
its niche. This time, however, no matter how hard he tried rubbing on
the surface with the rag, with the ball of his thumb, or with his fingernail,
the little block wouldn't budge. Desisting from his efforts after a while,
he sat on his stool and wondered whether it was worth satisfying his
curiosity or whether he should just finish his dusting and forget about
something so insignificant as two little joints in this four-foot, long
shelf Then he had an idea and going out to the stairwell in the verandah,
where the tools required for little household repair jobs were always
kept, returned with a small hammer and some quarter-inch nails.

Kneeling down on the floor once more, he tapped a nail into the
centre of the first block of wood and then, carefully pulling upon the
nail, worked the block free. Releasing the nail from the block with a
flick of his thumb, he put on his reading glasses once more and looked
at the little piece of wood in the light from the window. It was like a
cross or a T; the cross-bar of the T was somewhat more than one inch

in length where it was meant to fit against the sidewall of the wardrobe, while the perpendicular part of the T was shorter, only about half an inch long. The thickness was presumably the same as the thickness of the shelf, about three-quarters of an inch. As in all wooden joints, the sides where it fitted into the shelf were a darker colour than the exposed top or the bottom surface, and polished extremely smooth, indicating that something sharper and slimmer than the usual carpenter's saw was used to cut it. Or perhaps the tool was just a chisel; but after being cut the wood must have been sanded so carefully that it had fitted tightly into the corresponding and equally carefully cut and prepared shape on the shelf. And of course the supporting pressure of the sidewall of the wardrobe had kept it securely in place.

Mr. Osman turned the block over and over in his hand and felt its smooth sides with his finger and thumb, but couldn't surmise what its purpose may have been. It really didn't seem as if it was meant to replace a flaw in the wood, and he leaned into the wardrobe to look more carefully at the space where the block had come from. If there had really been a flaw it should have left some trace of itself at least along the lines of the joint. But there was none. Or was there? And Mr. Osman leaned further in to gaze down at the spot from directly above it. As he did so he caught a dull yellow gleam of something inside the cavity left by the block. It came from a brass plate set into the cavity. So that's it, he thought, as he felt the plate with the tip of his finger, the block was there simply to cover the metal joint which secured the bottom shelf to the base of the wardrobe. No mystery there at all; just the painstaking craftsmanship of the makers of the wardrobe. But as his fingertip probed the cavity, he distinctly felt a small hole on the surface of the plate. He withdrew his hand and peered closely at the spot where his finger had been Yes, there was a small hole there all right and ... did it look like a keyhole? It was a little too dark in the interior of the wardrobe to see properly.

Mr. Osman turned around towards his bed and reached for the electric torch that he usually kept underneath his pillow. He held it above the cavity and shone its beam straight down. Yes, indeed, it was definitely a keyhole. He could even see the little stem that old-fashioned locks had in the middle of their keyholes, which indicated that the key to be used here would be the cylindrical, hollow kind. So the thing was not a joint, it was actually a lock. A lock to what, for what? The wardrobe itself had a lock, in addition to the usual tiny

brass deadbolts set on the insides of the shutters. And each of the
drawers it contained had a lock. All of them were, of course, made of
brass and similar to this one in appearance. But what was this one for?
And what, he suddenly recollected, was conceded by the block whose
outline he had uncovered on the other side of the shelf? Another lock,
or something else? Picking up the hammer, he drove a nail into the
middle of the T-shaped outline on the right hand side of the shelf. This
one, however, was not as easily extracted as the first one. He needed to
drive the nail deeper and pull harder before it came away. Using the
torch once more, he saw that this cavity too, with its keyhole set into a
brass plate, was precisely similar to the other.

With the blocks in each hand and his eyes from one to the other of
the spaces they had vacated, Mr. Osman sat on his stool and
ruminated. Which part of the wardrobe did these two locks secure? As
far as he could remember he had never seen his father or his mother
using them. In fact, he was sure that his parents had never even been
aware that they existed. He and his wife had certainly not been, and
they had used the wardrobe for so many years. And besides, if these
were really locks, where were their keys? He had in his possession the
original keys of the wardrobe as well as of the individual drawers.
Suddenly, he felt mildly excited. Could they be, he thought, could they
possibly be locks to secret compartments built into the wardrobe?
Compartments that no one had known about all these years? But then,
where could they be? Underneath the bottom shelf, obviously.

He got up from the stool and, standing back a few paces, looked at
the wardrobe. Its original deep mahogany varnish had survived for a
long time but was dulled now despite the coats of polish applied to it
over the years. The grain of the wood showed, as well, minute fissures
on the surface that betrayed its age. In appearance, it was typical of
the furniture of late colonial times. The top had a ledge that projected
over the front and two sides — looking much like the cornices on
buildings of the period — with a series of convex and concave borders
carved on it. Above the ledge and flush with it stood a removable,
thickly carved facade, high in the middle but tapering away to the
sides, the upper edges of which were cut in two snakelike, undulating
shapes that met in the centre. Below the ledge, on the front and the
sides, were bordered panels three inches in height, with a floral vine
motif carved on them. The shutters, showing the inevitable dark
patches in the centre where they were most often handled, were each
bordered by the motif. The sides appeared to be constructed of four

rectangular but undecorated panels set into a frame, each of the same size, two on top and two at the bottom. The base was a full twelve inches high, its bottom flush with the floor. Like the top, the base had panels on the front and the sides, more than six inches in height, bordered by the same motif as everywhere else, though here the carvings were in deeper relief and had more elaborate borders. The space in the centre of the panel, bordered and enclosed by the motif, was plain and smooth, though little scratches and tiny indentations on its surface showed the wear and tear of the years.

It was on this central part of the panel that Mr. Osman rested his gaze for a long minute. He knew that, unlike many other closets, the wardrobe did not have much open space underneath it since its bottom, covered entirely by a single sheet of unvarnished wood, was almost flush with the floor. He remembered this from his childhood and also from the time that he had had the wardrobe brought into this room all those years ago. And yet its lowest shelf was clearly not as deep as the base — though the shelf was sunk a couple of inches into the base at the top it was still something like ten inches above the floor, leaving a lot of space unaccounted for in the interior of the base. No one, apparently, including himself, had ever wondered about this discrepancy. The height of the base had always been put down simply to ornamentation, to the design of the wardrobe. Old furniture of its kind always stood high above floor. Large four-poster beds of the period, for example, were sometimes three feet in height or even more, allowing bunks, boxes and household things to be stored underneath them. It was the base, Mr. Osman decided, that must contain the hidden compartment or compartments. That was what the locks were for. Access to the compartment was gained through those locks, which were set, no doubt, in what were actually lids or shutters.

Secret compartments! Concealed hiding places in the wardrobe! Unknown, undiscovered for all this time! Who would have thought — Mr. Osman paused and laughed at himself a little for the absurd way in which his excitement was increasing. So what if there were a couple of secret compartments in the wardrobe, he tried to tell himself soberly, they just provided more room for Marufa's use, that was all — and even then only if he could figure out how to open them. There was no reason to think that there was anything in the compartments, far less to think that there was anything valuable in them. His parents, his father at least, must have known about them but had probably simply forgotten to tell their children. And they must have forgotten because they had either never used them or had taken everything of value and interest out of them. That was the most likely explanation.

Nevertheless — a smile tugged at the corners of Mr. Osman's mouth — why not enjoy this small, childlike pleasure of discovery? Amer and Amena would surely share the pleasure, perhaps even Jalal and Marufa. It would be something to talk about, for a few days at least. He leaned into the wardrobe and looked down at the locks glinting dully inside their niches. He would have to get a locksmith, perhaps even a carpenter, to cut them out if the locksmith was unsuccessful. The latter thought was disturbing. No, he decided, he wouldn't be able to bear it if the wardrobe was damaged in any way. Maybe what he should do first was get all the keys in the house, especially all the old ones, and try and see if they fit. He could begin, of course, with the wardrobe keys. There were indeed, right here, a thick bunch of old keys, unused for ages, in a small wickerwork box in one of the wardrobe drawers.

But as Mr. Osman poured all the keys out on his bed among the papers and documents he had been sorting, the call to afternoon prayers sounded from the neighbourhood mosque and he turned in surprise to look at the clock on the wall. He hadn't realised he had spent so much time on the mystery of the locks. He would have liked to try the keys out immediately before calling Marufa to show her what he had found but, leaving them regretfully on the bed, he went to perform his ablutions in preparation for prayer. Returning to his room before leaving for the mosque, he replaced the little wooden blocks in their cavities and closed the shutters of the wardrobe.

IV

On his way back from the mosque in the hot, early afternoon sunshine be suddenly decided that he would not tell anyone else, for the moment, of his discovery. Later there would be time enough to tell Marufa, Jalal and the children. For the moment, he would himself make the most of it. Figuring out how to unlock the compartments — or indeed, he thought with a wry smile, finding out if there *were* any compartments to unlock — would be a few hours better spent than his usual routine of sleeping, eating and walking for exercise. Nevertheless, when Marufa called him for lunch as soon as he re-entered the house and while sitting at the table with her, he was several times tempted to tell her casually that he had found something interesting while cleaning out the wardrobe, something which he would like to show the children when they returned from school. In the end, he didn't, and when Marufa herself asked if he had finished sorting the papers, he answered shortly: "Not yet."

In his room after the meal, he found the floor swept and the papers and other objects that he had piled on the bed neatly put away on his writing table and the empty drawers stacked against one wall. Either Marufa or Milly must have done the tidying up so that he could, as he usually did, take a nap after his meal. Well, he thought, this afternoon there wouldn't be any siesta for him; instead he would solve the mystery of the wardrobe so that he could talk about it at the dinner table in the evening.

He took the bunch of old keys from their wickerwork box and examined them. A number of them, made either of brass or cast iron, looked as if they would fit the locks. These he took out of their rings and put them separately by on the bed. Taking out the wooden blocks from the wardrobe once again, he began to try and fit each key into the lock on the left side of the shelf. Several of the keys went into the keyhole but, when he turned them, they either turned completely round or wouldn't turn at all. Having tried all of them, he put the latter kind, the ones that turned completely round in the keyhole, back into their box and began to try the others again, slowly and patiently this time. When none of them worked, he went to the toolbox in the stairwell and returned with a bottle of sewing machine oil, a few drops of which he squeezed into the keyhole. Having waited a while for the oil to spread inside the lock, he tried the keys yet again. Some thirty minutes later he had to admit himself beaten, for the lock resisted all his efforts. He took out the block on the right side of the shelf, oiled the lock, and tried the keys all over again on this one but with as little success.

Lying down on the bed at last to rest his acting back, Mr. Osman stared at the ceiling and wondered what he should do. The easiest way to get the locks open would be, of course, to call a locksmith. He even knew one such locksmith, a man of about his own age, who had a roadside stall near the city bazaar and who would know how to go about making a key for these old cabinet locks that were once so common. But he felt reluctant to involve any workmen, outsiders who would be curious about the locks they were helping to open. He didn't want anyone to share the secret of the wardrobe with himself, not just now at any rate. Another option was to seek Jalal and Marufa's help, but he felt equally reluctant to involve them just now. Yet another was to go out and buy as many likely-looking old keys as he could find at locksmiths' shops in the bazaar. Yes, he decided, this was a better idea. He should try and get the locks open by himself. If he failed and found himself at wit's end, that would be the time to ask for other people's help. He would walk down to the bazaar that evening and look at the keys in roadside locksmiths' stalls; he would probably be able to buy a big bunch at very little expense.

He was about to drift off into his belated nap when he suddenly remembered that he had not tried the wardrobe keys themselves on the locks. He got up and fetched them from his desk-drawer. They were in a small bunch and there were only two among them, the two keys to the lock on the wardrobe shutters, that looked as if they might fit. They were of the right length too, and the first one slid easily into the lock on the left. Breathing a prayer and turning it he felt, to his surprise for he had not expected success, the levers turn smoothly inside the lock and spring back with a faint click. The lock on the right clicked open just as easily. Withdrawing the key, he stepped back from the wardrobe and looked expectantly at the panel on the base. Nothing had happened; nothing had changed.

Fool, he berated himself, did you expect it to slide smoothly open for your benefit like a magic door in an Arabian Night? Something else needed to be done, obviously. But what? He tried gripping the edges of the panel with the tips of his fingers and pulling. But it remained immovable. He inspected the other panels on the sides of the wardrobe. They looked just as firmly set as the one on the front.

Slowly, he sat down on his haunches between the open shutters, elbows on his thighs and both hands on his cheeks, and frowned long and hard into the wardrobe. Was it possible that there was no secret compartment, that the locks were just locks set into the base of the wardrobe? Or were there other locks, levers, handles, somewhere else in the interior that needed to be pulled, pushed or otherwise operated? He had emptied the wardrobe that morning but had seen nothing that could serve the purpose. There was the brass rail at the top left half meant for hangers, but it was simply a rail, a removable one that rested on wooden brackets that were screwed to the sides of the wardrobe. Apart from the rail, there were the brass handles on the drawers; but they too were just handles attached to the drawers, which were themselves removable. There were also the small deadbolts set into the shutters as well as the glass knob on the front of one shutter. But again, neither appeared to be anything else than what it was.

At length, failing to think of what to look for, he took the key once more and, inserting it into each lock successively, turned it clockwise and counter clockwise several times. As far as he could tell by the feel, the locks were certainly locking and unlocking. But that was all; the panel didn't budge, nothing in the interior or the exterior moved or made a sound. Mr. Osman removed the key, looked at it and at each of the locks in turn. He was feeling exasperated and a bad word he had not used since his youth rose involuntarily to his lips. Controlling with difficulty the temptation to spit it out loud, he replaced the blocks of wood in their cavities, closed and locked the wardrobe shutters and replaced the keys in his desk-drawer. Then he lay down on the bed with his arm resting on his forehead and stared at the slowly revolving ceiling fan above him. In less than a couple of minutes he was asleep.

V

He woke with a start to Milly's loud voice in his ear asking him if he wouldn't like his tea now. The wretched child, in spite of repeated admonition, never spoke quietly, and especially not when she was waking someone up from sleep. She had the habit of coming up close and shouting "Grandfather!" as if he was hard of hearing. She seemed to believe that a man of his age and appearance should by rights be stone deaf. Marufa had probably sent her into his room to see whether he had woken up from his nap.

"No, no," he said testily, blinking at her and waving her away, "when do I have tea before prayers? Tell Marufa I'll ask for it when I come back from the mosque."

The girl looked at him for a moment. "But it's almost dark now," she said. And so indeed it was, as a glance through the windows showed him. He must have overslept somehow. And missed his late-afternoon prayers too.

"Well, all right," he told Milly as he sat up on the bed. "Tell Marufa I'll have my tea now." It was almost dark but there was time still to catch the sunset prayers at the mosque.

Mr. Osman sat for a while on the bed after Milly had left the room. Strangely, he didn't feel rested though his sleep had been unusually long and deep. His head was aching a little and, as he moved his limbs, the joints felt stiff. Must be the result, he decided, of this morning's activity. Or perhaps simply of oversleeping in the afternoon, something he rarely did. Letting out a sigh for the lost vigour of his earlier years, he got off the bed and walked heavy-footed to the bathroom.

That evening he returned from his walk rather earlier than was his custom. He had forgone his planned trip to the bazaar to buy keys since he didn't need them any more, but after his return he had sat for a longer period than usual on the front porch, watching the traffic pass and listening to the talk in the street. The excitement of the afternoon seemed to have drained out of him and he felt listless and more than a little fatigued.

Later, at the dinner table, he debated with himself once again whether he should tell Jalal, Marufa and the children about the wardrobe. He had almost decided to ease the subject into the dinner-table talk when, emerging from his thoughts, he realised that the meal was being taken in unusual quiet. Amer and Amena, tired perhaps from a long school day, were speaking in monosyllables; Jalal appeared preoccupied and was eating quickly but abstractedly. Marufa was trying to make conversation but around her eyes and mouth there were what Mr. Osman knew were lines of strain. Her eyes, as they flickered towards and away from her husband, were dark with concern. Mr. Osman sighed inwardly. He knew what the matter was. Jalal had financial problems once again. Mr. Osman finished his meal without saying anything and returned to his room.

He decided to say his last prayers of the day at home instead of in congregation at the mosque. An hour later, when Marufa came in, he had just finished but was still seated on the prayer rug that he had spread on the floor in the middle of the room. Marufa did her round of the room quickly and was about to leave when he motioned to her to stay. He let her wait for a few seconds before asking, in the tone that he had used with her when she was a little girl: "Is anything wrong, child?"

"Wrong, Baba? Why no, there's nothing wrong. I only looked in to see if there was something you needed." She avoided his eyes and looked away as she answered.

He continued to gaze up at her from where he was seated. "Is Jalal in debt again?" he asked, trying to make his voice gentle.

She was silent for a few moments and then said: "Yes, but it's not serious."

Getting to his feet stiffly, he said: "I have some money in my savings account from my pension ...."

"No, Baba," Marufa didn't let him finish. "I'm sure Jalal won't need to ask you for more money. His difficulty is only temporary, he told me: He has money owing to him too — if he can recover it from his creditors there won't be any problems."

"Well, let him know that I can lend him some if he needs it."

Mr. Osman bent over to pick up the prayer rug from the floor and swayed a little as he straightened his back again. Marufa put out a hand to steady him and, with the other, took the prayer rug from him, folded it and hung it from the head of his bed.

"Yes, Baba, I will," she said, and left the room.

Mr. Osman sat at his desk for a while, resting his elbow on its surface and his cheek on his palm, looking sideways out through the window at the strip of starry sky that could be seen between the line of the porch ceiling and the wall in the front of the house. Marufa, he knew, had not been telling the whole truth when she had said that Jalal's difficulties were not too serious. Jalal, of course, had always had trouble of this sort, trouble from which he had needed to be bailed out by his in-laws. Perhaps this time, Mr. Osman mused, he would bail himself out. It was at moments like this that he felt his wife's absence most. Had she been here now she would have found out from Marufa exactly what Jalal's predicament was and, depending on its seriousness, would have either kept it to herself or told him what to do about it. Since he had never been able to speak to Jalal about the latter's personal or business problems, he could only do what he had just done — offer the resources of his not-too-large, and probably all too insufficient, bank account.

The sound of doors slamming somewhere in the house, indicating that Marufa was locking up for the night, broke Mr. Osman's reverie. He heaved himself up from his chair, lifted the mosquito net, fluffed up his pillow and lay down on the bed before using his bed-switch to turn off the single bulb in his room. Remembering his wife briefly had crowded his mind with memories of her. Resolutely, he tried to shut them out and to relax his body and breathe regularly in an effort to go quickly to sleep.

VI

It must have been some two or three hours later that he woke up. Traffic on the street outside appeared to have ceased, leaving a relative silence in which the *chhik-chhik-chhik* of the ceiling fan above him sounded quite loud. Moonlight was streaming through the two windows of the room that opened into the inner courtyard of the house. As he turned over on the bed, the shadowed outline of the wardrobe seemed to loom above him. He stared at it for a few seconds through the mosquito not and then, suddenly sleepless, sat up and climbed out of the bed. Switching on the light, he put his glasses on. Then he got the keys from his desk-drawer and opened the wardrobe. In a minute he had the bottom shelf cleared and the blocks of wood removed from their places. Light from the bulb was falling diagonally into the interior of the wardrobe, leaving a triangular patch of shadow on the shelf and he could just make out the brass sheen of the locks inside their cavities. He inserted the key that he had used a few hours before into the lock on the left and turned it. Then he did the same for the one on the right. Both, as before, clicked back smoothly.

He removed the key and spent a few seconds looking from one lock to the other. Then — he would never know what gave him the idea and made him do it — he leaned down and inserted his thumb into the cavity on the left so that it rested on the surface of the lock and pressed firmly. There was a dull click and he felt rather than saw something move in the wardrobe. Breath escaped with a rush from Mr. Osman's lips in elation. He turned and pushed the other lock down, this time with the tip of his forefinger. It took two tries before this lock too gave under the pressure with a satisfying click, and this time too he felt a slight movement as if something had suddenly come loose.

He straightened up and looked down at the front panel on the base of the wardrobe. Yes! He could hardly believe it. The entire panel, six inches in height and running almost the width of the base, was sticking out a quarter of an inch, like a drawer not quite properly shut. It was this that accounted, no doubt, for the movement he had felt. Mr. Osman kneeled down, spread his arms and grasped the panel on its two sides with the tips of his fingers. As he pulled at it carefully and evenly, the panel slid smoothly out as if on oiled rails. It felt heavy, considerably heavy, and appeared to be a solid six-inch thick, four-foot long block of wood. However, as he pulled it out and it tilted

downward a little, there appeared a gap between its top outer edge and
the rest of the panel. He realised immediately that the panel was not
solid; it only gave that impression because it had a thin, well-varnished
wooden sheet, covering its top like a lid. It was indeed a drawer, though
it had been concealed so well, and been locked so securely in place,
that its only visible part had been most excellently disguised as an
innocent decorative panel.

Having pulled the whole drawer out as much as he dared, Mr. Osman
grasped the lid-like wooden sheet's bevelled outer edge with finger and
thumb and lifted it. The whole sheet came free, revealing underneath
it a tightly packed mass of what looked like purple coloured cotton wool.
As he removed the lid and leaned it carefully against the wall, his
nostrils prickled to a smell, an exceedingly strong fragrance, that
suddenly made his head swim — it was a fragrance with which he was
familiar, a fragrance the vestiges of which had, some twelve or sixteen
hours earlier, sent memories of all those long past years chasing each
other in his mind. He turned and gazed in wonder and a sudden
realisation at the purple cotton wool — it *was* cotton wool — that was
packed into the drawer. Here was the origin of the odour that he had
for so long associated with Mother's wardrobe, the smell of *attar*, and
old brocade and *neem* leaves ... and something more ... yes, of course,
sandalwood. The smell that rose up from the drawer was of old amber
attar, overlaid with sandalwood. But there were other smells mixed in
it too ... camphor? — perhaps, though it was difficult to think of
camphor lasting such a long time. The smell rapidly filled the room
and was blown about by the ceiling fan. Mr. Osman passed his hand
over the bluish-purple, coarse cotton wool. So this is why, he thought,
the old wardrobe had never ceased to give off this ancient odour,
although the cotton wool that was permeated with it was packed
tightly into this drawer, almost sealed into it, the smell had constantly
escaped into the interior of the wardrobe and had refused to be
expelled.

What else did the drawer contain? he wondered. Was this cotton
there simply as some kind of insulation or packing material or was it,
seeing that it was saturated with aromatic substances, supposed to be
only a deodourant? He sat down on his haunches, took a pinch of the
wool and tugged at it. When only a few shreds of the cotton came away
in his fingers, he took a handful and lifted it. The whole mass of the
cotton wool came up like a mattress, two or three inches thick. Holding

up one end of it at a height of about a foot or so and peering beneath it into the drawer, Mr. Osman could not at first comprehend what he was looking at. The drawer appeared to be lined with velvet of a dark colour, with round brass buttons of varying sizes attached to it in straight rows. He pulled the whole mass of the cotton out and, laying it carefully flat on the floor near him, turned back to examine the drawer. Bending over it, he ran the tip of his forefinger along the velvet lining to feel its texture. Then he tried to grip one of the brass buttons. As he did so, the breath caught in his throat and shock ran through his body — buttons? — *brass* buttons? These weren't buttons! They were gold coins.

There were several rows of them and each coin appeared to be nesting in a round, velvet-lined groove of exactly its own size. Mr. Osman sat looking into the drawer in astonishment for a few moments, with his hand inside the drawer and his forefinger resting on one of the coins. Then, using his thumbnail, he eased the coin out of its groove. It came away with some difficulty, so tightly was it wedged into place, and as he picked it up he could see that beneath it in the groove there was another. Apparently, the grooves were deep and there was more than one coin in each.

With the coin he had brought out in the palm of his hand, Mr. Osman went to his desk, put on his reading glasses, and examined it under his table lamp. It was a coin all right and it was gold. It was, in fact, judging from the head engraved on it, a British sovereign of the time of Edward VII. Turning it over in his palm, he made out the words "Sydney Mint" and the date "1903." An Australian sovereign, then, but a sovereign without any doubt. A real solid gold coin worth — worth what? He had no idea what the current rates for "guinea gold" were.

Returning to the wardrobe, he worked a few more coins out of their grooves and, sitting down at his desk, examined them closely under the lamp. Darker in colour than the first one, these were of different sizes and obviously not sovereigns. The largest was a little less than in inch in diameter, neither as round nor as finely engraved as the sovereign. In the light of the table lamp he could make out Arabic script — or was it Persian? — on the coin's somewhat worn surface. This must be really old, he marvelled. Could these be Mughal coins, what used to be called *asharfis* in the old days? Possibly. He turned them over and over between his fingers, trying to read the inscriptions and looking for a date, but although he could recognise individual letters, entire words or dates were too difficult for him.

The inscription on yet another one he looked at closely was unmistakably in Devanagri script though angular and crudely cut. The language was not Bengali or he would have been able to read it. It was either Hindi or Sanskrit. As he laid the coins out on his table, he realised what they were. They were coins of the Indian princely states of British times and, judging from their crudeness, dated most probably from much earlier than the twentieth century. They were hand-cast, not machine-made. What were they called, these coins ...? *Mohurs*, *pagodas* and *fanams*, if he remembered correctly. How ancient were they? And were they really gold? He pulled open his desk drawer and looked for the magnifying glass that he sometimes needed to read small print. But though he rummaged through the drawer he couldn't find the glass. Amer must have taken it away to play with, as he sometimes did. Clicking his tongue in regret, Mr. Osman contented himself with arranging the coins into a row on the table and then gazing at them with his hands in his lap. They are coins and they *are* gold, he told himself a few moments later, and suddenly scooped them up in both hands.

And, he thought as he turned to gaze at the open wardrobe in wonder, there are so many of them that they are *treasure* — a treasure hoard! But, he paused as another thought chilled and sobered him, whose are they, whose is this treasure? Where did it come from? Who put it there? Had this hoard belonged to his parents? He could not believe it. How was it that his parents had never disclosed its existence to either him or his brothers? If they had accumulated these coins over the years — as admittedly it was a tradition among his father's generation to convert family savings into bullion or gold coins — they would surely have let their children know about it during their own lifetimes. Mr. Osman's father had been a stern as well as a taciturn and distant parent who had never been in the habit of either asking his sons' advice or taking them into his confidence about his affairs. But surely, if he had intended this wealth to be inherited by his children — as what else could have been his purpose? — he would have arranged for its safekeeping or its disposal long before his death. On two or three occasions before his last illness he had discussed the division of his property and assets with his eldest son, Mr. Osman's elder brother, but he had never mentioned that there was anything in his possession as substantial as this hoard. And neither was there any mention of it in his diaries, which Mr. Osman had read many times and which had lain in a drawer of the wardrobe for years.

VII

No, Mr. Osman decided as he stood in the middle of the room with the smell of amber *attar* swirling around him, this heap of gold could not have belonged to his parents. And, evidently, no one else in the family had known about it. The wardrobe would never have become an old and unwanted piece of furniture if anyone had. The coins must have been hidden in it from long before his father bought it. In fact, so cleverly concealed was the hiding place that it was highly probable the wardrobe had been specially built for the purpose.

So whose were they then, these coins? The obvious answer was that they must have belonged to the original owner of the wardrobe. Mr. Osman searched his memory, and seemed vaguely to remember his mother talking about his father having bought the wardrobe at a sale of some kind, an auction, on a business visit to Calcutta from where he had had it crated and shipped by rail to their home. What kind of a person could the owner have been? Some Marwari merchant of the city? A rich landowner, a *zamindar*, Nawab or Raja, who had prudently stored away part of his revenues and rents in gold? Or maybe an English Sahib, a Colonel or Major or District Collector, whose hedge this was against an impoverished retirement in England, and who had this wardrobe custom-built for the express purpose of hiding his perhaps ill-gotten gains? Whoever it may have been, it was a wonder that the wardrobe had been sold with the treasure inside — perhaps because the owner had died and no one else had known about it. That would explain the auction his mother had talked about. The family or the next of kin may have sold off the personal effects of the deceased owner. It was another wonder that the gold had remained undetected, undiscovered inside the wardrobe for so many decades.

As he stood there, he suddenly realised that there might be a clue to the ownership of the coins in the drawer itself, a document or letter or something else. Pulling out the drawer as much as it would go, he passed a hand over the surface. There was nothing except the coins. He tried to pull up the velvet lining at one corner. But it was stuck fast. He turned to the wad of cotton next, passed his fingers through it and, picking it up, shook it violently. Nothing. Could there be something inside the casing of the drawer? Could he take the drawer out completely and look inside the casing? He tested the weight of the drawer by pulling it horizontally a little. It seemed to be extremely heavy, and he doubted whether he could remove it from the wardrobe by himself. There was nothing, then; no clue to the original ownership of the coins — unless it was the little brass plate affixed to the shutter which gave the name of the makers of the wardrobe. He looked up at it: "Hoosein and Hoosein, Cabinet Makers, Calcutta and Bombay." Did the firm still exist? If it did, perhaps, even after all these years, they would have the name of the person for whom they had built the wardrobe.

Mr. Osman sat down on his stool in front of the drawer and reflected. Should he try to discover who the owner had been? Although he asked himself the question, he knew that this was next to impossible. More than half a century had passed since his father had bought it in a city that was now in another country. He had himself never been to Calcutta and knew that he would not want to go now. And even if he did, he would not know where to begin looking. But was it absolutely necessary for him to find the original owner of the wardrobe? Finders keepers, he thought. Had these coins been found in the ground somewhere they would have been treasure trove. In this case, besides, his father had bought the wardrobe with the treasure inside and it had then become his personal property. Technically therefore, the treasure had belonged to his father. This line of reasoning made Mr. Osman feel a little better, but some of the doubt still remained in his mind.

He stood before the open drawer and began to count the rows of coins. When he had finished, he still stood there, looking down into the drawer and the coins that still looked like brass buttons. After a long moment, he took a deep breath. The excitement of the past half-hour had left him feeling a little dizzy. His whole body seemed to be tingling and felt damp, as after a hot bath. He took up the purple cotton pad and put it back where he had found it. Then, after replacing the wooden sheet on top of the cotton, he carefully pushed the drawer shut. When he had felt and heard the twin clicks as the locks engaged, he looked at the front panel of the wardrobe. The drawer had slid smoothly and firmly into place with hardly a crack between its edges to show that it had been opened.

In a few more minutes he had replaced everything that he had taken out of the wardrobe. The floor of the room, he noticed, was dusted with tiny purple shreds of the cotton. Finding a rag, he went down stiffly on his knees and carefully swept all trace of it away. As he stood up and looked about him, the air in the room suddenly seemed close and dense despite the whirling ceiling fan. He switched the fan and the light off and, opening the door as silently as he could, stepped out into the little adjoining porch that faced the street.

VIII

It was cooler outside on the porch and he stood for a while breathing in the slight and soft northern breeze. To his right, above and beyond the street light, the sky was dark and punctuated by stars. The dawn was still sometime away. Unfolding his canvas deck chair, Mr. Osman sank down into it and stared unseeingly out through the steel grille that surrounded the porch.

He felt tired, his forehead and arms were sweaty, but thoughts crowded his mind. Although he had no idea how much the coins were worth, this much he realised that they amounted to a small — or even a large — fortune. What should he do with it? Share it with his entire remaining family? Keep it for himself, give it to Marufa? She was, after all, the worst off among his children — she was, indeed, the worst off in the whole extended family. If anyone deserved this windfall — this unlooked for, unexpected wealth — she did. She, who had so patiently and uncomplainingly put up with the relative poverty of her life so far. And moreover, it was because of her, her request to him to be allowed to use the wardrobe, that had led to his discovery of the secret drawer. The money that the coins would bring would pay off Jalal's debts, the debts that only the previous evening had brought the lines of worry to Marufa's face, those lines which Mr. Osman always hated to see in her still youthful face. It would provide for a better education for Amer and Amena than the one they were now getting.

There was no knowing how much the coins would fetch if they were sold. Perhaps there would be enough for them to get rid of this house and move to a nicer area of the city, to the outskirts, on the edge of the countryside, away from the noise and the crowds of this street, to live a better life with rather more comforts than they had now. After that there might even be some money left over for him to indulge himself ... in what? In all his life he had had few aspirations, few ambitions. He had worked at his job, kept himself and his family in moderate comfort, provided for the few luxuries that his wife and children had asked for. He had wished for no more, and now, in his old age, he could not think of what he would like to do. Perhaps, he thought as he looked out into the darkness, he could travel — beginning first with a trip to Calcutta to see if he could discover the identity of the original owner of the wardrobe? Or maybe he could go once again on the Hajj. He had gone the first time soon after his retirement, making the journey on a crowded ship. This time he could go by air, as everybody else did these days, and stay longer ... but would it be right to perform the Pilgrimage on money found in this manner?

He shook his head in the darkness and admonished himself: these decisions were for afterwards. He should think about what he should do right now. How should he break the news about his discovery to Marufa, Jalal, and the children? He felt a little thrill of pleasurable anticipation as he imagined himself calling them into his room and dramatically revealing the pile of gold to their astonished eyes. How would they react, what would they say? He could imagine Marufa exclaiming in wonder and astonishment, with her hands on her cheeks, as she usually did when something pleased her or when she received surprise presents. Amer and Amena would probably want immediately to get their hands on the coins, to feel them and look at them closely — and, he suddenly thought, they would want immediately to run out and tell all their friends about the treasure found in their house. Whereupon rumours would spread in the neighbourhood and people would come in to ask about them. No, he should probably tell Jalal and Marufa first. There would be time to show the children the treasure after the three of them had decided what to do with it.

What to do with it ... that question kept returning. A ripple of anxiety went through him suddenly. Money, especially a lot of money, always brought trouble and disagreement into a family. He had seen friends and relatives suffer from the effects of the division of inheritances and common property. Would his discovery of these coins result in anything like that? Would his elder daughter and his son, both of whom lived abroad, insist on their shares? And what about his own elder brothers and their families, who could also claim ownership of the wardrobe? Would they have anything to say about the gold found in it? Would this treasure, this heap of gold, bring unhappiness and discord into his family?

Mr. Osman closed his eyes, leaned back into the canvas back of his chair and tried to stop thinking. If only, if only his wife had been still with him. She would have known how to deal with these problems. The thought sent a pang through his heart of longing and loneliness. She should have been here, he found himself saying with silently moving lips, she should have been.

But he had had long practice in suppressing memories of his wife, memories that brought only pain and no solutions. He rose from the chair and, grasping the cool dew-damp bars of the grille, looked up and down the street to stop himself from thinking further. In front of him, across the street and a little to the left, there was a roadside motorcycle workshop, shuttered only with bamboo fencing, where a single bulb still burned though there was no one to be seen inside. Beside the workshop was a row of three small betel-nut and cigarette shops. In front of these, he could make out figures asleep on the ground. The breeze had freshened somewhat in the last few minutes and was now rustling leaves on the roadside trees. The eastern sky was still dark but he could sense that the dawn was nearing. He felt lightheaded, probably from lack of sleep. The breeze, though cool, had not dried the sweat on his skin. Time to get back to bed, he thought. Or maybe he should wait until the *azaan* sounded and go to bed after offering his prayers.

Folding up the deck chair he had been sitting on, he went back into his room and closed the door to the porch. The light that he switched on seemed to flood the room with blinding brightness, and he raised a hand to screen his eyes from the bulb. As he did so, his head swam with dizziness and the room seemed to tilt and sway. He momentarily had the unpleasant sensation of standing in empty space and felt at the same time his knees buckling. Something hit him on the back of his head. Moments before he lost consciousness he realised that he was lying on the floor, looking up at the ceiling.

IX

His eyes opened to bright sunlight falling in a rectangle on the whitewashed wall. Someone was shouting or quarrelling somewhere nearby. Rickshaw-bells and hawkers' cries floated in the air.

He was lying on his side. In front of him a woman in a cotton-print sari was standing with her back to him, doing something at a table. He stared at the sunlight on the wall and then shifted his gaze to the woman's back. She appeared to be rearranging the things on the table, tidying up. It was Marufa.

He had been asleep and had dreamed incessantly. He had dreamed of Marufa too. But why was she here, at this time of the morning? He tried to ask her the question but only a low, hoarse whisper escaped his lips. His mouth was dry and his throat ached.

The whisper was nevertheless loud enough to make Marufa turn quickly around. She looked at him for a second with widened eyes and then kneeled swiftly beside his bed. "What did you say, Baba?" she asked in a high-pitched voice. "What did you say? Are you awake, Baba? Do you know who I am?"

Mr. Osman rolled his tongue in his mouth and swallowed painfully. "Yes," he said hoarsely, but more clearly than before. "Why are you here? What's happened? What time is it?"

Marufa's face broke into a smile and she put an arm over him. "You *are* awake, Baba! You're all right, aren't you, Baba? Nothing's happened," she said delightedly and then immediately contradicted herself. "You've had an accident. You fell down and hurt your head. But you're all right now. You do recognise me, don't you? I'm Marufa, Baba." She moved her hand to his face and laid it on his cheek. "You had an accident," she said again.

Accident? Hurt his head? Mr. Osman tried to turn over on his back but Marufa restrained him.

"No, Baba," she said. "Don't move right now. Lie still. You've hurt your head. There's a bandage on your head. And there's a saline needle in your arm."

Mr. Osman looked down at the tube attached to his left forearm and raised it a little. His arm ached and he could only move it slowly and in jerks. He felt his forehead with his other hand. There was indeed a bandage all over his head and down beside his ears and under his chin. Accident?

"Don't move, Baba," Marufa said again, pressing gently on his shoulder. "Don't move right now. I'll call the others." She rose and shouted excitedly for someone before coming back to kneel at his bedside again.

Amer came to stand beside him but only had time to ask, "How are you, Grandfather?" before being sent away again by his mother. In a few minutes, during which Marufa continued to talk, Amer came back with a young man in a white coat and a stethoscope round his neck.

"How are you, uncle?" the young man asked cheerily before pushing Mr. Osman gently onto his back. He proceeded to apply the stethoscope to Ms. Osman's chest, shine a flashlight into his eyes, and tickle his feet. "How are you feeling?" he asked again.

"My arm hurts and there is an ache in my throat," Mr. Osman told him.

"That's all right, that's fine," said the young man. "The aches and pains will go away in a few days. Now I want to see what you can do. Can you raise your arms?"

"Yes," said Mr. Osman, but the man made him raise his arms two or three times, then his legs, bending them at the knees, and finally told him to try to turn his head from side to side.

"I think he's all right," said the young man to Marufa after Mr. Osman had gone through these movements. "He's very lucky and I think he'll probably be back to normal very soon. But he should be under observation for a few more days." The man smiled at Mr. Osman, patted him patronisingly on the shoulder and left.

On the man's departure Mr. Osman finally asked the question that had been bothering him for the past several minutes. "Where am I, Marufa?"

Marufa leaned close to him. "You're in the hospital, Baba. You've been here for some time. And we were all here with you. Jalal and Amer and Amena. And Uncle Naseer was here for quite a long time." This was Mr. Osman's cousin. "And yesterday a lot of people came to find out how you were. Almost everyone from our neighbourhood came."

"But how did I get here?" Mr. Osman asked. "I don't remember coming here."

Marufa held his hands in her own. "We brought you here, Baba. In an ambulance. When we found you lying on the floor we called a doctor and he said that you should be admitted to hospital. You were unconscious."

She said slowly, as if trying to make him understand: "You had an accident, Baba. You fell down from your bed and hurt your head. You were very sick — you were unconscious for more than three days. The doctors thought at first that you must have had a stroke, but they weren't sure and they said at last that you must have had a serious concussion. They said that if you didn't regain consciousness by yourself they would have to try some other kind of treatment. Thank God, you're awake now, thank God you are talking."

Mr. Osman passed a hand over his eyes. He said, after a few moments: "I don't remember falling down from my bed. I don't remember coming here."

Marufa said gently: "How can you, Baba? You were unconscious when we found you on the floor that morning. And you were unconscious all this time. Since day before yesterday, you would open your eyes but wouldn't respond when I talked to you. The doctors told me to keep talking to you all the time and to call out to you. I've been doing it since then, but you wouldn't reply and it was only this morning that I was beginning to think that — " she choked off the rest of her words.

"I was asleep," Mr. Osman said weakly, in his still hoarse voice. "I was asleep. And I heard your voice in my sleep. And I dreamed of you, and of Jalal, and the children. I was talking to you about something. About something very important. But I can't remember what it was."

He looked up at her appealingly, and at Amer who had reentered the room just then. His voice rasped in his throat as he said: "And I don't remember having an accident. I don't remember falling off the bed."

"On Wednesday, Grandfather," Amer said. "No, not Wednesday, the day after — Milly found you lying on the floor in your room early on Thursday morning. You had lost a lot of blood. You must have fallen down and hurt your head against the corner of Grandmother's wardrobe."

"Grandmother's wardrobe!" Marufa cried out. "That wretched wardrobe! If only I hadn't asked you to clean it out for me. It's all my fault. You tired yourself so much doing it — that must be the reason that you fell and hurt yourself."

Mr. Osman looked up at her again. "Mother's wardrobe? Did I clean it out for you? Why?"

"Because I asked you to, Baba. Because I wanted to use it for some of my things, my winter clothes. You spent all Wednesday morning rearranging the things in it. Don't you remember?"

"No," Mr. Osman said slowly. "No, I don't remember anything like that. But I think I dreamed of the wardrobe too. There was something I wanted to tell you about it — "

"It doesn't matter, Baba," Marufa interrupted him. "Don't talk too much now. You'll remember everything once you're all right. The doctors did say that your memory might be affected because of your concussion. But they said the important thing is that you recognise all of us and remember our names. And you do. You recognised me as soon as you regained consciousness. That's the important thing. I'm sure when you've recovered fully all of the things you've forgotten will come back to you. But now I want you to stop talking and rest. The doctor who came just now said that the specialist will come and see you when he makes his rounds in the afternoon."

The specialist came that evening and poked his body all over with steel instruments and made him go through all sorts of complicated movements and joked with him and told him he had nothing to worry about, that his memory would, just as his daughter had told him, come back to him eventually, and all that he had to do was look to his diet, take plenty of exercise and not allow his blood pressure to rise. It wasn't a stroke this time, apparently, but it could have been.

But Mr. Osman did not remember even months later when he had resumed his constitutionals and his five times a day walk to the mosque for prayers. The wardrobe still stood in its corner as before, though it was packed now with Marufa's winter clothing, but he could not remember what it was that he had dreamed about it.

"Don't worry, Baba," Marufa would occasionally tell him soothingly on her evening visits to his room. "It will all come back to you one of these days. I'm sure it wasn't anything really important."

To Marry or Not To

Shahid Alam

Every year, for the last twenty-three years, Niaz Kamal went to Bangladesh to get married. He began this annual ritual in 1977, when he was twenty-eight, and by the year of his latest venture he was fifty-one. Of course, he failed. Which is why he tried again and again. And every year, as he added to his age, his prospective bride's was reduced, even if it was by a day from that of the previous year's. Ha Jin's Lin Kong returned every summer to Goose Village to divorce his wife, Shuyu. Niaz Kamal's labours were no less strenuous than Lin Kong's was. In fact they were more, far more. For one thing he travelled the greater distance — from London to Dhaka. For another, every two years he would make an additional trip — to the United States — to look at another pasture. Not to mention frequent trips each year all over Great Britain. You must admit that there was greater mileage logged there than in Lin Kong's straightforward destination. And both kept failing in their respective objectives.

Niaz was a Bangladeshi who had settled in England. Soon after graduating from Dhaka Medical College in 1975, he had gone to London to pursue higher studies in surgery. In those days people from the new country, old civilisation, born out of bloodshed and privation and struggling in fearful poverty, found it much easier than onwards from a decade later to obtain a visa from Britain. The exodus from Bangladesh began as a trickle and then became a torrent that the British government felt compelled to hold back and reduce to a dribble. Niaz was lucky to be in the vanguard of the migration. He was twenty-six when he left and looked remarkably unchanged at fifty-one. Of course, there were changes, the hair had thinned out for one, but even plastic surgery cannot be expected to completely push back the encroachments of a quarter of a century. And Niaz never sought assistance from a fellow-surgeon of a different specialisation. He was good-looking then; he was good-looking after twenty-five years.

Of medium height, big boned and compactly built, he fancied himself a ladies' man and with good reason, too. Women found him attractive. Square-jawed with a firm jawline that embraced a strong square chin, he did justice to the character that that kind of a face is popularly supposed to denote. A pair of large, liquid brown eyes were generously set apart and were under the benign protection of a pair of arched dark eyebrows. A wide-bridged short nose broke the regularity of the fine features, but a proportionately sized mouth with sensuous lips made up for that disharmony. A broad forehead displayed perpetually quizzical lines and started a head of fine wavy black hair that was always carefully coifed. It was styled in the fashion of the day and, while it was full without ever being luxuriant in the earlier days, after twenty-five years, strips of skin on the head could be discerned if one looked closely at it. But the hair was brushed and styled with so much care that it hid more than it revealed. Niaz was a fop. He always groomed himself well. Stylish clothing and expensive shoes adorned him. He was much lighter-skinned than the average Bangladeshi and better built too. A faint aroma of cologne wafted around him, except when he was at work. Then he would be surrounded by a heavy smell of the operation theatre.

Niaz was the eldest son of a prosperous businessman. Before leaving Bangladesh, he drove a Japanese Datsun that his father had bought for him two years earlier. By the time he was as old as his father was when he had gifted his son the Datsun, he owned a Jaguar and a jeep. Plus a four-bedroom house in Essex, where he worked. He was considered a competent surgeon who would never rise to the level of brilliance. He was reputed to be a playboy who could be expected to land a suitable wife. That is, by the many people who barely knew him or only knew him as a charming, intelligent man with good looks, a nice house with all the accessories of comfortable modern living, a stable profession and a good steady income. The few who were close to him, mostly friends who went back to his school days in East Pakistan and who had also migrated to Britain, thought otherwise. They were cynical and, with them, he has a butt of their private jokes. They were aware of his expected bride qualities and each year they went through the ritual of finding a suitable bride with him. They themselves had long been married with grown children. One or two had divorced and one or two had become widowers. But Niaz Kamal went on being a bachelor for whom his age froze at twenty-four.

"He's mad!" would be a constant refrain from his close friends. That included the few he also had in Bangladesh, the US and Canada.

"That fucking asshole can never get married." This from a close friend in London was not intended to be malicious, but actually indicated the problems of him finding a suitable bride.

Some of his old friends explained Niaz's situation as a virulent outcome of a failed love affair in Dhaka. He was, for the only time in his life, deeply committed to a medical student a year his junior. He was then in his fourth year of study and planned to marry her as soon as she had graduated. She fell short of some of the attributes that he subsequently demanded of any prospective bride. Sharmin was only pretty rather than beautiful. Even by Bengali standards she barely cleared short, instead of being tall or at least a respectable medium height. And she had a half inch of adipose tissue around the waist. But she had a pedigree family background, had English-medium schooling, was smart in appearance, intelligent, and reasonably erudite, had at least comfortably well-off parents and was a Muslim.

The attribute of family background in Bangladesh does not necessarily connote wealth. It is a nebulous concept of a gentry whose forefathers possessed acres of land or who were of a certain religious familial descent, and were respected for belonging to it by the members of the community they lived in. The fact that many of the landowners had gained their property through the pillage of a rapacious ancestor was forgotten as time added layer upon layer of respectability to succeeding generations of that long-dead plunderer. A first class education and cultivated etiquette gave them the polish that was expected from a good family. Quite often, the originator or an immediate successor adopted a surname that carried the weight of good breeding, and the stamp of impeccable background is set upon the members who have subsequently been born into that family. Niaz Kamal belonged to one of those families and expected no less than that his bride's matched his. The Muslim attribute came later, when he had settled in England.

Niaz was a mild womaniser before he met Sharmin. And even while he knew her. He had only talked off and on with her for two years since she had entered medical school, but had shown no amorous inclination. He had other interests. Then, in her third year, he discovered her through the eyes of an eternal lover and, by his final year, he was planning for a fairytale marriage that only the inevitable Grim Reaper would end. And then, in her final year, the world came crashing around the young intern. Sharmin had decided that her future did not lie with Niaz. She had no idea with who it was going to be — she would let the future take care of that — but it was definitely not going to be with him. She found him a pompous ass and a big bore and decided that she would go berserk in having to put up with lifelong pomposity and boredom. And Niaz's world lay in temporary ruins. His grief lasted a long time, but, eventually, he got over it. By which time he was set to go to London. And turn into quite a womaniser with a big psychological scar that, his closest friends said, prevented him from finding a suitable bride. That he took refuge behind a wall of finding faults with a prospective bride to reject for fear of rejection himself. That he set bride qualities at lofty heights in order to attain the near-impossible and someone far better than Sharmin, or to find shortcomings that would make it easy for him to reject candidates.

And there was no shortage of parents who were willing to show him their daughters. Irrespective of the reluctance of some of the daughters in wishing to get married to the much older man when they could have any number of equally, or even more, qualified younger men, or even not to get married at all until they were ready to. Irrespective of his reputation as a playboy which the parents were aware of. That aspect would come out along with his other qualities when they made extensive inquiries about him. They would gain a son-in-law of whom they could boast about to relatives and friends as belonging to a well-off illustrious family. In addition, he was possessed of good looks and superb health, had excellent manners, was a specialised surgeon with good income and property in — and this was the apex of their justification — England, no less! The U.S. would have been a shade better, but it was still England, no less! So what if he was a bit long in the tooth, had a randy reputation and if their daughter was not exactly dying to get hitched to him. They conceded that there was truth in the young lady's argument that if she was going to have her marriage arranged, then these days there were a number of young Bangladeshis with good educational qualifications and sound jobs in the United States, so cherished, and in the U.K. no less! But, never mind, would any of those precious young men combine all the qualities that were concentrated in the person of Niaz Kamal? And furthermore, he was more established than any of them. How did they know? They just did. After all, he had far more years to progress in his profession and acquire property. Exactly! He did not have many more years left in his

profession. Then he would retire, potter about and die, leaving her a
widow at a relatively early age. Now she was being silly. Look at his
physical condition. Plus, he was a specialist doctor and knew how to
take care of himself. And he would be less likely to leave her than any
of the younger men. And, anyway, they were only looking out for her
best interest and future happiness. There was no harm in at least
seeing him and giving him a long sighting. And so she did.

If you have been given the idea that in each case the parents were
the ogres forcing their preferences on their poor, helpless daughters,
then quickly get rid of it. There were several instances when the girl
willingly wanted to have her first and, hopefully, only, marriage to the
good doctor. Oh, yes, the good doctor also stipulated that he would not
even consider a divorcee or a widow. After all, his future wife would be
landing him — a fresh first-timer at the altar — so why should he end
up with a jaded second-timer or, Heaven forbid, a devastated multiple-
timer? So, previously unmarried young women tried to get him to look
favourably in their direction. They found him eligible for exactly the
same reasons that the parents did, although their order of priority over
his qualifications often differed. For them, his family background was
of less importance than that of his profession and residency. He offered
a chance to get out of the familiar destitution of Bangladesh and into
the world of plenty, however much they might be living in isolation
from the mainstream society of that world and be restricted to that of
their own familiarity — that of the expatriate Bangladeshis.

When Niaz landed in Britain, shattered of heart, even though a
year had passed since it received its massive jolt, he was determined to
mend it in the enticing atmosphere of London. He hooked up with a
few Bangladeshi and Pakistani students. Some of them were studying
to become Chartered Accountants to belong to a respectable profession
and earn a lot of money; the rest were studying to become specialists in
medicine or surgery to belong to a respectable profession and earn a lot
of money. And none planned to go back to their countries expect as
visitors. All intended to acquire British citizenship. In course of time,
all did. Most contemplated marrying white British women. Expect for
one or two, all had their wishes come true. And those one or two
married white continental West Europeans and declared them to be
better in all aspects of physical beauty and sexual performance than
the British women. By the time Niaz had made his latest foray for a
bride, expect for one or two, all had their marriages survive. These one

or two had got divorced and their ex-spouses were fairly evenly divided between British and Continental West Europeans. There were cultural incompatibilities in their failed marriages that could not be surmounted, that was for sure, but there was also philandering on the part of the South Asian men that came with proof to the knowledge of their spouses. The intact marriages all had gone through periods of culture and tradition problems, but compromise, understanding and sheer luck prevented the degree of strain that would have unravelled them. And there were philandering by some of the men here, too, but their spouses only heard vague rumours that they laughed off or did not hear about at all.

Niaz was one of the few who was ambivalent about marrying a white woman. These men preferred a countrywoman, at least for not having to deal with the problems and complexities of differences in tradition and culture. Niaz, however, initially, was more interested in women, period. He began his womanising with a vengeance as a reprisal against the woman who had ditched him. Sharmin, back in Dhaka and busy with her internship, did not get to hear about it and, even if she did, would not have been affected. Through the labyrinths of his hurt mind the message travelled that he could thus find healing and gain revenge on his lost love. So he went on the prowl. And landed women of diverse ethnicity and religion while going through his studies and, then, undertaking his annual ritual in finding a suitable bride. He did not stop, only occasionally slowed down, even after he received his specialist's degree and started a busy work schedule. There were British women, an American or two, a few European tourists, Pakistanis, Indians and Bangladeshis. In repairing his heart he damaged or broke others'. He was never in love with any of them; some of them were with him. They suffered when they were discarded, some in silence, others volubly, but who only succeeded in giving voice to their bitterness. He was not moved one bit. Others were in it for some fun and played his game without any fallout at the end of it all. No bitterness, no recrimination, no anger, no sorrow; just permanent parting of an ephemeral liaison.

He got the idea of marriage in his conversations with his flatmate, Khalid, a Pakistani of Kashmiri origin, who was studying to be a Chartered Accountant. He was about to take his final examination when a chance encounter got him to meet Niaz and easily convince him to move into a recently vacated room in his flat in West Hampstead.

He only rented the flat; a Bangladeshi immigrant with a flourishing "Indian" restaurant business in Brick Lane, a small Bangladesh in London, owned it. The imminent Chartered Accountant and the specialist surgeon of the not-too-distant future got along very well — a Pakistani and a Bangladeshi of well educated, upper middle-class background finding familiarity with each other in an alien environment that both were determined to one day call home. Funny, the countries they were then citizens of had fought an acrimonious bloody war only five years ago that witnessed the emergence of one as a sovereign country out of the shrinking body of the other. The two people were deadly enemies then, but the passage of time and the instinctive urge of expatriates of broad cultural and ethnic similarity to band together to cope better with the trials and tribulations of a different, sometimes hostile, environment acted as a centripetal force for them. The same instinct to present a large front to combat the bigger issues of living and trying to integrate in the overall society worked, and continue to work, even more strongly at a sub-cultural level. Then the Bangladeshis find greater ease in spending a lot of their time with, and living in proximity to, other Bangladeshis, the Pakistanis with their people, the Indians with theirs, and, so, Banglatown in Brick Lane, Bradford, South Hall, Birmingham are spread across England.

Khalid was aware of his flatmate's skirt-chasing activities. He was not one so inclined, but accepted Niaz's with good humour. He had a steady girlfriend, an English undergraduate student, who he planned to marry as soon as she graduated in a year's time. Khalid was religious without being dogmatic, was liberal in outlook, had many Indian friends, but was fiercely anti-Indian because of Kashmir. He preferred that Kashmir became an independent country, but, if that did not come about, then that the entire territory should become a part of Muslim Pakistan.

"You people became independent. Why shouldn't we?" He would ask for his friend's sympathy and approval for his conviction. He got those, but Niaz was more inclined to talk about women. Khalid was a good listener and was also a boisterous participant in the stories of his peccadilloes, but, after a time, he found that the stories had become a monotonous merry-go-round.

"Why don't you get married?"

"Why? I'm having too much fun!"

"Are you really? Then why do you keep saying that your parents are looking for a bride for you?"

"They may look."

"But you've never said you don't want them to look."

"Eventually I have to get married."

"Why don't you go to Dhaka and at least take a look at the girls your parents like?"

Thus was born the idea of the annual pilgrimage. Exactly at what point Niaz decided that he would only marry a Muslim girl of South Asian, preferably Bangladeshi, origin, he could not say — the idea probably grew on him — but it was not too long after he had become a Fellow of the Royal College of Surgeons. Then the significance of his Dhaka visits became more crucial.

"Why not marry a white?" Khalid asked when he heard the story of another failed mission. By this time he had become a Chartered Accountant, found a very good job, gotten married to his English girlfriend and moved into a good-sized apartment. Niaz visited them when he found time to get away from his busy surgical duties and latest amorous interest.

"I think I'll stick to our kind." What he did not say out of sensitivity to his friend was that he thought that whites did not make as good wives as South Asians, and he needed a good wife.

Niaz tried hard to find a Bangladeshi or a Pakistani expatriate. There was one he particularly wanted to marry. She was the daughter of a very rich Bangladeshi business tycoon who could afford to send her to study Economics at Oxford. And she was intelligent enough to first, gain admission to, and then, do well at, that venerable institution. She was not a striking beauty, but was pretty enough, and possessed all the other attributes that he was seeking in a suitable bride — expect one — but he overlooked that until explanation time arrived. By the time he met her he was forty-six, she was twenty-four and had recently graduated from the London School of Economics with a Master's degree. She had started work at a big multinational corporation in London. He was introduced to her at a party and decided, after a few more occasions of meeting her, that she was going to be the wife of his dreams. And he said so to his friends until one day they heard: "I'm not going to marry her. She's not of the right family."

"But you knew her background."

"I thought about that. Hers is just too inferior." He was referring to her father who started as a low-level official in the government food department. That is when he made his money by siphoning off from government-imported rice, wheat, sugar and other food items and selling them on the black market. In a few years he had made enough to resign from his low-status job and start a business enterprise that grew and grew and grew and catapulted him to the top rung of society. Now Niaz brought up his rags-to-riches via the stealing route factor and his humble family background of peasants and artisans.

The grapevine is a powerful, quite frequently devastating, tool in the life of Bangladeshis, whether at home or abroad. Inevitably, the young woman got to hear about Niaz's decision to reject her and the weighty reasons that went behind it.

"You must be joking!" she shot back at her informant. And told her a wholly different story. She did not even give him a consideration when he, boldly but gracefully, announced his intention. No, she did not find him repulsive and the age difference was not a factor; in fact, he was always courteous, although always a bit full of himself. She could not marry him simply because she was in love with someone else, a Moroccan, whom she was planning to wed. But she was angry about his reference to her family origin.

"Who does he think he is — a prince? Why doesn't he try marrying a princess? See if she'll have him!"

Niaz's friends believed her version when the story got back to them courtesy of the ubiquitous grapevine. Some did so purely out of spite for his timeless marriage attempts in between endless philandering. A few were jealous of his successful womanising and were glad to have someone shut him out. Others were aware of her affair with the Moroccan. And all were confirmed in their beliefs when, not long after her clarification and rage, she married her Moroccan.

"Well she had to get someone. She couldn't have me," was Niaz's philosophical explanation to the bearer of the news of her marriage. And got busy looking for the next suitable bride.

Niaz had everyone believe that he had rejected every prospective bride on grounds that she did not match up to his exacting standards. And everyone believed him because they thought he was insane. He could only be crazy to have set such demanding standards in the first place. That way, they reasoned, he would be rejecting almost anyone who came into his view. They started to believe that Niaz was not serious about marriage, that he was afraid of it, that he did not really know if he even wanted to get married, that, in fact, he would remain a bachelor till death. They were not sure, however, if he would at any time give up trying to end his bachelor status up until his demise. They began to suspect that he was playing a charade to feed his monumental ego in seeing prospective brides. That he was only letting them have the satisfaction of taking a look at the most eligible Bangladeshi bachelor and drool, that he was fooling with them if the opportunity so presented, that he had no intention of marrying any of them. They were wrong about his desire to tie the knot.

They were also mistaken in thinking that he did all the rejection. The Oxford and LSE alum placed that myth to rest. They resorted to a grapevine that stretched to Bangladesh to find out more and were pleased to discover that almost as many rejected him as he did them. Now, that was good. The bastard was not a universal pick there, after all. He needed to have that big balloon of an ego pricked. And they were going to do it, slowly, obliquely, in the devilish way they knew how. Some of the women let themselves be seen to please their parents and, having done filial duty, promptly rejected him. He was either too old, or too suave, or too full of himself, or had too much of a reputation as a playboy, or was a combination of all of those or some. Some had boyfriends they were not willing to give up; others, although unattached, were not inclined to an arranged marriage, and a few, who gave him a chance, eventually found him incompatible. Part of that irreconcilable variance stemmed from their different social outlooks. Niaz had just become too Western for their taste. He got to know about this determinant of his rejection, went back to London and announced: "She's too eastern for my taste."

"But that's what you're looking for."

"Yes, but she can't be that traditional. How can she cope with this society if she doesn't have a Western outlook?"

So Niaz spread his net wider in the United States and every corner of Great Britain, and added Canada, to find an Easterner with a Western mentality. And found rejection. Because the Western mentality of the Easterner born and brought up in those countries applied their values to turn him down. Particularly since they belonged to the community of expatriates with decent family background and wealth. Niaz would not compromise on his standards for a suitable bride, although he would once in a while bend them just a little. But there were not many with all those attributes in the Bangladeshi Diaspora, and they had the world to choose from. Or, at least a world of their own choosing.

In Britain he tried to branch out into Pakistanis and Indian Muslims. Here he had a smaller pool to look into because the women of those communities, while together presenting a much larger population than the Bangladeshis, had their own men to select from. Here, too, Niaz stood by his standards, although the crucial criterion of family background he had to accept on the say-so of his Pakistani and Indian friends. In one or two cases he was accepted, but a primordial instinct that goaded him to take up the challenge to marry a Bangladeshi made him retreat. And after he withdrew, he regretted his decision and could not figure out why he had taken it. And delved right into a fresh round of wife hunting. And the age differential between him and the prospective bride grew with each year. And the requirement that she be a Muslim grew stronger. Niaz did not drink, not because of any religious conviction, but he did not smoke either, and he abstained from both for reasons of maintaining a sound health. But, except for Eid and the occasional Friday midday prayers, he did not discharge any fundamental tenet of Islam either. Besides not being a devout Muslim, he was as secular as any person was. Yet, when it came to selecting a wife, he stipulated that she had to be a Muslim and, as the years progressed, pinned subtle degrees of devoutness to the religious attribute.

Then Niaz reached the age of fifty and celebrated it quietly with a few selected friends. He was in between girlfriends at the time. Soon after, he went to Bangladesh. This time he was determined to get married. He did not. More accurately, he could not. He had ignored the consequences of time moving relentlessly forward. Of course, there would be plentiful young women of his benchmark to assess. And, of course, there were. But not all for him. Most were not for him. He did get to see a very few though. All between the ages of nineteen and twenty-four. This time rejection all came from their side. Niaz made a quick exit for England.

A small party was going on at an imposing house in Dhaka not long after he had left. In attendance were his childhood friends who had made it big in Bangladesh and chose to remain there. The talk meandered around to Niaz's latest round of failure.

"Your friend is sick," thundered a woman to her husband and the other men in the room. "He saw a friend of my son. She's only nineteen! My son thinks he's a sick, dirty old man." She sounded and looked outraged. Her son had completed his freshman year at an American university and was home for his summer holidays. The girl was studying at another American university and she, too, was home for the holidays.

No one disagreed with her comments. A few tried to joke their way out of an uncomfortable atmosphere, but did not succeed.

Then, one of the men, who had studied with Niaz in high school, his face clearly showing worry, blurted aloud his private thoughts: "My God, I'm not giving him my daughter's address." His daughter was also nineteen and he had sent her to study engineering at a good university in London. She could do very well in that big city without a guardian uncle to look after her and show her around.

Niaz was back in England, getting over his despondency. The summer was making its seasonal swan song in resplendent glory. That made it difficult to keep up a mood of melancholy. Niaz was thinking that there were more and more Bangladeshi women going over to study in the U.S., Canada and Britain. And the number would be growing each year.

An Ilish Story[*]

Khademul Islam

It is December 1972 in Dhaka (then Dacca). A brilliant mid-morning on a back verandah in Rayer Bazaar. My mother and I are comfortably perched on old cane *moras* watching my maternal grandmother about to gut a fish. She is seated behind the dark, curved blade of an old *boti*, holding down its scarred, wooden stock with her right foot. The sharpened edge of the blade glints. A small, stained *pati* (reed mat) is spread beneath the *boti*. By her side, on the coarse red cement, is a small wicker basket. She is a small woman with a white, stiffly starched sari like a crackling cloud around her. I haven't seen her since I was a child. Our family, my parents, I, my brother and sister, had escaped from Karachi, from the old West Pakistan, to Dhaka, to the newly-risen state of Bangladesh barely a month back, and were staying with my *mama* (maternal uncle), till we could find our footing. I look up at the sky bordering the verandah roof, at the day glowing with the same liquid light in which we, five refugees lugging three suitcases, had crossed the Indo-Bangladesh border at Benapole. My grandmother had come down from Chittagong to visit with us, marvelling at her grandchildren's growth and clucking sympathetically at the stories of our flight from Pakistan.

"*Ilish mach*," (hilsa fish), she had informed me with a smile, holding the fish up in the air. From the Padma. "*Taja* (fresh)," she had added, pointing to a startlingly clear, protruding eye. And indeed, the sleek body, silvery as a sitar note, faintly bluish-green on its back, had winked in the vivid sunlight. It is a medium-sized *ilish* ("They're small in the wintertime"), the downward slant of its mouth and the angular line of its lower jaw giving it a vaguely determined air. I cannot remember the last time I had seen one. Born and raised in dry, dun-coloured, sprawling Karachi city, all this, fish, rivers, relatives, Dhaka's sudden swathes of green grass and toy-sized post offices, is new to me.

---

[*]Published in *Six Seasons Review 1:2* (2001).

My grandmother is talking about 1971. Every Bengali in 1972 talked about 1971, about the war, refugees and subsequent release from the daily horror.

"1971 was 1947 all over again," she says as she holds both ends of the fish with her hands and vigorously saws it back and forth across the blade. Fish scales fly in all directions and a few sizzle upward, float momentarily at the top of their arc, aquamarine and topaz spangles, before gliding down on the cement. In 1947, during the Partition, my grandparents had fled from Calcutta (now Kolkata) along with other Muslims. Whole *paras* (neighbourhoods) slaughtered in a day, my mother had said. Babies thrown over walls. Trembling adults and crying children fleeing pell-mell.

She then cuts off the small dorsal fin on the gray, denuded body, brusquely ripping through tough cartilage and tendon, leaving a thin scar, a bloodied line, on top. Then snips the smaller lower fins off, *tchk*, *tchk*, till the tiniest stubs are left.

"Down the road from our house," she continues with an upward glance at us, the irises of her eyes black as amulet string, "there was a Hindu household." Her hands are betel-nut brown, turmeric-stained, a working matriarch's hands, ceaselessly directing, ladling, tucking in, handing out the daily bazaar money, smoothing out, folding a *paan* leaf, picking.

She neatly fits the blade under the crescent moons of the gill covers and shears them off, exposing the glutinous, intricate balsa wood fretwork of bone, spotted with scarlet moss and lichen, that knits together fish head. The gills, serrated flaps laid on top of each other, are a distinct, flushed maroon.

"*Taja*," she says again and nods approvingly, the corona of sprung hairs around her head stirring with the motion. Behind her against the wall are two empty flowerpots and a red earthen bowl with drained rice starch for crisping her saris. Their shadows, peasant-dark doubles, are sharply etched on the peeling yellow limewash. A column of ants is marching up the sides and round the rim of the bowl.

"They were long-time residents of our *para*. We would allow them to use our big pond for bathing," she says, scraping away the last few small scales near the deeply Vee-d tail. Her words are in sync with her moving, working arms, spilling out, then halting, then spilling again.

"Well, you know, Chittagong is a conservative place, and our *maulvi* was a Peace Committee member." Peace Committees had been

Bengali groups, largely in the rural areas, fostered by the Pakistan army for propaganda and terror. She turns the fish upward and makes an incision just below its throat with the tip of the *boti*, a precise surgical cut, then gingerly draws out tiny fish sacs and glands, gray and yellow snot strung on liquid lines like a surreal *dhoba's* wash. The first flies appear.

She then grips the fish solidly with both hands, one clamped over the mouth and the other around its middle, and cuts its head off, the flesh on her upper arms jiggling with the effort. A snapping sound as the spine, after an initial resistance, gives way. Red specks spatter her spotless right knee. Ash-coloured threads, supple links to an external world of water and weeds, are visible inside the hollow stem. The mouth gapes, baring tiny teeth. She trims the head with casual, familiar flourishes and puts it in the basket.

"One night — well, it was two o'clock in the morning, we heard screaming and shouts of *narai takbir*," she continues, referring to the Muslim rallying cry during the 1947 communal riots.

She holds the *ilish* lengthwise along the blade, grasping it by the twin prows of its headless neck so that its back is towards her, and slices open the soft white underbelly with one single, fluid, upward motion. She then brings the fish closer to her and peers inside.

My mother, too, leans forward to look. "Eggs?" she asks.

"I don't see any," my grandmother replies. "They get eggs only during the *borsha* (rainy) season." My mother waves her hands to ward off the flies.

She pulls out the slithery guts from the marbled, moist cavity with practiced fingers. Dark strings coated with clotted blood. Out come micro bags and pouches, pearl and umbra, to be deposited on the mat. Her agile fingertips worry inside the gaping, boat-shaped abdominal hole, checking and rechecking for detritus. For life, wet, humid, mucous-laden.

"The next morning we heard that they had been attacked and killed," she says with another glance at us, pushing back rimless spectacles with the back of her right hand, careful to keep the fingers clear of the lenses. "They said the *maulvi* himself had slit their throats." Her voice ends on an accusing note.

"Who said?" asks my mother.

"Their immediate neighbours."

A silence, in which a breeze sighs through torn, dusty leaves. She deftly turns the fish over and under in her hands, scrutinising her handiwork. A painter surveying an almost finished canvas, assessing shades and tones. Then, slowly, almost dreamily, she slices the fish into proportionate, heart-shaped pieces, bullying only through the spine and translucent rib bones, and plops them into the basket. The tail lands right by the head. Teardrops of blood, instant rubies in the hot bright gush of sun, well up from the chunks of pale pink flesh. The *boti* blade, like her fingertips, is streaked with blood and slick traces of gummy matter. Fishy secretions, around which the flies happily buzz.

"Where's the *maulvi* now?" my mother asks.

"Oh, he's still walking around, hale and hearty."

She had used the word "*jobai*," the language of Qurbani Eid, the day of ritual sacrifice of animals that I have been steeped in since childhood. It specially means to slit the throat. In Urdu, in Pakistan, it is the sharper, metallic "*zaba*." On Eid day, scared, wild-eyed cows would have their hooves tied and brought crashing down on to cement courtyards or bruised grass, and then the *mullah* would step in with his *kalma* and his newly whetted knives. *Mullah's* hands, nails bitten to the quick, raised in supplication or stroking a beard, an index finger reverently running along a line in an open Qu'ran as if to underline its surging rhythms. Hands that ran orphanages, bathed the dead, performed marriages, went door to door on Qurbani Eid plying their trade.

The cow would draw air through its mouth in great heaving gasps only for it to vent noisily through the ripped, open gullet, dewlaps flapping, and as this noise would fill the air above our heads, we the children in our festive new Eid clothes (the littler girls spangled in flickering *zari* and silk hair ribbons) would stand in a circle and watch as arterial blood, red, viscid, slippery, would first spurt and then seep into the earth. Beneath Karachi's peerless, fabulously blue summer skies.

I look at my tingling palms, at my grandmother's cheeks, still smooth after all these ruffled decades, at the chipped tomato of my mother's toes. Bengali skin, tenderly being warmed by a saffron sun. Our flesh, the mysterious, particular, almost prim denseness of live tissue, its sinuous declivities, the cells and membrane stitched together, really, by faith and prayer.

What unmakes us, makes us.

Later at lunch, with sugary squares of siesta-time light streaming in through thin white curtains and my grandmother's hair still wet from

her bath, my *mama* notices that I am giving the fish curry a wide
berth.

"You're not eating the *ilish*?"

"Not today."

"Can't sort out the bones, eh?"

"No. I think I need more time."

A pause. Another round of rice and *ilish jhole* (curry broth) for
everybody except me.

"You're hardly eating at all."

"I'm not very hungry."

"So how do you like our Dhaka?"

"*Bhalo* (good). *Khub bhalo* (very good)."

Sunset

Razia Sultana Khan

The sky was a scream of blazing colour: red, purple, orange, yellow. Every time the sun set, a different combination went into play. No two skies were ever the same. Shathi looked down, overpowered by the beauty, and her glance caught the little black suitcase beside her.

Shathi was sitting in the little park a few blocks from her house near Ramna Thana in Dhaka. She had been excited when they had found the new apartment near the park. I'll be able to do my jogging here, she had thought. And the first couple of months she had faithfully kept to the routine. Shamrath had joined her in the beginning but gradually she had come alone. And now she perceived how alone she had been all along.

The bench that Shathi was sitting on faced a pond, and, in the light of the setting sun, it looked deep and mysterious. A flash caught her eyes as a tiny object flicked out from a spiral of waves and a gauzy dragonfly plummeted into the water. Soon the rings marking its grave blended into the whole. There was a stretch of lotus leaves with the tight petals hiding their vivid pink and magenta colours. They only bloomed for the morning sun and some mornings there was a riot of colour and she would wish she had her paintbrush and canvas and resolved to have it with her the very next time. Invariably she would forget again.

Once she had actually lugged her canvas and brushes to the site. It had taken a while to set up the whole thing and by the time she was ready she could no longer ignore the ring of people, mostly young girls and boys selling soft drinks and peanuts, surrounding her. Although they kept a respectable distance whispering among themselves so as not to disturb her, she had been too aware of them to get much painting done. That effort was sitting at home, tucked away unfinished, behind a bookshelf,

After her marriage Shathi had tried to keep up her one passion, painting, but their one-bed apartment did not allow for much space.

The bother of putting everything away after each session was too much. Then, one day, she had left her stuff in a corner of the living room meaning to work on it the next day, and, while Shamrath had not said anything, he had made a point of sitting outside on the balcony that evening. After that she made sure she put everything away before he arrived home.

Shathi had led a protected life but received a good education. Her parents had not worried about what she studied as long as she got a degree, hoping that would ensure a good marriage. And it had. Shamrath was a junior executive in a bank and expected to move up fast. He also had good looks and could be charming, and both her parents had fallen for that.

Shamrath was ten years older than Shathi, but that had not bothered her mother. Age did not matter with men — or so she believed. Her father, or *Baba* as she called him, had not been too pleased about the age difference but had to submit when her mother triumphantly pointed out the eleven-year difference between *their* ages. And they had been together now for twenty years? He was silenced in the face of such strong opposition, keeping the fact that he wanted a different life for his daughter to himself. So, at nineteen, Shathi had found herself a married woman.

Ma, Shathi's mother, had been sixteen when she had married, young by today's western standards but of the "right age" for Bangladeshi girls a couple of decades ago. Tall and slim, with a grace that caught people's eyes wherever she went, she was definitely a beauty. Her new husband saw the look in their eyes and imperceptibly squared his shoulders. Her girlish exuberance and bubbly nature fascinated him in the beginning but gradually wore him down. He had hoped she would grow out of it as she got older, and only years later did he realise that it was not her immaturity but her character that made her behave that way.

Ma's interest lay primarily in pretty clothes and jewellery, and she could spend hours shopping. As a child Shathi had accompanied her on numerous occasions because Ma never went shopping alone. Baba would invariably accompany her, but he was always in the periphery and not really in the picture.

"Keep an eye on him so he knows where we are," Ma would say, and Shathi had felt like a fulcrum keeping the two extensions together.

Once Ma was in a sari shop, her presence invaded everyone else's space. As soon as she was seated on the carpeted area or the low stools — depending on what the shop had — the senior salesperson would politely ask her what she desired. Ma would say a few incomprehensible magic words, and he would nod in perfect understanding and bow reverently, acknowledging the maestro. He would, in turn, whisper a few directions to his assistants while Ma nonchalantly made herself more comfortable. Her eyes would glow and she would give a sigh of contentment.

Most sari shops in Dhaka have an open carpeted space in front of their shelves on which to display saris. There would be a flurry of activity and excitement, and within seconds junior salesmen (they would all be men) would appear with packets of saris balanced between their hands. They would scatter them with expert abandon, and the saris would land in a perfect fan shape, a rainbow of colour.

There were silk saris and cotton ones, *jamdani* and the very fine muslin ones. The silk saris would range from the soft pure Mysore silk to the Rajshahi raw silk ones, from the gossamer-like ones that could be drawn through a ring (so they said) to the stiff, glassy ones that rustled when one walked. Ma's eyes would flick over them, and she would casually point to the ones that had caught her fancy. The senior salesman would unerringly pick those out of the lot and motion for the others to be taken away. Some he would set aside, having seen her eyes linger on them just a moment longer than the others. Those would be brought out later.

The senior salesman would motion to his assistants, and they would each delicately pick a chosen sari out of the pack, remove the transparent covering and swish the sari open of its folds. In a matter of seconds the sari, or at least half of it, would be draped around the live mannequin with the multiple creases fanning out in front and the *anchal* flowing behind, like a scarf. Ma's body language, a slight smile, a faint nod, or the half raised index finger, would mark her approval, and the senior salesman would smile and murmur something about her extreme good taste. The sari would be folded back into its original folds and set aside.

By this time another "model" would take the place of the previous one on the "stage." There was something incongruous in the very male, slim, dark model, with a five-o'clock fuzz further darkening the lower part of the face, one knee slightly turned in before the other to add curves to the flowing material, which Shathi found very appealing. She could have watched them for hours. Decked in brightly glamourous saris, their masculine features impassive, now turning one way, now the other to show the saris to their full advantage, they would have graced any catwalk. Shathi had laughed out loud the first time she had seen them, and Ma had been quite cross and flashed her an "I'll-deal-with-you-later" look.

Once in a while Ma would narrow her eyes and gaze at the sari with a far-off look. The salesman would turn to the model who would quietly fade away and another would appear. Once her choices had all been displayed, the ones that had been set aside as "maybes" would find their way on to the models and Ma would smile demurely, aware of and not at all unhappy at his manoeuvre.

Sometime during the display a boy would appear balancing a tray, with cups of coffee or bottles of cold refreshing drinks, and Ma would mutter a mild protest and then vaguely look around her. Her eyes would fall on Shathi. This was a signal for Shathi to go fetch her father. If she had done her job properly, he would be easily found and requested to come in and have a drink.

As soon as Baba entered, his eyes would instinctively go to the pile of saris at Ma's side. Ma would smile imploringly at him and yet there would be a glimmer of worry in her eyes. Baba's reaction normally depended on the size of the pile and sometimes he would forget the presence of the salesmen, and say, "You're not getting all of them, are you?" Ma would flush, and Shathi would turn away and look at something else.

The salesman would offer Abba coffee with the most perfunctory and servile bow and mention in passing how popular these saris were in India or how the last customer had bought a dozen of them in one sitting. At such times there seemed to be some kind of unspoken understanding between the salesman and Ma, and Shathi would feel she was watching an alien adult world quite outside her comprehension. After a few sips of the aromatic foaming coffee, Abba's frown would lighten, and Ma would release her breath slowly and again that look would pass between the salesman and her. All that remained after that was for Baba to pay for the saris. From this point onwards, Ma would detach herself from the whole financial incident and give her attention to Shathi. She would look at her daughter lovingly and ask her if she were bored and would like an ice cream or a chocolate and watch her face light up.

Abba had indulged his wife in the beginning but when he realised that she had little control when it came to buying saris, he tried to dissuade her, first gently, then quite sternly; but somewhere along the way he realised she had a way of getting what she wanted.

With the instinct born of innocence, Shathi, even as a child, had realised that when Ma opposed something it would not happen. Somehow this had made Baba more endearing despite the fact that Shathi had been conditioned to be afraid of her father. It had taken years, long years after her marriage, for that fear to evaporate and condense into love and respect. One incident she recalled fondly. She was a First Year student at the College of Fine Arts.

Baba was in the kitchen getting a cup of tea in the morning one day, as Shathi rushed in to get some breakfast on her way to study with a friend.

"No class today?" he asked mildly. Shathi never had time for breakfast and was usually up and out without anyone realising it.

"We have an exam. But that's later."

Baba looked at her for a moment, then left the kitchen with his cup of tea.

Shathi opened the fridge. The only edible thing seemed to be some leftover *chapatti* from last night. She took one out, put the *pitha*-making utensil on the gas cooker with some water and, sliding the thin *chappati* on top of the perforation, covered it with a lid. The steam would soften the bread and make it tender and edible. Although the *pitha* pot was meant to steam the dumpling-like rice cakes Bangladeshis were so fond of, it had a myriad other uses. Shathi had learnt one of them from a previous live-in domestic help they had.

During *Shab-e-barat*, the night of blessing, well-to-do Muslims distributed *halva* and *chapati* to whoever came to their door, hoping to get Allah's blessing for their one-day's charity. Their maid would join the hordes of half-naked children and beggar women to collect the food. Then she would dry all the bread she had collected — sometimes as many as sixty or seventy of them — on the balcony under the sun. The evenly toasted buff disks looked like rows of saucers — waiting. Every time Shathi passed them, she stopped to admire them. She wondered how their perfect circles had been achieved. Which mother, or wife, or daughter or daughter-in-law had sat there hour after hour, patiently making those perfect discs so that the rest of the family might get their share of blessing?

A couple of days was all it took for the moisture to be sucked out and for them to turn into hard little plates. The maid would then carefully pack them one on top of another, almost like a stack of paper plates, place them all in a jute sack, then take a week's leave and visit her family in the village to present them with this bounty.

"But how do you eat the hard things?" Shathi had asked curiously.

The maid had smiled affectionately at the young girl's ignorance and replied. "We steam a few for our meal each time. They become as tender as a baby's cheek."

Shathi tried it the very next day, and it did work.

Now, as Shathi waited for the bread to soften, wondering what else she could have, she peeped into the dining space. Abba sat slumped with his cup of tea in front of him. Probably cold by now. She wondered what he did, all alone in the mornings. Ma didn't get up till much later.

On a sudden impulse, Shathi said in a loud theatrical whisper, not wanting to wake Ma up, "The omelet is almost done, so don't leave the table." She opened the fridge to take out a couple of eggs.

"You'll be late," he started to say and then stopped.

Shathi sneaked another quick look. His slump looked a little more comfortable. He was going to wait.

Once the food was ready, Shathi skillfully manoeuvred the kitchen door with her back, while balancing the plate of hot onion omelet on one hand and the plate of steaming *chapati* on the other. She placed the platters on the table and went to get a glass of water. Ma was very particular about always having a glass of water ready with the food. When Shathi returned with the water, she saw that he had cut the omelet into bite-size pieces with a spoon and was tearing out a piece of the hot bread with his right hand. He folded the egg into the bread and popped the large bundle into his mouth. Shathi bit off the words "Wait, it's hot!" He was the older one. He should know. Hadn't t he said that to her often enough? "Wait for the food to cool. It's not going to run away."

His face squirmed with the intensity of the temperature. Probably the taste too. Had she forgotten the salt, or put in too much green chilli? She sat down cautiously on the edge of the chair. He moved the food around in his mouth, cooling it with his breath, as it floated inside, and then swallowed it. He didn't speak. He was ready with the next large mouthful before this one was down. And he had been leaving with only a cup of tea! Almost choking, he reached for the water. That's why Ma always said. "Have a glass of water ready, whenever you're eating."

Shathi watched her father with mixed feelings. At this moment he was a far cry from the fearful person whose one piercing look used to make her squirm. She took in his thin, angular face. Very, very different from that young rotund face that smiled back in the big monochrome picture hanging on the wall of the bedroom. The dark-haired man looking back at the world from behind square, black-rimmed plastic glasses had confidence, and the camera had captured the slight smile which reflected that. Next to it was another picture of a beautiful, shy girl demurely looking at the camera. Who were these people? When had they changed?

Shathi sat opposite her father, quietly watching him as he ate. A blob of egg stuck to the left side of his chin, a line of shiny oil showing its path of descent. Patches of unshaven hair on his chin stood out where he had missed. Maybe he needed a new razor. She wondered vaguely who bought his razors. In the morning light the harsh lines on his sunken face stood out. Baba bent his head, trying to catch a piece of onion escaping from the omelet in his mouth, and she noticed the shine on his head where the thinning hair, carefully combed back, had parted. Some awareness made him look up at that moment and their eyes met. Shathi looked away guiltily but not before she took in — out of the corner of her eye — how his hand went up to try to coax the straying strands into place. A wave of tenderness shot through her and she mumbled, "I'll get you some hot tea," as she turned to slip into the kitchen. Her hands itched to smooth the shiny spot and her heart said, "It's ok, Baba. It's ok to lose hair. It happens to everyone."

"No," he said, stopping her. "Wait. I want to talk to you. We never seem to have time nowadays."

Shathi sat down tentatively, as he hesitated. Her childhood fear surfaced. What had she done now? Her movements of the last few days scrolled through her mind, while she waited for him to continue. He turned to check the bedroom door — the one that opened into the living room — and something in his demeanour told her that Ma was up. Shathi pretended to be engrossed in her cup of tea, but Ma's eyes must have taken in the remnants of the omelet and bread, because she said sweetly as she passed on her way to the kitchen. "How nice; father and daughter having a cozy chat." Shathi realised, they probably did look like two guilty children — why guilty? And "don't let me stop you. I was just wondering who had come so early in the morning."

Shathi stole a look at her watch, "I'd better go. I'll be late." Her stay would only worsen the situation and cause him more embarrassment than support.

Used to working ten hours a day, Baba's recent retirement had come as rather a shock. He had lost the only space he had. The chores that had occupied his weekends expanded to engulf the remaining days. Shathi had thought he enjoyed doing those little chores: polishing the brass table lamps and the endless lines of statuettes and figurines, until one day she overheard him say, with a look of fatigue and disillusion, "Isn't there an end to all this stuff?" He was then polishing the set of silver crockery which they had probably never used in their lives. By that time he had become shrivelled, a physical realisation of a state of mind. He had also lost interest in most things. The only pleasure that remained seemed to be his daughter's visits, but Shathi was too involved in her new life and only had time to pay cursory visits. She wished... but now it was too late.

During the week that he was in hospital she had left everything to be at his side, but he had been unaware of what was happening around him. The doctors said he was suffering from neglect.

•   •   •

Ma always dressed up at home. Shathi's friends sometimes remarked on that, albeit a little enviously: "Shathi's mother is always 'at home.' She never has to dress for visitors no matter when you go." Shathi's mother took it as a compliment, smiled and let it pass. She liked looking after herself but there was another reason as well. A compulsion to always look her best. She had inherited this from *her* mother, Shathi's *Nani*.

Nani had been thirty-five when, after fifteen years of being "happily married," she had a bad miscarriage and been quite ill. After spending two weeks in bed, she had been rudely brought to her senses by her husband telling her that he was thinking of marrying a second time. So she would have someone to look after her, he had hastened to add.

"Of course, you would be the senior wife and be in charge of everything," he had further consoled her. It was Bakul, the young live-in maid.

Nani had dragged herself out of bed the following day and gone to her mother's house with the two youngest children, one and a half and three. Her mother had consulted with Nani's father and they had sent her back. Now was not the time to leave him alone; she was just creating a vacuum. She had been forced to swallow her pride and come back, unbidden.

Those had been difficult times. She had gone to one *pir* after another. One gave twisted paper packets of "blessed sugar grains," which she was told to put in the *pan* which he was so fond of having after his meal. Another gave her a *tabeez* which she had to hide in the cotton of his pillow. And all this time she had prayed. How she had prayed!

Something must have worked for one day, about a month later, Nani went into the kitchen to find the maid gone. Also gone were four of Nani's best saris. Things had slowly gone back to "normal" but Nani had learnt her lesson and made sure her daughter did not have to learn the same lesson.

Shathi had heard all this long after her own marriage and had finally understood why Nani always took such good care of herself and dressed so well, even at home. By the time Shathi's grandfather had died, it had become a habit.

In the beginning Shathi's own marriage had seemed to work. Delighting in their physical discoveries of each other, they had only added up the plusses. Young, avid and naïve, she had given everything to the marriage and expected as much in return. She had accompanied him to the houses of his relatives and friends. But she had gone alone to hers. Shamrath enjoyed gambling. Only he didn't call it that — playing cards is what he did. Every Friday evening found her alone at home while he went with his buddies to play. Sometimes, if it was a family gathering, he would take her. She had been happy to accompany him and learnt to play the different games: gin, rummy and even poker and all the others that she couldn't even recall now. She thought of the hours and hours spent sitting in the group dealing the same cards; no conversation except what was in relation to the game. So repetitive, so meaningless.

She *had* tried to adjust — and adjust some more. What else was there to do? Good Muslim women in Bangladesh got married and stayed married. She couldn't very well blame him. He had remained the same. It was she who had changed: from a naïve shy girl, conditioned to be non-assertive, to one sensitive to her likes and dislikes as well as to her rights. But she had tried, and the last ten years were a witness to that. And things would probably have continued in that state had not ....

No, it had not been another man. Actually it had taken very little. Just like it takes very little for a full-blown rose to disintegrate or a ripe fruit to drop. In the end it had taken — very little.

It was Friday and she was expecting guests for lunch: a few of his friends who had recently arrived from the States. Shamrath casually told her the night before that there would be eight of them and to cook something nice. The next morning was warm and humid. Feeling depressed at the thought of spending the whole morning in the stuffy hot kitchen, she had come to a quick decision. She would get some *biryani* from Hajibaba's. As anyone in Dhaka knows, Hajibaba's makes the best *biryani* in town. Its secret seemed to be in always having a short supply. They would start selling at 12:30 and by 1:30 the bottom of the huge copper pots would be visible.

Shathi often got meals from there because cooking, which had never really excited her, now seemed very tiresome indeed. Yet it was something that had to be done. She would have been happy enough with a sandwich or some fruit but he needed a regular meal for lunch as well as for dinner. Rice and lentil soup and some sort of a curry: fish or chicken or beef. As regular as clockwork. The only variety allowed would be *polao* or *biryani*. So once in a while she would take the long ride of almost 30 minutes — more, if the traffic was bad — from Ramna to Hajibaba's in Old Town

On that fateful day she'd gone to pick up the packets of *biryani*. She had timed herself well but the ever-increasing traffic of Dhaka had been more daunting than usual and it was well after 12:30 when she reached Hajji's, hot and sweaty.

One of the waiters saw her worried look and came towards her with a smiling face. "What would Aunty like?"

Shathi was taken aback. It was customary in Asian culture to refer to other women as "Sister" or "Aunty." But people usually referred to her as "Sister." To have suddenly graduated from that to "Aunty" upset her. She looked at him directly, and an innocent pair of bright eyes met hers unflinchingly while he waited to serve her.

Putting her chagrin aside, she said: "I'd like ten packets, please."

He was gone before she had finished her words. She looked around as she waited. The basic wooden tables lining the aisles leading to the kitchens were mostly taken. There were all sorts. The wealthy, dressed in their white *pajama* and *kurta* or jeans and T-shirts and the not-so-wealthy in their *lungi* and *ganjee*. The only thing they had in common was that they were all men. It was amazing that even in something as basic as eating, women were left behind. She instinctively looked further on, where a cloth partition divided the "family quarters" from the rest. But today the curtains were drawn and the seats occupied by men. It was Friday.

"Here you are, Aunty." Bright Eyes was back and he had called her "Aunty" again. She let it pass, noticing the inquisitive eyes of mostly everyone else in the place on her, and paid the cashier for the food. Now to get a rickshaw and head back home. No empty rickshaw came to her rescue, however, and she looked, irritated, at the cars parked along the lane. They should have been able to buy a car in ten years, but no, they never seemed to have any money saved. If only he would stop gambling .... But then he didn't gamble. He played cards.

Then, she saw a rickshaw with the driver casually lounging in the seat.

"How much to go to Ramna Thana?"

The rickshaw driver's eyes lazily swept the street, from one end to the other. As her eyes followed his, she saw, to her chagrin, that not *one* empty rickshaw could be seen. Satisfied that she had also noticed, he casually offered, "Twenty taka." This was twice what she would normally pay and Shathi felt her temper rise; but, weighted down by the packets and with the rivulets of sweat pouring down her temples, she acknowledged his advantage and gave in.

Balancing the packets on the seat of the rickshaw, she awkwardly hopped into the empty space. As the rickshaw moved forward, she adjusted the packets in the space beside her. The dry leaves made a reassuring rustling sound. She liked the way Hajibaba's packed the food in dry-leaf semi-spheres. The leaves, about half the size of a girl's palm, all seemed identical. The crisp brown leaves were placed one on top of another and caught with bits of twigs. The thought of young boys or girls sitting indoors hour after hour dovetailing the leaves into each other fascinated her. She hoped there were girls too — there were so few jobs which they were allowed to do. And this was not really a job. She would have quite liked doing something like this, something artistic. Even thirty years ago, these leaf parcels had been very common in Bangladesh, for packing food for take-aways. But now — all you got were polythene packets. Hajibaba's was probably the only restaurant in Dhaka which still had these leaf packets.

As the rickshaw weaved its way through the traffic she allowed her thoughts to ramble again. Perhaps if they'd had children .... She grabbed the packets as, with a jolt, the rickshaw hit the one in front and came to a stop. She tensed for the jolt from the back as the one behind them hit them. Why could they never stop before hitting each other instead of after?

She craned forward to see where they were. Loud music could be heard competing with each other from different restaurants. The rickshaws were all huddled up in an unruly mass at the Chawk, the centre of Old Town. In the cacophony Shathi tuned in to the melodious voice of Farida Parveen — a line from an old song.

The rickshaw moved on and the voice faded, but she was back in her childhood — her father was singing the song to her mother. She must have been about four or five but that picture had stayed. Tall and handsome with a shock of black hair; and her beautiful mother, blushing and laughing, pretending to evade his embrace. They had laughed quite a lot then. When had the laughter stopped?

She tried to shut out the picture. His death six years ago was still too recent. Thinking of him unsettled her — it was too close. Why had things gone so wrong for him? For a moment she saw herself in his place — the same meaningless existence.

The party was a success. The guests enjoyed the *biryani* but were appalled that she had gone and gotten it herself. "You should have sent the driver," someone said. If her movements were a bit automated no one noticed or mentioned it.

He was in the living room, smoking, when she came out with the black suitcase. "I'm leaving," she said.

His cold, puzzled eyes followed her. They seemed to say, "Where will you go? Where *can* you go?" But he was silent as he deliberately put out his cigarette end in the already overflowing ashtray.

She turned around and left the house, knowing that no matter what, she would not return.

So now Shathi sat in the little park where she had planned to go jogging. The sun had vanished but the glow was there. She breathed in deeply as if to absorb the muted colours and watched the glow darken and the warmth of the embracing wind cool. She glanced at the black suitcase beside her. Had she remembered to pack something warm?

Men, Women and Lovers

Syed Badrul Ahsan

In the cold haze of dawn, Firoz was not quite ready to begin the day. Besides, he was not supposed to begin anything. It was the weekend, a time he needed to be with Fati. Firoz always looked forward to the weekends. The difference between him and other men was that while all those others chose to be with their spouses and children, he made it a point to slip away from home and go looking for Fati. He knew he was committing adultery. What sane man, he often asked himself, would desert his wife once a week to be with his mistress? That was the way he looked at himself. In the early days of his marriage — and Firoz did not quite remember if he had been married twenty or twenty five years — he surprised himself by the alacrity with which he went to other women. He was afraid every time he held in his arms a woman not his wife. The fear sometimes turned into trepidation when he remembered, even as he pressed his flesh against the woman he was with, that she was someone else's wife. But in all this time, the surprise and the fear had all given way to a sense that such were the ways of the world. He had been an adulterer for as long as he could recall. What made the feeling of guilt less pronounced in him, assuming of course that he did indeed feel guilty, was his knowing that the woman he was with at a given time was doing precisely the same. She too was an adulterer. He gave his head a quick shake at this slip up in grammar. No, his women were adulteresses. That was how he corrected himself.

He heard the rustle of paper nearby and almost instantly stretched out his left hand to touch Fati. He ended up touching the empty space that was the other half of the bed. Fati was not there. He was not surprised. It had always been this way. After a long night of passion, it was always Fati who awoke first and started the day off. This morning it was like any other. She was seated at the table by the window, already busy scribbling away. Firoz watched her out of the corner of his eye. The pale sun cast a whitish screen on her ebony skin. It reminded Firoz of all the tales of pharoahs and their queens he had read about. In his consciousness, it had regularly been an image of Nefertiti that he associated with Fati. No, Fati was not an Egyptian. So what? She was a Somali who had never dreamed in her life of ever making her way to a place like London and becoming something of a writer. Firoz sometimes thought that a long strand of pain lay hidden in her. In her screams of ecstasy, there was something of escapism. Was that scream similar to the fearsome howls Fati had let out when the local militia commander in Mogadishu raped her at gunpoint one night when mobs went about stripping homes of goods and women of clothes? No pain can be more consuming than a loss of country. It was something Fati had told Firoz on the day they first had coffee together on High Street Kensington. She spoke that day about the savagery she had gone through. Her infant child had been snatched from her and sliced in two with a machete wielded by a child soldier. Her husband, a journalist, had been forced to run all through the town centre by the gunmen of the warlord Farah Aidid. When he finally collapsed, sweaty and dusty, he begged for life. It did him no good. The goons simply hacked him into pieces. "He was a rather good journalist, you know", Fati often told Firoz as he sat sipping tea one morning in her kitchen. He understood. But what did he understand, really?

Fati's voice pulled him back from his reverie. "Slept well?" He knew he had to be grateful to this woman for all the good she was doing for him and to him. Men like Firoz were never content with what life had on offer for them. He knew he would ditch her someday, as soon as another woman took his fancy. That was something about him, some sense of raw power that drew women to him, a facet of personality that often left him mesmerised at his own ability to do such wonders. He had always liked his mistresses, though not all those women were happy to be called by such demeaning terms. It was Fati who had once told him, as they walked past the tube station at Kentish Town, that she was his lover. Anything less than that, she said with a smile rooted in fierceness, would mean a swift end to the relationship. Firoz had not responded. If there was a response, it was that sheepish, helpless grin that spread across his face as she said those words to him. Deep down, though, he knew Fati was like the others, a mistress. As for lovers, Firoz did not have time for them. More pertinent was this feeling in him that a married man could not morally or ethically have a lover, that indeed that there was a point in life when men and women could fall in love and damn the world beyond theirs. That kind of love, he made a quick mathematical calculation, came to people in their twenties and thirties. Firoz counted the years since he had been born. This morning, watching Fati at her writing, he smiled at the thought that he was fifty-two. Fati was thirty-five.

Outside the window, the grey morning turned greyer with the rain beginning to knife through the air. The pale sun was no more on Fati's face.

Sujata was not in much of a mood to get out of bed that morning. For some strange reason, the prospect of reading the Saturday issue of *The Guardian* did not much energise her. For years she had been reading *The Guardian*, or more precisely its weekend magazine section. Narrow it down still further. It was actually the book review section that Sujata loved going through. It was her feeling that book reviews gave her an opportunity to understand the works without having to spend money on buying them and then reading them. That was opportunism, a crass kind of it. Sujata knew it as well as anyone else. But her reasoning was simple. Once she had read a review, she saw little reason to read the book it dealt with. As she once told her son, a young man who periodically seemed to make bizarre connections between poetry and physics (he was always explaining the one in terms of the other), she knew that reading a book after she had read a review of it would inevitably create a kind of prejudice in her, to say nothing of the superfluity it would entail. Why ruin her own sensibilities like that? Her son had tried to argue back, but stopped when he looked into her eyes. They had a way of suddenly shutting out people, of telling them they should drop the subject because Sujata was not willing to talk about it any more.

But this morning it was her backache that kept her pinned to her bed. Fortunately, the day being Saturday, she would not need to go to work at the Indian retailers she had been employed with for so many years. A long time ago, when she first came by the job, Firoz had remonstrated with her. "Am I not here to provide for the family?" He had asked, in something of anger and pain. He clearly loved her. That much was certain. She had not answered his question, one reason being that she had already answered it quite a few times. She needed to do some work. She could not mutate into a housewife like everyone else she knew from the wider South Asian community. She kept teasing him with that Hillary Clinton remark about staying home and baking cookies. And every time she did that, Firoz had walked out of the room in a huff.

The bastard. Sujata muttered, almost wanting to scream out the expletive. Or was it an expletive? She knew she had used far stronger terms about her husband when she first became aware of his wayward behaviour. Once, when he came back to London after a trip to Dhaka, she asked him, without so much as batting an eyelid, how many times he had f....d Mira, the friend she had once introduced to him and who had then become her husband's lover. Firoz had been shocked at the vehemence of her question and yet he had not been able to muster the courage to protest. He knew as well as Sujata that he had indeed been to Bangladesh to see Mira. He had spent good time, quality and quantity wise, with her. This morning, as the backache seemed to go all the way up from her hips to the nape of her neck, Sujata muttered, louder than before, "Bastard". This time, though, she was not being abusive of her husband in relation to Mira. She simply missed him. Every time she had a backache, she missed Firoz. He knew nothing about dealing with back pain, but he would find in Sujata's predicament an excuse to rub oil on her back, run his hands up and down her as she lay on her stomach, and then find the means of going all the way down to her posterior and the entire length of her legs. Sujata had always had a plump figure and Firoz loved it. It was the legs he marvelled at. He found them seductive as much as he spotted the baby-like in them. Massaging Sujata then turned into a gentle, insistent message from him: he needed to play games with Sujata the woman, with Sujata the baby. She kicked his hands away as soon as she felt them insinuating their way to the hollows of her thighs. And she turned, her back now on the bed. Just as she began to tell herself that she had stopped Firoz's depredations, stopped him in his tracks, she found herself the victim of a new onslaught. He dropped his whole weight on her and had his mouth lock itself into a long kiss with hers. She struggled to get out of it for a few long seconds. Then something strange happened. She kissed him back. And right there in the middle of a dismally steamy afternoon, they made love and remembered the first time they did it, at Firoz's friend's place on Elephant Road in distant Dhaka. At the time, Sujata and Firoz had little plan to marry.

A tentative smile came over Sujata as she remembered it all. On a visit to Calcutta in the early 1980s, she spent a whole day on College

Street looking for a book Firoz had told her about. No, he had not asked her to go looking for it. But she loved him, loved the way he talked and delivered all those lines from Shakespeare. The first time they had met, she thought he looked a bit like Woody Allen. And he had found her unusually intelligent and, more to the point, forthright about her opinions, on everything. And he liked the buxom side of her, though he tried to keep his gaze fixed on her face. He was beginning to fancy that body, the riotous movement of her breasts as she walked by. She knew he was watching. And every time she walked in that jaunty, almost western manner, he went home and composed poetry on her. On College Street, she stared through the questions of the booksellers as she remembered all that. It had been springtime in her life and Firoz's. They had become lovers, had got drenched in the monsoon rain on Dhaka streets and had furtive dinners at corner tables in the Chinese restaurants, playing footsie all the time.

Sujata had come back from Calcutta with Kuldip Nayar's *Distant Neighbours: A Tale of the Subcontinent* for Firoz. He was thrilled and went around telling everyone in town what a great woman Sujata was. And Sujata knew she had never been loved this way before. She had had boyfriends before, but Firoz was the only man she had known who took any interest in books. They had the money; he had the brains. She needed both those amenities, as she called them, in life. But since the possibility of a combination of the two did not appear likely or even feasible, she settled for brains. The brains, at one point, walked out on her, at least on the weekends. The weakness of the flesh in him had yanked him away to the darker regions of desire.

A soft knock on the door signalled the end of Sujata's recollections of life's more charming phases. It was her daughter, eighteen-year old Urmi asking her if she could come in. "Just a minute", said Sujata, as she tried to pull the blanket up to her neck. Her children had never seen her naked. She would keep things that way.

Fati made her way out of the station and waited to cross the road. It was raining somewhat and she had no umbrella with her. She had never used an umbrella. An umbrella, she had convinced herself, was a typical British way of handling the weather and looked good on the English. She was not English, she told herself. It was one way of saying that she suffered from no pretensions that came through people of other communities trying to adopt English customs even if they did not go with their mannerisms and language. There was another reason why Fati did not use an umbrella. She loved the feel of rain on her smooth, jet-black skin. The rain had a way, almost lyrical, of streaming down her cheeks, along the corners of her mouth, before making its way to her long neck. And what a neck it was! Fati remembered she had once been told by her first lover in London, a huge hulk of an Englishman who looked like a wrestler but was really a college lecturer, that if she had not been Somali he would have taken her for a Tutsi.

"Ah, Tutsi", Fati had said then, almost in a whisper. As the Englishman watched her, somewhat in the manner of a predator (he was, if not holding her in the middle of the night, forever devouring her with his stares), Fati told him, half-seriously, "Do you realise, Bryan, that you have just made a connection between two brutalised civilisations?" Bryan was too dense to get the meaning. She waved away the thought of explaining it all to him. It would be a waste of time anyway. At the back of her mind, though, she tried juxtaposing the levels of battering that the Tutsis of Rwanda and her own Somalis had gone through. Suddenly, she did not know if she was a Somali or a Tutsi. Maybe she was both. Perhaps she was neither. She could not be a Tutsi because Rwanda was not her country. And Somalia? It had died from self-inflicted wounds a long time ago. She sighed, as the traffic lights turned green. She went over to the other side and began walking briskly towards Gower Street. That was where Waterstone's was and this being her day off work, she would go looking for some paperbacks to buy. As the drizzle and the wind blew through her hair, she felt a certain tinge of freedom. Firoz the lover from Bangladesh was not with her. For once, she was happy, nearly ecstatic, not to be with him in her room trying out all the varieties of *Kama Sutra* he had been teaching her on the weekends. She marvelled at Firoz's animal sexuality. Age was not holding him back at all. But all that womanising had really come in the way of his scholarly life. He hardly ever talked of books any more. Fati felt a slight pang of sadness. If that was the way their affair went on, Fati saw little hope for the future. Or could it be that she was really not interested in being in love with Firoz any more? She had little time to dwell on the answer, for she was already inside Waterstone's. She made for the periodicals section first.

Urmi went through her regular pattern of buying at Walthamstow. It was a weekend market she had been coming to for years together, since that first time when her parents had brought her here in a pram. She was now eighteen, felt twenty-eight and wished she could be free of it all. She knew her father had acted in lowly fashion toward her mother. He had let all those other women come in the way of the family that should have been there. But he had been good to her, to her brother. Which may have been a reason why she had not been able to condemn him the way everyone else did. Of course he had sinned. Of course he had shamed all of them before their own kind. Firoz, she knew, had made himself an outcast before the Bengali community in London. But he was a good man nevertheless. His heart was in the right place, wasn't it?

In the right place? Urmi shuddered. What was wrong with her? If her father had his heart in the right place, what about her mother? These were the thoughts she played with as she entered the butcher's. It was full of Pakistanis, a second generation that had found life's plenty in that butcher shop in Walthamstow. The youngest among them, of Urmi's age, brightened up as he saw her step into the shop. "What will it be today, memsahib?" He asked her. With a flourish of his right hand he pointed, all at the same time, to ribs, thighs, brains, liver, indeed everything. Urmi smiled. The effusiveness of these men in the meat shop always overwhelmed her. Today, through the image of that hand in a flourish and through her quiet smile, she could not help wondering about the war her father had waged long ago against the fathers of these cheerful, busy young men. Bengalis against Pakistanis, she nearly said it out loud. And yet she and these young men, it suddenly struck her, had never talked of that war. Was it because it was forgotten history? But how could it be forgotten if her father recalled it at almost every point of his life? Then what was it — a distance in geography, with Pakistan and Bangladesh nestling in their own troubles somewhere far away from these young who had come of age in a country they now called their own?

Urmi walked over to the ribs corner. The Pakistani young man, in parallel motion, accompanied her. Other buyers were coming in and Urmi could steal snatches of quite a few languages. Pidgin English, Punjabi-flavoured Urdu and Sylheti Bengali were the ones she could decipher.

Sujata sipped tea downstairs as she struggled to weigh the options of which of the two *Guardian* book reviews, one on a work of fiction and

another dealing with a new biography, she ought to be reading first.
The backache had eased somewhat and yet could come back without
warning.

Unknown to Sujata, Firoz had got down from the tube at Covent
Garden, to do nothing in particular. He felt lonely. And he missed her.
Strangely enough, he did not miss his Somali lover at all. For her part,
Fati at that moment was thoroughly immersed in a piece by Boris
Johnson in her Waterstone's corner. She chuckled at the man's witticisms.
How can a man who is young, who is a journalist, politician, husband
and father of five all rolled into one, have so much humour stored up
inside him? Fati wondered. She did not want to think of her murdered
baby in goon-infested Somalia.

And Urmi? She had just fallen in love, in that Pakistani meat shop.
The young man with the flourish had given her the message in the deft
way he had willed his fingers to brush her hand as he held out the
packet of ribs. The fingers smelled of beef. Her hand smelled of beef.
But she was happy. She hugged herself, closing her eyes as she did so.
An elderly English couple smiled at her in benign fashion when she
came to.

Revelation

Farhana Haque Rahman

"**B**eware the jinn, Nitu, for they are everywhere."

"Jinn? What are they, Bua?"

They were sitting in the kitchen, watching Ansar Chacha, the cook, slice up onions and peppers for dinner, which was going to be *bhoona gosht* or maybe chicken curry, her almost absolute favourite. Her absolute favourite though, would be, she hoped, coming as soon as the night guard Torab Ali returned from the *mundir dokan*, the open stall just down the street, made mostly from flattened tin cans, where the thin brown man in colourful shirt and *lungi* sold all kinds of forbidden delicacies. He would be bringing Bua some *paan*, ground betel nuts and lime wrapped in a betel leaf, which she would pound to a pulp in a bamboo cylinder and suck rather than chew, since she only had four teeth. Even though Fatima Begum was born in a small village in Laksham and not Dhaka, Bua knew just everything about everything because to Nitu she was at least a hundred years old.

"Haven't you been listening? I told you: jinn are everywhere. Some of them are nice, but most of them are up to mischief — or worse. Ansar Chacha, I have told you a hundred times that the *shahib* likes them chopped very small."

Nodding, the cook reached for another onion and continued chopping.

"A little girl must always be on her guard."

"What do they do, Bua?" Nishat squirmed in anticipation, for Bua's stories were always interesting, a lot more interesting than the ones Miss Twiddle made them read in second grade. She didn't like Miss Twiddle, a mean English lady who looked like the stump of an old banyan tree and often made the girls cry — sometimes even the boys. But Nishat loved Bua, who although she rarely smiled — maybe because she had only four teeth — often would protect her from Mother's wrath and would sometimes, when Mother was not at home,

---

* Revelation was earlier published in the *New Age* Eid special 2003.

allow her to have a *dal puri* from the *mundir dokan*, the deep fried puffed bread stuffed with lentils, especially delicious because forbidden.

"It depends, Nitu. If they like you, if you're good and do everything Allah and your parents tell you to, they protect you. Remember the story I told you about the man in my village whose house was saved in that terrible flood? Well, it was just because a good jinn was watching over him. Ansar Chacha, how often must I tell you not to put so much chillies in the *dal*?You will be in trouble with Begum Shahib and I will be in trouble too."

"So they protect you?" Gazing at Bua, Nishat wondered if perhaps Bua was a jinn.

"Some do, most do not." Bua leaned across the table, eyes intent. "Listen to me, Nitu. Do you see those big trees out there in the garden?"

"Yes." Nishat looked out the window.

"What do you see?"

"All those beautiful birds and chattering monkeys, and that peacock, his feathers up like a fan, chasing a female peacock." She had always wondered why the male peacock had such bright colours, while the female one was so plain; not like real people, the women are always resplendent in gorgeous saris.

"And up high in the trees?"

"Well, just lots of branches and leaves."

"And in the leaves?"

"Just leaves." Her tummy was starting to rumble: would a *dal puri* be coming soon?

"Listen, let me tell you, Nitu, there are more than leaves up there. There are jinn — terrible, horrible jinn — that are crouched there waiting for a young girl foolish enough to walk underneath alone."

"Waiting for what?" She felt a cold shiver go down her spine.

"For a foolish little girl, of course. And when she walks below them, they reach down with their long arms and great big claws, grab her hair and snatch her up. And that is the end of her!"

"Oh Ma! How scary!" After a moment's hesitation, she asked: "Is that why I have my hair cut so short, so that the jinn can't grab it?"

"You are bright, Nitu, and will be beautiful too if you listen to me. When you are older, your hair will be allowed to grow long and thick."

"Then the jinn won't grab me?"

"Not a jinn but a man. I pray for a fair, handsome man who wants you for his wife. But until then, don't walk under those trees. There,

there, Torab Mia is here. A bit of *paan* for me and look, a *dal puri*. Do you think that might be for you?"

"Bua, I think that you are the most wonderful person in the whole world! Hmm, it's delicious, as always." She looked up. "The jinn, the nasty ones, do they grab little boys too?" There were times when she wouldn't mind at all if one grabbed her four-year-old brother; he could be such a pest, especially after a hair cut when he would have a temper tantrum and demand that Bua somehow fixed back every strand of his hair!

"No, just foolish little girls."

"Oh." She took another bite of the *dal puri*, a small bite so that it would last longer. "They're just up in the trees?"

"Oh, no. Didn't I tell you that they are everywhere?" Bua had sucked and chewed the *paan* until it was almost gone. "There are some that look just like people but have their feet on backwards."

"On backwards? That must look very silly." Nishat giggled.

"They are nothing to laugh at, Nitu. They drive people mad."

"How do they do that?" Nishat shuddered.

"They stare into your eyes and turn your brains inside out."

"Oh." Nishat glanced at Ansar Chacha, relieved to see that his feet were pointed in the right direction. "Why do they do that?"

"Who knows why jinn do anything. They just do it. Now run along and brush your teeth so that your mother won't smell what you have been eating."

"It was really, really good!" Giving Bua a quick hug, Nishat hurried to the bathroom, where she gazed at herself in the mirror as she brushed and re-brushed her teeth, wondering if Mother would ever let her hair grow out. Wondering, too, why the jinn in the trees only snatched little girls. Maybe because they were more precious than little boys? She would have to remember to ask Bua. She rinsed off her toothbrush and was about to go to her room to read "Goldilocks and the Seven Dwarfs" for the tenth time, when she heard a commotion in the direction of the kitchen and rushed to see what the trouble was. Bua, Ansar Chacha and the rest of the servants were gathered there, peering out of the door into the garden and talking excitedly. Approaching Bua, who was standing to one side shaking her head and looking wise, she tugged at her sari. "What's happening?"

"No, no, no. This is not for you, Nitu. Now run off to your room and think about how fortunate you are."

"Please, please, tell me." Releasing her hold, she started to wiggle through the crowd by the door, but a firm hand on her arm stopped her.

"No, you don't. You stay right here!"

"But I want to see!" She tried to struggle free, but Bua's grip was too strong.

"It is not for you to see."

"Then at least tell me what is happening."

"If I tell you, will you go quietly to your room?"

"Well, all right, all right, if I must."

"A jinn has just driven one of the guards mad, and they are taking him away. I think it is Torab Ali."

"The jinn?" She was dying to see its backward feet.

"Of course not. The jinn disappeared long ago. The guard. They are taking the poor crazy fellow away."

"Can't I see him, just for a minute?" She had never, ever seen a crazy man, except perhaps on her way to school that old man who sometimes shuffled along the side of the road, waving his skinny arms, cursing everyone around and sometimes muttering to himself.

"You may not! What if the jinn saw you, looked into your eyes and turned your brains inside out? What little of them there are. Now hurry off or I'll tell your mother."

Back in her room, sitting cross-legged on her bed, fists clenched, Nishat pursed her lips, pondering. Bua could be really mean sometimes. All she wanted was a quick look, maybe even to get a glimpse of the jinn with funny feet. She banged her fists on her knees, trying to think of some way to get back at her. Suddenly, staring at her fists, she had an idea. All the servants were gathered in the kitchen, so there was no one around to see. With a low giggle, she scrambled off the bed, crept silently down the hall, carefully opened the door to the side of the house and, glancing around to be sure that there was nobody there — and no big trees close enough for a jinn to reach down with its claws — she stepped outside. For a moment she stood gazing at the side of the house — more than once she had carelessly brushed against it, the chalky red paint coming off, much to Bua's annoyance, on her clothes — then clenching a fist, pressed the side of it on the wall and studied the result with a giggle of excitement.

It did not take long to touch the wall with the side of her other fist, then dash inside to press first one then the other on the white plaster of the inside wall, one above the other as far up as she could reach, hurry out again to dirty her thumbs, come back in to leave thumbprints next to each fistprint, then stand back to admire her work, which looked remarkably like a trail of red footprints. Unable to suppress another giggle, she ran into the bathroom to wash her hands, taking care to leave no stains in the bowl, then tiptoed into her room, closed the door and got into her bed to wait.

After what seemed like a very long time, she heard footsteps passing down the hall, then silence, then a shriek that sounded just like Bua, followed by running feet, then another silence, then a babble of voices hurrying past. Getting off her bed, she quietly opened her door so that she could hear better.

What she heard above the chattering was Bua's voice. "You see! Everything I have told you is true. Allah have mercy on us! The jinn was here, right in the house, walking backwards up the wall! Quickly, Rahela, wash them away immediately, before the Begum Shahib returns! Hai Allah, I must go immediately to be sure that our little girl is safe!"

Nishat just had time to close the door and scramble back into the bed before Bua burst in, eyes wide, her wrinkles etched with concern.

"What's happening out there?" Nishat tried valiantly to look alarmed.

"Come with me and I will show you!" Grabbing her hand, Bua almost dragged her down the hall and into the room. "There!" She pointed.

"What is that?" A babble of voices answered.

"A jinn!"

"It was walking up the wall!"

"Bua knows!"

"She told us."

"The same one that drove the guard mad!"

"I hope it's still not here!"

"Hai, hai, Allah protect us!"

"All right, all right, enough!" Bua had an arm around Nishat's shoulders, holding her close. "Rahela, I told you to get a bucket of water, soap and brush and clean them off. The rest of you go back to what you should be doing. The Begum Shahib will be returning soon. And don't breathe a word of this. There is no need to scare and distress the family more than necessary." Bua turned to Nishat, her face stern. "Don't you open your mouth either, Nitu. Your mother and father will be upset enough about the guard, and they will not be happy with me when they know that you saw the footprints of the jinn."

For a moment, Nishat hesitated, all eyes on her. It would serve Bua right for not letting her see the crazy guard, but then she looked up into those ancient eyes, so wise and wonderful in so many other ways, felt her arm around her shoulders, remembered the *dal puri* and all those others she had defied Mother's orders to get for her. No, she couldn't do it, not with all the others there to hear, to snicker at Bua behind her back.

"I promise not to say anything, Bua."

And she never did, although even when she was much older, with long, thick black hair, she would feel a tremor of apprehension whenever she walked under the branches of a tree.

The Mapmakers of Spitalfields*

Syed Manzurul Islam

t was Friday afternoon and we were at the Sonar Bangla Café. There was a long queue, but that didn't surprise us. It was always jam-packed at this time of the week with regulars looking for a moment's respite from the toils and traumas of the week. Between gossiping about the playback song numbers and the dance routines in the latest videos, and between humdrum news from faraway home and savouring the spicy delicacies on offer, they drifted into another world. We sat squashed in a comer, under a painting of a boat coming straight down from the horizon, where the sun had just risen above a hazy line of trees. Badal was trying desperately to break through the cacophony of noise and catch the oarsman's song blaring from the loud-speaker at the far end of the cafe. Shafique, in between spoonfuls of *halva*, was glancing furtively at a gourd which was protruding from his knitted jute shopping bag. I was leaning against the chair to fork a piece of *kebab*. At that moment, the front door flung open and two blond men in white overalls came following the cold wind which galloped through the length of the cafe. Sensing danger, everyone ducked into their shells, except the oarsman, who went on singing until he scaled down from the breathless heights he had climbed. Jaws tight, the two paced the whole length of the floor in their purposeful red doc-martens, looking for someone or something out of the corners of their eyes. Abruptly, they stopped behind a man wearing a flannel suit and a broad-brimmed hat, then went to the front of him to scrutinise his face. They shook their heads as they walked towards us. They leant over our table, inscrutable, except for a knowing twist of their lips, saying nothing, but like well-trained bloodhounds trying to sniff out an odour of a clue. We knew their game, so we too kept our mouths shut. Seeing that we hadn't lost our nerves, the smoother of the two produced a photo from his pocket and laid it on the table. While he questioned us with the utmost politeness, his companion

*Anthologised in Syed Manzurul Islam, *The Mapmakers of Spitalfields* (London: Peepal Tree, 1997).

stood impassive in his towering bulk. When he saw that his smooth companion wasn't getting anywhere, he lifted his heavy eyelids, giving us a menacingly inquisitive look with his pale blue eyes. We shook our heads and said we hadn't seen the man in the photograph before. Nor had anyone else in the cafe. The bloodhounds didn't look very pleased. Mr. Smooth lost his cool. He screwed up his eyebrows and thumped the table. Mr. Nasty thrust his bulk forward to redouble his menace.

— *It's too bad, mate,* said Smooth, *the whole business stinks. I know the game you're playing, but it sickens me, really it does. How far would you go to protect your own kind, eh? For God's sake, the geezer's a lunatic. An absolute nutter, you know. Have you ever seen the way he walks, have you, huh? We can't let him roam the street like that, you know. We want to take him in for his own good.*

We still kept our mouths shut. Suddenly becoming thoughtful, as if he had hit upon something, Smooth paused to scrutinise my face.

— *What they call you?*

I gave him my name.

— *Don't play games with me, mate. You know what I mean. What they call you around here?*

I again repeated my name. He snapped the photo off the table and they left together as hastily as they had come.

For quite some time after they left, the silence wasn't broken, until someone nervously struck a match and many of the regulars reached for their cigarettes. We didn't want to hang around, so before the other customers could emerge from their shells and break into a cacophony of feverish questions and improbable answers, we hit the street. It was only four in the afternoon but already getting dark. We looked in both directions to make sure the guys in white overalls weren't around and headed east along Hanbury Street. We walked briskly in the cold. Shafique, as he always did when nervous, whistled out of tune. Badal, between puffs of his cigarette, looked thoughtful. But I knew he was dying to ask me about Brothero-Man. We didn't talk as we walked on, but I shuddered at the thought of the two men in white overalls catching up with Brothero-Man. When we were passing Spelman Street I thought I saw a silhouetted figure emerge from an alleyway and disappear into the maze of high-rise flats. Was that Brothero-Man? But I wasn't so anxious for him now because I knew they wouldn't be able to catch him at this hour. He had this thing about twilight and dawn. Each day, at those uncertain moments between day and night, he applied himself most skillfully. Not only did he outflank their hesitations with the supreme subtleties of his craft, but went onto a different plane altogether. Now that it was twilight they would be lucky to catch even a faint glimpse of his shadow. Yet, he never hurried, always laid one foot in front of the other with the utmost precision as he went back and forth, sketching delicately, with the skill of a miniaturist, a map at the very heart of this foreign city.

We walked together as far as Commercial Street. Finally Badal's nerves got the better of him, and, just before we parted, he asked me:

— *He isn't really mad, is he?*

I almost said — *Why do you ask me? How should I know?* — but I didn't say anything. Anyway, he didn't push me for an answer. Badal and Shafique said goodbye and went towards Whitechapel Station. I came back the way we had come. I wanted to find Brothero-Man and warn him about the mad catchers in white overalls.

Soon I found myself at the side of the high-rise complex that lines the middle section of Hanbury Street. When I looked up I saw the faint outlines of saris and lungis, festooned, fluttering from the washing lines. I couldn't help laughing, because they looked as dashing at the task of flying the flag as the Union Jack had done in the olden days. Suddenly I saw some garment, cut loose by a gust of wind, floating like a kite. I watched it disappear into the darkness. Even before I reached the concrete playground in front of the tower blocks, I could smell burning spices escaping through crevices in doorways and windows. Within, the whole building oozed spices, an aromatic aura which made it seem like a secret zone in another country. I could have closed my eyes and still reached the tower blocks by following the trails laid by the spices. Looking at the clothes hanging on the parapet, I thought of Brothero-Man and his meticulousness for colours. For instance, if white was the chosen colour of the day, then the obligatory white flannel suit would be matched by immaculately polished white shoes and a white broad-brimmed felt hat. The only contrast, apart from his own skin, would be added by a violet tie. Then he would be ready to walk the streets like a tip-top man. Irrespective of the season and the weather, he came this way every day, and more than once, to look at the washing lines, to breathe in the burning spices, and laugh, baring his gold teeth. Nights had their own routines, but in the day he would sit on the parapet, watching the children playing games and singing rhymes. How he loved the rhymes — oh what sweet rhymes they were. Those Bengali ones, learnt from the hums and lullabies of their mothers,

were mixing with the *hickory dickory dock* of those English ones. At
first the children used to throw stones at him, pull his jacket from
behind and scream at him, *Mad mad mad, there goes a stark-pagal-mad,
who is madder than the hatter-mad.* But soon they came to accept him
as a permanent landmark in their playground, like the parapet on
which he sat. Mind you, unlike the parapet, Brothero-Man had bottomless
pockets, bulging with goodies beyond the children's wildest dreams.
When they were most absorbed in their games, Brothero-Man would
tilt his broad-brimmed felt hat over his face, pretending to have fallen
asleep. But the children knew it to be the signal for a more enchanting
game and they would come rushing towards him. Seeing the children
out of the corner of his eye, he would push the broad brim to the back
of his head and say, *Litile brotheros and little sisteros, abracadabra,
are you ready for Alibaba's magic-jadu show?* Then he would conjure
up, with a deft play of his fingers, the latest models of toys, expensive
sweets, and even puppies and kittens from the bottoms of his pockets.
He would hand them to the boys and girls with a grin on his face. Ah,
he was happy then — my brothero.

Before I could emerge from the depths of thought that Brothero-Man
always demanded of me, I had already crossed the poorly-lit playground,
and was facing the lift. It, as usual, wasn't working. So I took the
stairs to the seventh floor. It didn't bother me much because I was
used to walking. Munir opened the door. I asked him if he had seen
Brothero-Man. He hadn't seen him around lately. Overhearing us,
Soraya came rushing from the kitchen. Yes, she had seen him that
very afternoon on his usual spot on the parapet, watching the children
play. As usual every Friday, the theme of the day was yellow. But it
was a new outfit, Soraya told me, and how handsome he looked in it.
Before I could ask about little Tariq, he was already next to me, but
sensing the serious tone of our conversation, he stood silent. I was
rubbing his head but not paying him any attention. A bit offended, he
tugged at my jacket, looked at me with his huge dark eyes and asked if
I had any sweets for him. I rummaged in my pockets but found nothing.
He pulled a face, went to his mother and stood staring sadly at the
floor, holding onto the edge of her sari. When I promised that I would
take him to see giraffes tomorrow, he looked happy. He smiled saying
loooong neck — and went back inside.

Soraya offered to make me tea. When I said no, she asked if I would
try some rice bread she,had already made. I declined this too, saying I

was in a hurry. She looked concerned, but didn't ask me any further questions. I had taken my leave and was almost out of the door when Munir asked me why I was looking for Brothero-Man. I told him about the guys in white overalls. Knowing Munir well, I didn't expect him to be sympathetic but I was surprised when I heard him say:

— *You know, it wouldn't be a bad idea if he goes in for a while. Let's face it, the guy's utterly mad. Look at the funny way he dresses. My God — the colours! Tell me something, how can a sane person walk about all day so aimlessly? And where does he go? Absolutely nowhere. And his talk, God, the amount of rubbish he talks. Honestly, I can't make any sense of his babble; I'm not even sure whether he speaks Bengali or English. You might not agree, but I think he needs treatment. The people you saw in white overalls must be professionals. We've no reason to be worried about them. I'm sure they came only to help.*

Soraya bit her lips with bitterness, as if something had finally snapped between herself and Munir.

— *I can't believe I'm hearing these things from you, Munir. What's happened to you? Have you eaten your head or what? I thought at least you'd be able to tell the difference between a mad man and a wise man. Have you bothered to listen to him? If you had, I'm sure you wouldn't say these things. Oh Allah, what nonsense I'm hearing! You think him funny-like because he dares to speak the truth like the prophets.*

I was saddened by the widening gulf between them. But what could I do? So I left them to their arguments and once more took to Hanbury Street.

The Sonar Bangla was buzzing again with regulars. Even from outside I could hear the oarsman's song. A lonely shore had no doubt prompted him into full flight, dared him to climb an unattainable scale. I walked past quickly, slipped across the road and went into the youth club. There the wacko guy Jacko ruled the scene like an absolute monarch from the jukebox, funking BAD BAD beats. All around the joint, Bengali youths, all them styling in cool leather jackets, hung around hyped on black-Afro-man's vibes. Between quick shuffles of their feet, they cued on the green tables, and crossed over to the other side. Where did they go? Harlem, Kingston, or just Brixton down the road? It didn't matter to Brothero-Man. God, how he loved the place. If you could fathom his mumble, you would have heard him saying, *Goodly goodly delectation, look-look, dhekho-dhekho, such a first-class scene.*

From where they got the knack, nobody knew, but these youths had mastered martial arts to the black belt class. And kick for kick they faced the skin-headed boys in uni-jacks. Brothero-Man had a real thing for the boys. He once told me, *Brothero, do you hear what them farty-wurty mouths say? Them say how the boys have gone kaput — neither here nor there — lost in the shit-hole of a gulla-zero. What a fucking-wukking talk that is, brothero. What do you say, eh? Laugh, brothero, laugh. Sure, them don't got the brain, even the goat shit size. Aren't they everywhere, brothero, aren't these boys everywhere? Hey brothero, you're looking at tiring miring biring the king Brick Lane piring.* When the boys at the club heard Brothero-Man talk like that, they would laugh. *What the fuck you're on, Brothero-Man? We don't dig you right.* Sure, the boys at the club thought him a bit crazy, but they had a soft spot for him too. When Asad saw me from the table, he hurried with his shot and came over.

— *What's up?*

I told him about the guys in white overalls. He went quiet, shook his head.

— *I tell you something: the fuckers are playing with fire. If they touch him, things will burn. And they'll have a riot on their hands.*

He went back to his table and blasted the cue into the pack, scattering the red and the yellow balls in disorder across the green baize.

Surfacing from the youth club I continued ahead, around the corner into Brick Lane. Suddenly I felt the cold like an icy syringe digging deep under my skin. But I had to keep looking. I put my hands, bluish from the cold, into my pockets, flung the long scarf over my head and walked on. Along the way I remembered the first time I had met Brothero-Man. How long ago was beside the point, but it was memorable for being one of those rare sunny days in winter. I remember waking that morning, opening the window and letting the soft sunlight drape me with the fragility of muslin. Unwisely, I put on only a light jacket and almost in a dream set off down the Brick Lane way. Before I could get my bearings, Brothero-Man had already leapt on me from nowhere on the springs of his legs. *Good morning-salaam. Welcome, brothero, how do you do-doo, brothero?* I must have looked at him with puzzlement, if not with fear, but even then I could sense that he was a brother. Almost immediately, before I could reply, he had left me, though he paused a second to look back and smiled at me, showing a glint of his golden teeth. I looked on as he, apparently untouched by the cold, melted into an alleyway. Later, much later, I learned that he had been walking these streets for the last twenty years. Before that, nothing was certain. But few doubted the rumour that he was a *shareng* on a ship from the Indies. He must have been one of the pioneer jumping-ship men, who landed in the East End and lived by bending the English tongue to the umpteenth degree.

There are many who date the day he took to walking as the beginning of his madness. But others mark it as the beginning of that other walk when, patiently, and bit by bit, he began drawing the secret blueprint of a new city. It wasn't exactly in the likeness of our left-behind cities from the blossoms of memories. Nor did it grow entirely from the soon-to-be razed foreign cities where we travellers arrived with expectant maps in our dreams. What do you say, brothero? Surely a strange new city, always at the crossroads, and between the cities of lost times and cities of times yet to come.

I was still walking along Brick Lane and entered once more the zone of spices. But this time the tempting scents from the rows of restaurants were overlaid with gentle aromas from the sweet shops and smells of leather from the sweat shops. Ambling towards Aldgate East Station, I paused to look at the mannequins in a brightly lit sari shop, their plumpish bodies wrapped in the latest styles of silk, cotton and synthetic saris. I knew that Brothero-Man would have lingered here with his eyes fixed on the mannequins. Then he would have taken his hat off to comb his hair in the reflection of the window. Often, when the shop was open, he would go inside and run his fingers along the rows of saris. It would please him to see the fluttering colours and hear the secret melodies in the rustles of silk. Sensing Brothero-Man's presence, the owner of the shop, Zamshed Mia — who never usually spent an idle moment not making a profit — would look up at the spy monitor and stay there rapt for minutes on end. These moments never failed to bring tears to his eyes because he'd never seen so much tenderness in a man's caress before. Desperate to repay him in some way, but not knowing what to do, one day he offered Brothero-Man one of his most expensive saris. He told him that perhaps he could send it to his beloved. Brothero-Man flung the sari in his face and told him that his beloveds were right there in the shop window. After that he gave Zamshed Mia the full treatment of his foul mouth. Zamshed Mia didn't understand exactly what he meant; such mysteries, he thought, were beyond him. From then on he would only look in silence at the miracle of love in the black and white video monitor. I wondered what topographical details the map-maker had been noting here, and moved on.

Not far from here was a popular newsagent, selling imported books, magazines from Bangladesh, and Bollywood videos. I entered the shop, picked up a copy of the weekly *Natun Din* and went up to pay Kamal at the counter. I asked him if he had seen Brothero-Man. Of course, he had been there in the morning, as he always was, ever since the shop opened. He'd browsed through the latest magazines, Kamal said, and asked for his favourite songs to he put on. He seemed his usual happy self, but while reading a news item he had gone quiet and muttered to himself in his fucking-wucking, obscene language. Kamal told me, too, that two guys in white overalls had also recently been in his shop, asking questions about Brothero-Man. They'd told him that they would hunt him the whole night. Whatever it took, they wouldn't leave without him.

— *He's a bit funny-like, I admit,* Kamal said. *But my old man thinks he got some kinda special power. He sees some deep meaning in his walk. I don't dig all that, but he's harmless, ain't he?*

I was, once more on Brick Lane, walking its littered pavements. Night had fallen some hours ago and even the groceries with incredibly long hours were closing. But the flutter of cab lights would go on for the whole stretch of the night, and the restaurants and pubs still had a few profitable hours left to run. I wondered why the guys in white overalls were so desperate to catch Brothero-Man before the end of the night. Perhaps they'd got wind of his secret map-making. Yes, but why couldn't they wait any longer than this night? Then it occurred that perhaps they had a hunch that he was on the last leg of his survey, and one more night would complete the map. Surely, they would do anything in their powers to prevent that.

I felt a renewed urgency to find Brothero-Man before the guys in white overalls. I was moving briskly when I saw one of the regular tramps of the lane, soaked in alcohol, emerging from a dark recess. He staggered towards me, rubbed his mouth with his trembling hand and strained his half-closed eyes as if trying to tell who it was. But his drunkenness and the darkness of the Lane prevented him from recognising me.

— *I'll let you in on a secret, Guv. You're looking at the real Jack the Ripper. How about it? Give me a fag, will ya?*

I didn't have any cigarettes, so instead I put a twenty-pence piece in his hand. He looked well pleased. I left him and headed towards the Haji Shahab's grocery. It was closed but the lights were on. Through the glass front I saw the Haji counting what looked like a lot of money. The takings must have been good because he had a grin on his paan-red lips. When I knocked on the glass door, I saw panic in the Haji's eyes. He dropped the money in the till and slammed it shut. He looked around, holding onto his long hennaed beard until he saw me. Only then did he look relieved and the grin came back to his lips. He opened the door and bid me a warm salaam. He locked the door behind us and offered me a cigarette. Twirling his beard he said:

— *Where is your friend, country brother? What's his name — the one who calls everyone brothero? I tell you something, no one looks at my fish like him. Only Allah knows why he looks that way. But I'm sure they aren't ordinary looks. What do you say, country brother?*

I said I hadn't seen him for the last few days and was looking for him desperately. The Haji said that Brothero-Man had been there that morning, as ever devouring his fishes with his eyes. It was one of his rendezvous — a necessary stop in his walking routine. The last time I'd come, I remembered, I was with him. Together we'd stood in contemplative silence looking at the fishes. We were so absorbed that at first we didn't notice the Haji standing just behind us, rubbing his portly belly. We were somewhat startled when he spoke.

— *Oh, what do you say, country brothers? They're as desirable as houries, eh? If you gobble them up like this, with your hungry eyes, my customers will get bad stomach, no?*

Brothero-Man looked at him fiercely and gritted his gold teeth.

— *Look at him, brothero, look what a nasty piece of fussing-wussing gob. I'm telling you, brothero, he was sure raised on hog-shit. Look, how he hides his wickedness under his beard. And his portly sack, look at it, how it hangs over his nasty thing. Who knows, brothero, how many bastards he raised with that thing. Sure, him's as greedy as a shit-eating-hog. Always fussing-wussing, I tell you, brothero, him eating too much rice. Hish, mish, bish, I'm the king kish.*

I had never seen the Haji looking so scared because he couldn't quite decide whether Brothero-Man was a mad man or a holy man. In his confusion he offered Brothero-Man a cigarette. He took it, lit it and stormed out. Much later, he told me that the Haji had his own value because, like the fishes, he was good to look at.

I told the Haji about the two men in white overalls. He shook his head and said that they would make a grave mistake if they touched him, because only Allah knew what would happen to them.

— *I wouldn't be surprised, if they were ruined for generations, country brother.*

I was back on the street and once more I was walking along Brick Lane. When I was passing the mosque I couldn't help but stop, because Brothero-Man would have stopped here. Of course, I didn't go in, because he never went in. Almost like clockwork he comes five times a day and stands outside. He stares at the gloomy facade of the mosque and chats with the regulars who go in for prayers. Once, one of these asked him why he never went inside the mosque. He paid dearly for asking that silly question because Brothero-Man was in good form that day.

— *Inside / Outside what a fussing-wussing talk. Have you any idea, you shit head, where that mosque be? Right in me inside. Well, well, now tell me, you mother-fucking donkey, how can I go inside of the inside? Bawk bawk bawk not knowing how to talk.*

It was late and the last prayer of the day had been said some hours ago. I stood in the cold wind that blew across the Lane and looked at the mosque. It was still there, my brothero, always there.

Where could I go from the mosque? Oh yes, I could always go and see my friend the poet who lived across the road. So I crossed the road and walked ahead and within seconds I was outside his door. I pressed the button and waited. Suddenly I saw a blue van braking abruptly and skidding a little on the icy road. Out came the two guys in white overalls, walking slowly towards Commercial Street. Did they have a lead on Brothero-Man? I knew that they'd never find the pathways through the secret grids of his map. But if Brothero-Man — for some strange reason — wanted to be found?

My friend the poet opened the door. I climbed the dark stairs behind his rumbling bulk and ancient odour. He once told me, between a roaring laugh and dropping ash from his cigarette, that he cultivated that stink as a protection against his enemies. We all laughed but there was some truth in it. If you weren't seasoned in his friendship, you would puke the moment you went anywhere near him. But now the stink made me forget, at least for a brief moment, about Brothero-Man. Back in his room, the poet resumed his reclining posture on the divan and lit a cigarette. Closing his eyes, he blew smoke into air already densely clouded with smoke from hundreds of cigarettes whose butt-ends littered the room. Before I could open my mouth, the poet told me to allow him some time, because he had something on his mind. From the way he looked I knew he was spinning a new verse, so I kept quiet. I sat on the chair facing the divan. He finished his cigarette, lit yet another with the butt-end and withdrew into himself as if I wasn't there. Between patting his thigh and picking his nose — and always that cigarette — he went on mumbling to himself. Suddenly he came out of his thoughts to tell me how wonderful tea would be. Before I could respond, he had already resumed his thoughts. Dutifully I went to make the tea. When I came back with it, he barely acknowledged me. I resumed watching him. Suddenly a pack of huge rats, raising a deafening uproar, zoomed diagonally across the room and disappeared in the pile of rubbish heaped next to the cooker. I told the poet what I had seen. He told me that I must be imagining things, because he hadn't seen any rats; surely there couldn't be any here. Yet I noticed that as he lit another cigarette, dug his elbow deeper into his pillow, he pulled the tattered sheet of his divan, protectively I felt, over his feet. Perhaps feeling a bit guilty for keeping me waiting, he said — *Are you doing nicely, my friend?* — but soon he went back to his poetic meditation. I didn't want to disturb him because I knew he was thinking of Brothero-Man. How could you mistake the way he was curving his lips and blowing the air. He wasn't so much mimicking Brothero-Man as he was riding with him in the same galloping motion. Then I heard him as the mumble got louder.

> Boy, wasn't he there?
> right there, under your very noses
> an invisible surveyor marking cities
> as if through dense forest and uncharted savannahs
> like a white horse with a long flowing mane
> galloping through the veins of your city
> flickering the icon of his body
> & charting
>
> but you look through a microscope
> right into the very depths of his pocket
> 'there there,' you say, 'the map ought to be there.'
> how little you know that sizzling of a body
> dancing a pure force in twilight
> sprinkling ink like rubies along the way

& between walking feet and clicking eyelids
wearing a parchment of a map at one with his body

now you will seize the body
you do that as you please
he laughs, glinting his gold teeth
seeing the floating mirror of his body
stamping space in the speed of his trails.
my lords and ladies, I am afraid
he has bitten off a chunk of your land
& grinning gold with his teeth

I heard a sharp cry from the street below and jumped to the window. I cleaned the steamed-up panes with my palms and looked down to see what was happening. The mist was so dense and the street-lights so dim that they were no more than drops of yellow in a bowl of milk, but there was no mistaking the van even though I couldn't see the colour. Just in front of the van stood three figures in silhouette. Two of them seemed to be barring the way of the third. From their size I could tell that two of the men were the ones in white overalls. But the third? Since they were looking for him, who else could it be but Brothero-Man? The two guys in white overalls seemed to be talking to him, but he suddenly thrust his hands between them and pushed them aside as if cutting through water like a breaststroke swimmer. He began to walk away and then broke into a trot. The two men turned around and ran after him. One of the men in white overalls, the one of towering bulk, lurched forward and grabbed Brothero-Man's jacket collar, while the other man, the thin and tall one, stood in front. Perhaps he was still trying to persuade Brothero-Man to come voluntarily. He, though, jerked himself free from the man who was holding him from behind and head-butted the man in front. This I concluded from the way the man in front was holding his head. My brothero certainly knew how to take care of himself. Now he began to trot again, with the man of towering bulk trotting after, grabbing for him, almost flying through the air. Brothero-Man seemed to be trying desperately to stay upright and shake off the man of towering bulk. But the thin, tall man came around and grabbed him by the neck. Brothero appeared to elbow him fiercely and drag the man of towering bulk along the pavement. The tall, thin man was hitting Brothero-Man with a truncheon-like object. He fell to the ground, curling up. Then it was all over and the two guys in white overalls were dragging him towards the van. I shouted to the

poet that they were taking away our brothero. He jumped off his divan
and we ran out to the street. As we reached the van, a policeman came
out of the station, which was just opposite. He focused his torch on the
scene and at last we could see clearly what was happening. The two
men were indeed the mad-catchers in white overalls. But the third
looked like a policeman. It wasn't Brothero-Man. I cursed myself for
not realising that it wasn't his style to fight that way. The third man
was Jamir Ali. It was common knowledge on Brick Lane that one day,
possessed by the evil bobby-spirit, he had stopped speaking and gone
mad. He made himself a police uniform, bought a real-looking helmet
and stood outside the station, as if he was a real policeman on duty. He
wasn't struggling now, but all the same they dragged him into the van
through the back door, and slammed it shut. They told the policeman
with the torch that there were others still roaming the streets who were
madder than the one they'd caught. Then the thin, tall mad-catcher
looked at me suspiciously.

— *You can be sure he won't get away. We're here to round up all the
loonies. We've our job to do, you know. But specially him — the real Mr.
Crazy. We'll get him by the time the night's up. We aint buffoons, we
have our information. We know he's planning something crazy at dawn.
We can't let that happen, can we?* He was about to get into the van but
came back to look me up and down closely.

— *What they really call you around here, eh? You don't fool me,
mate, we're watching you. But one piece of advice: if I were you I'd stop
this walking nonsense. Why did you have to come all this way here to
do your bloody walk? It sickens me, it really does.*

They drove away, turning the corner into Fashion Street. The poet
went back to his flat, and I walked on looking for Brothero-Man. On
the way I met Allamuddin Khan — a deadly serious fellow, all-round
guru and a nonconformist *par excellence* — buzzing like a queen bee
through the haze, surrounded by his young followers. At first he didn't
notice me, he was so absorbed in his wise-man role. I caught the name
Vatsyayana and thought perhaps he was pep-talking the boys on the
delicate art of seduction. Suddenly seeing me so close, he froze with a
start. Then, he said abruptly, as if to regain his composure:

— *We must finish our talk on the metrical form of Rabi Thakur's
work.* He remained silent for a while, and then smiled wryly. But he
was soon back to his old form again, laying on all sorts of esoteric
wisdom to the bafflement and admiration of his followers. I thought if
the two mad-catchers in white overalls got to hear him he'd be in real

trouble. I told him about them and Brothero-Man. Allamuddin Khan, despite all his wisdom, looked shaken.

— *For argument's sake, even if he is mad, what the hell they think they are up to? We have been living all our lives with so called mad people, even eating from the same plate. And certainly living in the same house and the same neighbourhood. It never bothered us. Anyway who can tell who is really mad?*

He wanted to come with me but I told him that I would rather look for Brothero-Man on my own. Anyway, he told me that he and his boys would go round looking for him too.

I slipped my hands deep into my pockets, turned my lapel to cover my neck and walked on. I hadn't gone far when I paused in front of what had been Naz Cinema. Sadly, these days it stood only as a monument to that bygone celluloid age. At this time of the night its entrance looked dead except for a few tramps who lay huddled up in cardboard and rags. But during the day, a different form of life unfolds in its precincts. Ever since the cinema had gone bust, there had been a bazaar here. At the centre of this bazaar was the stall of righteous things. And at the hub of this stall was the black-beard-and-no-moustache presence of the master of righteous arts himself — Mulana Abdul Hakim. As I stood there I remembered how Brothero-Man had rescued me from the trap so cunningly laid by the Mulana. I was green then in Brick Lane. It was a Friday afternoon and I was passing the bazaar when I saw the Mulana for the first time. Seeing him in his righteous pose against the display of Qurans, calligraphies of divine words, velveted prayer-rugs with images of Kaba-Sharif, toupees and tabiz, I sensed trouble. I looked away and quickened my pace, but the very moment I felt his salaam swoop down on me I knew I was trapped. I had to return his salaam and approach his stall. Whatever you might think of him, you had to agree that nobody had a tongue as diamond sharp as the Mulana. God, how he mows his customers down in a flash with a regular swipe of it! Then the poor wretches feel only too happy to buy his righteous merchandise at double its proper price. No sooner had I reached the stall than the Mulana unleashed the flourish of his tongue. First, he put me on the hair-thin bridge that one must cross to reach the gate of heaven. Underneath the bridge lie whipped up the full horrors of hell. I was balancing most unsteadily on that hair-thin bridge as he made me feel the heat of everlasting fire and hear the hiss of swarming serpents down below. The whole game was to do with righteous debt. If you were found short you'd really had it; no amount of trapeze skill would see you across the bridge to the gate of heaven. Sinner that I was, my legs shook. I had the distinct feeling that I had almost slipped from that bridge, though I still wasn't prepared to part company with the few pounds I had for the week if I could help it. In desperation I looked around for someone or something to rescue me from the spell of the Mulana. Just to my right was a stall selling Bollywood posters, but the plumpish heroines in seductive poses and wearing bathing suits were powerless to rescue me from the hair-thin bridge. As I dug into my pocket, I knew my pounds were as good as gone. I could see the impish smile breaking on the Mulana's lips as he spat out paan-red saliva, waiting to conclude yet another triumph. But then, as if from thin air, Brothero-Man came to my side. Mulana Abdul Hakim went pale and silent. Not daring to look at him and without saying a word, he offered Brothero-Man a paan from his small tin box. Brothero-Man snatched the paan off the Mulana most disdainfully and put it in his mouth. Then he turned his back on the Mulana and grinned, baring his gold teeth.

— *Brothero, what's this bastard son of Iblish telling you? Can't you see he's a con-man fellow. Most wicked, you see. Always fussing-wussing with his foul talk. Come, brothero, let's run from his ass-like face. Ya ya ya Allah, what a bad-smelling fellow.*

I didn't look back at the Mulana as we walked away together. After that the Mulana didn't bother me any more, but Brothero-Man, despite what he said, always came back to see the Mulana several times a day and chew his paan. Perhaps, with his long black-beard-and-no- moustache, like the Haji, he was good to look at, especially in the setting of his righteous props. But who knows what meaning the Mulana held in Brothero-Man's secret scheme of things. Perhaps, as my friend the poet once told me, in order to stamp his body on the face of this foreign city, he needed all these signs.

Hearing me pass, a tramp peered from his cardboard box and asked me if the sun was already up. His friend next to him, the genuine Jack the Ripper, woke up to see what was happening, took a swig from his bottle and once more insisted on his identity. It was well past midnight and I was running out of time to find Brothero-Man before the mad-catchers in white overalls. So I hurried along from Naz Cinema, crossed the road and arrived in front of a pub, which had long since closed. Even on my first day in Brick Lane, this pub had struck me as an oddity. It was as I stood looking at it for that first time that Brothero-Man appeared, as he did on so many occasions, by my side.

— *Brothero, just like me, this place is not what it seems. You see, it's an either-neither place. But most interesting. You've to lift the veil-bhorka to see the face. You know what I mean, brothero?* He disappeared quickly again. Well, there's no doubt that behind the veil of a pub it was a different place. Most unlikely and almost hard-to-believe but it was a solid thing. You mustn't laugh when I tell you that the landlord was a puritanical turbanwallah, who served halal beer with samosas to a castaway clientele who outdid one another in bah-bah over oriental striptease.

Through the rows of cash & carries, the unisex hairdressing salons and then more groceries and restaurants, I finally arrived at the mouth of Brick Lane, its name announced on a black-rimmed white plaque. But where was Brothero-Man? I knew that he wouldn't walk beyond this point because it was the border line of his territory — and sometimes a territory which had to be defended. In fact, it was once a war zone. Yes, those were the days of cropped-headed-bovver-boots selling *Bulldogs*. They came like a pack of hyenas in broad daylight to raid Brick Lane. They drew blood, oh yes, they drew blood, and marched away watched by many panic-stricken eyes. But those were also the days when the workers surfaced from the twilight zones of sweatshops and from the steamed-up kitchens at the backs of restaurants. No matter what the danger, they stood their ground behind the barricade. But always in front, before the assault of the enemy, was Brothero-Man. He stood immobile in the chosen colour of the day with a giant rattan-stick in his hand. Then he was a commandante, my brothero.

Since he wouldn't go beyond this point, there was no need for me go any further. So I turned back. When I looked at the horizon I suddenly became aware that the markings of *our* city were no more than tiny dots in the sea of their strange city. There were the tall glass-faced skyscrapers of the city of London. Even in the mist and darkness they loomed menacingly over Brick Lane. Every time Brothero-Man looked up to see the skyscrapers, he became restless. He walked with renewed urgency as if constructing a battlement to safeguard his territory against an advancing enemy.

On my return leg, at the corner of Old Montage Street, I met Asad and his boys in leather jackets. They were patrolling the streets against the raiders of the night. They told me that they hadn't yet seen Brothero-Man but they had come across the two guys in white overalls.

Some of the boys had wanted to teach the guys a lesson but Asad had dissuaded them, by reminding them of the power of the law. The boys moved on and I continued on my way. As I passed Chicksand Street, I saw the mad-catchers pissing against a wall. I slunk away like a cat. I was once more following the beaten tracks of Brothero-Man. First, along Brick Lane, and then the alleyways that merge onto it, but always checking and rechecking the spots he would have stopped and looked at. But he was nowhere to be seen, and as a man without fixed abode, there was no home that I could check. Nor was there any spot where he slept because he hardly ever slept.

— *So little time, brothero,* he once told me, so *little time for all the tasks that need completing before they come for you. How could I waste time in a rubblishy-wubbishy thing like sleeping.*

I went back to the tower block in Hanbury Street, took the stairs again, and arrived at Munir's and Soraya's flat. It was nearly two o'clock. When I rang the bell, Munir came bleary-eyed to open the door. Soraya was just behind, looking anxious. She asked me if I had found Brothero-Man. I said no, but that the mad-catchers were still looking, evidently determined to get him before dawn. Munir asked me if I had eaten anything. I said I wasn't hungry, but Soraya disappeared into the kitchen and came back with a plate of rice with an assortment of left-over curries and dhal and a saucer with two green chillies, pieces of onion, and some salt. I ate sitting on the sofa. Munir picked up an old newspaper and turned the pages absent-mindedly. Soraya looked cold and sad; she cupped her chin, hiding her mouth and stared down at the floor. Without lifting his face from the pages, Munir told me how much Tariq was looking forward to going to the zoo. Both of them insisted that I should spend the night at their place. But I said no, I had to go to my friend the poet's place. You see, every day like clockwork, between two and three in the morning, Brothero-Man never failed to show up at the poet's, bringing him curries and rice. With a grin he would produce biscuits, cakes, bananas and oranges out of his pockets. By this time of night, the poet would be so hungry that he would eat at a furious pace and Brothero-Man would always say — *Sorry, brothero, I'm so late.* Then they would talk and laugh together until dawn when the poet fell asleep on the divan. Brothero-Man would pull the blanket over him and set out to walk yet another day.

When I rang the bell, the poet came rushing because he thought I was Brothero-Man. He was very hungry, pacing the room, puffing his cigarettes.

— Why doesn't he come yet? I'm so hungry today, my friend. Do you think something might've happened to him? If they take him what will become of me?

I sat on the corner of the poet's divan, waiting for Brothero-Man. An hour had passed. The poet was getting desperate; he was pacing the room, now and then looking through the window, still oblivious to the quarrelsome rats that had now taken over the room. God, he was so hungry that he even rummaged the pile of rubbish from where the rats had come. But he found nothing that he could eat, so he began licking some sugar from an almost empty packet. When he'd finished this, he burped loudly.

— You take some rest, my friend. When he comes I'll wake you up.

I thought of little Tariq — how he must be dreaming of going to see giraffes. I mustn't be late for that. Yes, I could do with some rest.

I lay on the poet's divan and looked up and saw the green and brown patches on the ceiling. The patches of mould were dancing in intricate geometric patterns. I couldn't take my eyes off them because the sudden loops of their curves and the crisscrossing play of their lines were etching the passageways through which so many had come to map the new city. Armies of men, women and children marched shoulder to shoulder like columns of ants. Undaunted, they pushed their way through the mazes, but many lost their way and perished. Some, though, had found their way through the mazes and floated on the deep pools of their toils to arrive at the golden city they had mapped in their dreams. The rats had gone quiet, but the poet was still walking. I could hear the movement of his feet on the loose planks of the floor, making creaking noises. They had a rhythm like the lullabies of wind against the broken latch of the window.

the poet is calm now after his dinner he lights a cigarette slumps back into the pillow at the far end of the divan Brothero-Man pulls the chair very close almost breathing into the poet's face they are happy now they are whispering to each other and laughing pressing their hands against their mouths because they don't want to wake me up they are so considerate my brothero how nice he looks today in his immaculate white flannel suit and a crimson tie polished white shoes and his golden teeth but no broad-brimmed hat today just as well because a white pagri with a long flowing tail suit him most handsomely he is so happy now sweet smile breaking loose on his clean-shaven face sweet smell of just a touch of musk by and by the time has gone the poet

*wants to embrace him to say goodbye but Brothero-Man will have none
of it it is too theatrical too much fussing-wussing he breaks into a huge
laugh takes out a smooth green apple from his pocket and offers it to the
poet saying take care of yourself brothero wipe that silly sadness off
your face you'll see me again sure you'll see me again but in a different
way now the poet extends his languorous arm to receive the gift gently
touching the sinuous hand that offers the apple perhaps despite himself
he can't prevent a drop of tears clouding his eyes but Brothero-Man
doesn't have the time for all that now he needs to walk how he needs to
walk because the dawn is breaking through the mist its soft light
streaming through the windows with a promise of a perfect morning
without any ceremony then and just as he has been doing for years
Brothero-Man sniffs the air and lands on Brick Lane almost immediately
he takes in his stride the empty thoroughfare the alleyways his nimble
fingers habitually counting the crystal beads on his tabiz, and one by
one he remembers Mulana Abdul Hakim's stall Haji Sahab's grocery
Zamshed Mia's sari shop Turbanwallah's pub the minaret of the
Mosque children singing rhymes in the playground odour of spices
claiming the alleyways boys cueing on the green table the purring of
machines in sweatshops and so much more but the two men in white
overalls have already taken to Brick Lane they sniff the air sensing
Brothero-Man's presence they pick up their pace pursuing him through
alleyways like men possessed with a mission of pivotal importance they
lose him for awhile so they run wildly and emerge on Brick Lane again
through Hanbury Street whatever the mad-catchers might think
Brothero-Man is not one for running away it's simply not his style
within minutes he comes back to Brick Lane via Old Montage Street
now heading towards the mad catchers in white overalls he's already
passed the threshold and the supple movements of his feet have reached
their unreachable perfection whirling and almost floating through the
air the tail of his pagri fluttering like a sail caught in high winds
finally they see each other fifty paces apart the two men in white overalls
pause a second then rush madly to catch their mad patient but Brothero-
Man is not running away only advancing most delicately towards them
in slow motion and melting in the ether first his torso then his hands
then his legs and neck though his white shoes and floating pagri and
his golden grin glide on their own through the air and almost touch the
mad catchers at the corner of Chicksand Street before vanishing
completely leaving the two men standing mute and frozen.*

In the morning I found the poet sprawled next to me on the divan. He was snoring raucously, an orange filter still squashed between his smoking fingers. I opened the curtains and let the soft sunlight drape me with the fragility of muslin, then drew them back again so the sun wouldn't wake the poet up. I hit the streets. I don't know why everybody seemed to be staring at me as I walked through the lane. I went to a comer shop to buy some sweets for little Tariq because I knew he would demand them as soon as he saw me. When I tried to pay, the shopkeeper wouldn't take any money. He just shook his head in silence, not daring to look me in the eyes. It was getting late so I didn't waste any time trying to pay him. Soon I was on my way to Soraya's and Munir's flat, to pick up little Tariq. He would be all worked up to see the giraffes. Still, there was time for a quick stop at the Sonar Bangla for a cup of tea. As I entered, a hushed silence descended on the café. I went to a lonely corner, sat facing the painting of the boat on the horizon. But the oarsman wasn't singing any more. I was still puzzled to see that people were staring at me with the same melancholy eyes as they were in the street. Then Lilu walked in from the kitchen with a cup of tea in his hand. He set it on the table in front of me, leaned over and whispered in my ear.

— *Brothero,* he said, *two mad-catchers in white overalls were looking for you. You got to hide, brothero, you got to hide.*

The Last Letter

Neeman A. Sobhan

She looks at the envelope as if it were a clandestine letter that she has discovered, written to her husband by another woman. She has come upon it quite by accident, clearing her husband's old desk in the basement before asking him if she can give it away for her neighbour Claire's garage sale next weekend. It was in the bottom drawer under some old travel brochures: the familiar white envelope.

For the first blurred moment, Rina cannot recognise her own handwriting. The envelope, addressed ten years ago to her father, Professor Nizam Ahmad, in her own rounded hand, stares back at her, alien and mocking. She listens intently to the slowly increasing roar in her heart like she was reading a thermometer: the mercury climbs to a raging fever. Listen, she tells herself, calm down, it is only an envelope containing a letter that you once wrote to your father now long dead, and which, for some reason, never got mailed. These things happened all the time: lives and letters got mislaid, or death overtook love. She quietens her breathing. It's okay. Of course, it will not be easy to swallow this new fact that her father never got to read her famous letter, when all these years she had thought otherwise. Imagine, she had spent an entire decade under a delusion!

Now, the temperature falls; a chill settles over her heart. This is a malicious cosmic joke played on her by fate, a cruel prank in which she feels the inexplicable complicity of her father. How like him to have died abruptly, rudely, while her important letter to him was in the process of being mailed. Showkat must have forgotten or delayed mailing the letter and by the time he got around to it, it was too late; she can see that now. And since then, the letter has been hidden all these years, the evidence buried to spare her. She doesn't blame her husband; she blames her father, for dying so inconveniently, allowing her no time to send him the most beautiful letter she has ever written, her first and last to him.

"It's not fair, Abba. It's so unfair." The feeling rather than the words scream and echo inside her. Unemotional and uncommunicative to the end, this then was Abba's goodbye to her: the final turning away, the last rejection. Rina walks numbly around the careful elegance of her suburban home in Potomac, Maryland, touching objects as if by experiencing their solidity she were establishing her own reality usurped and sucked a moment ago into the unfinished world within the white envelope in her hand.

She stops at Tanya's door. The lavender walls of an appropriately girlish, American pre-teen's room are hung with the regulation posters of music and movie icons. Rina's own contribution to the décor is a stiff doll dressed in a sari, which Tanya has indulged her mother by accommodating on her bookshelf, knowing that this is only symbolic of her mother's feeble attempt to transplant a Bangladeshi environment in an expatriate life.

The more Tanya outgrows Rina's manipulations at retaining some links with a Bengali past, which is only Rina's past, the clanging chains of *her* childhood and not that of Tanya who was born American, the more precious that rusted cultural coil becomes for Rina. But beneath the pleasurable aspects of such an anchor, like the food, the music, the old movies, the saris and the happy memories with which she moors her everyday life into a safe haven, lie the tangled, choking weeds of unsorted relationships, the terrifying emotional under-tow of the past that can easily unravel her hold on her slippery sense of self if she doesn't take care. Today it threatens to plunge her at the deep end.

Rina walks into her own study and confronts the enlarged, black-and-white framed photograph over her desk. The greying man, good-looking in a thin-lipped way, wearing a suit from the sixties, looks sternly at the camera. For Rina's younger sister Nina, their father had been exactly as this photograph depicts him: unresponsive, untouchable, removed. Rina has harboured some illusions, but today, years after his death, she feels him slip back into the photograph. She has lost him again.

Resting her head on the desk, she looks up at the Abba who till yesterday had been the father-that-received-the-letter and thus was dead but immortalised, transformed by his daughter's love. Today he is deaf, dead and gone. And she must dip into her memories to bring him back. Abba is not hard to remember because there is so little of him to remember. She can count on her fingers the exact number of times he smiled at her, recall vividly the occasions on which he lost his temper at her, the few times he praised her and the exact words he used. She safeguards the rare memory of being asked to press his forehead, or was it Nina's memory? Then why does *she* remember the tautness of his skin, the bristle of his eyebrows? Sometimes when she is with Nina, she asks her to corroborate other vague incidents so she can add it to her personal notes.

She has kept this diary assiduously because, since his death, Rina has started to write a story about Abba, to bring him to life in her own way. "What is there to write about?" This is typical Nina, suppressing a yawn during one of her weekend morning phone conversations with her, and which is related not to Nina's late hours at her New York office but to her lack of interest in their "dried out, cold fish" progenitor. But Rina is undeterred, persistent about fictionalising Abba. In any case, she has for a long time been telling Tanya selective stories about the grandfather Tanya has never known but whom, Rina is determined to believe, she would have learnt to love. It calls for some exaggerations; after all, it is not easy to conjure up the real Abba for storytelling, especially to make him interesting to her easily bored daughter.

With Nina she frequently explores the question of what Abba had really been like. "A bitter, laconic man," Nina supplies. "Come on, now," Rina shakes her head, writing aloud: "A man of few words, who disdained the 'frills and laces' of social conversation." "Whatever. Okay, unsocial and friendless," Nina volunteers. Rina counters, "I'd say he had few friends, but those he had respected him for his honesty and straightforwardness." "Yeah! Mention that he also lost a job and countless friends for the very same reason." Nina had always been Ma's natural confidante whenever their parents fought, which was often.

"You didn't have to be so damned open about your disapproval, you know. Apa is so hurt. She is after all my only sister. Of course, these things don't matter to you, living in a world of your own." Ma's voice would be barely controlled. Abba's tone was icy: "Your Apa knows very well that I think her son-in-law is a pompous ass who should be kicked from his present position." "Why can't you at least keep quiet ...?" "Listen, Razia, you know I refuse to suffer fools. If I embarrass you, then kindly leave me out of the next family-get-together. I would prefer it and it would solve your problem." And with that he would walk out leaving Ma seething. Her soft approach was even less effective: "I only worry about you...." "Then kindly refrain from doing so." She would continue unheeding, "Don't you realise that you make enemies with this unrelenting attitude of yours? One has to learn to be tolerant ...." "My dear, I choose not to and that's that."

Often, after a flare-up causing a much-anticipated outing to be cancelled, Rina would think that had she been in Ma's position, she would have walked out on a husband like Abba. After her marriage to Showkat, so warm and caring, she often wondered what had kept her mother in her marriage, apart from minor compensations like her being adored by her in-laws. Ma always said that Abba was just not cut out to be either a husband or a father, and this, Ma's acceptance of Abba, was the closest thing to the concept of love she could fathom in her parents' marital life. There was no other evidence; Nina's and her own existence seemed aberrations.

But Rina refused to accept Ma's verdict of Abba being a solitary man as easily and blithely as did Nina who ignored her father. All her childhood long, Rina set about seducing her father's affections. She remembers especially Abba's evening walks around the garden. The others left him alone but she steeled herself for the violation, approaching him hesitatingly: "Abba?"

Silence, mortifying. Maybe he hadn't heard. "Abba, I had something to ask you...."

He stopped in his tracks and Rina rushed into her practiced speech. "There is the school debate coming up...."

"What's the subject?" She had his attention, and now she had to be careful about the topic since on this depended much. If it was not intellectually stimulating, Abba was quite capable of grunting "rubbish" and walking on.

"So, which side of the issue are you supporting?"

"Well, Abba, (she repeated his name as often as she could) I haven't decided yet. I thought, Abba, that you might help me."

"I'll give you both sides."

He would clear his throat and an animated lecture would follow. This Abba, confronted with an abstract concept, would suddenly come to life, his voice sonorous, his face animated. The man that emerged was not her father, but the dazzling reason she would have stayed in a marriage had she been the wife of this acerbic but brilliantly lucid professor.

Often, there was no debate, nor was there a special writing assignment, nor a difficult chapter before an exam; since the only appeal to his attention, if not his emotions, was through the intellect, she armed herself to the teeth and lay siege to his mind. Even though she knew that to him she didn't exist individually but generically as a one-person class, she enjoyed her exclusive moments with Abba. He never looked at her with any real interest, except once, when she opposed his views and spoke passionately, and there had been the flicker of amusement in his eyes. Had Ma already tapped that source? Were their on-going fights their secret and last conjugal resort? These thoughts came to her only incoherently as she learnt to hold her father's interest by carefully provocative intellectual opposition. It was hard work, and he forgot her as soon she was dismissed.

Sometimes Rina had tried to act boyish, wondering if Abba missed a son. Or she played the obliging, sweet-tempered daughter to the hilt. In fact, she never tried harder to woo a man in all her life as she tried the entirety of her growing up as she set out to dazzle her father, getting her stories and poems published in newspapers, becoming the editor of the school magazine, the college debating champion and winning writing competitions and scholarships.

Years later, the one question that Rina often asked herself was whether she had actually ever loved Abba? After his death she wept with a sense of void, though unable to pinpoint where she felt the loss. These bouts left her exhilarated and a little embarrassed too, because she felt it gave the deliciously false impression that she had been wrenched from a particularly close father-daughter relationship, the kind enjoyed by her cousin Mona and her "papa." Showkat knew Abba so little that he accepted her weepy moods as natural. Only Rina knew that Abba himself would have been embarrassed and would have asked her to "kindly snap out of it." In moments like this she doubted she ever loved Abba except as an idea and a challenge, and yet hate and yearning, anger and acceptance, admiration and resentment all loomed large and real. Of course, she knows that hers has been a massive case of unrequited love.

Her most important gift to him, which he took for granted, had been her decision to study his subject, English Literature, rather than what she really wanted: Psychology. He had once proclaimed that she had a flair for writing. At that time she had not realised the despair hidden in that admission until years later when she started to read some of her father's fiction and found them surprisingly disappointing. She had expected them to be arid, but not dissatisfying. She realised then that Abba, the clear-eyed realist, had known for a long time that his writing was barren, that he might have been a brilliant critic but was a sterile artist. Since then, her awe for her father had turned into protective tenderness. His unfinished novel had been left untouched for years, and she had often tried to imagine the agony of working on something one had lost faith in. Her father's books, precious for their clues to his bitterness, had freed her from blaming herself for his lack of love.

Now, her eyes drift to another framed object on the wall. Abba had once corresponded with the great Bengali poet, Tagore. This letter, famous in the family, used to hang high on his study wall. Abba never mentioned it, but Rina had regarded it as a mystical talisman, denoting the accessibility of greatness. Years later, when she got possession of the letter — being the literary one in the family — she finally read it. It consisted of a few kind words by a great man writing to an adolescent acolyte. "Your work shows much talent and promise of a full flowering in the imminent future. My best wishes." Rina had spoken so much about the letter to Tanya that finally, when it was framed on her wall, she was glad that Tanya's Bangla was non-existent, and she merely pointed to the signature: "See, that says 'Rabindranath Tagore. Shantiniketan.'" "Cool!" Tanya had obliged. If it weren't an heirloom, she would have thrown it away, and, with it, Abba's torment.

But Rina had really started to see her father as human and capable of emotional pain only since she got married. It happened with the one incident after her wedding when he took ill and was hospitalised. Showkat had already left for Boston, and Rina was ready to join him. It was the day she went to say goodbye to Abba en route to the airport.

On the way she had speculated about the farewell: would Abba touch her head in blessing; would he pat her hand; or say something terse but memorable? When the time came and she found herself alone with him, he did nothing. She just stood by his bed for an awkward five minutes, waiting for him to say something but the room was stony with his silence. Finally, she cleared her throat and said: "So, Abba, I'll be off." He merely nodded. Stunned by this failed moment, Rina walked off blindly, almost running into her mother in the corridor. She ran to the car, bursting into tears of rage. When Ma joined her, Rina noticed her wiping her eyes. She said: "Your Abba was weeping like a child, his face turned to the wall. He wouldn't speak to me." For a moment, Rina was blank, and then her heart sang out, a surge of triumph hitting the highest notes again and again: "weeping like a child!"

Throughout the flight, she trained her mental camera over the scene of Abba breaking down, from many angles. In Boston, she fought the loneliness of the early days by reassessing her past relationship with her father on the basis of that one glimpse through a crack in Abba's door. This new perspective and the physical distance finally gave her the temerity to write a letter to him. This was the most important letter she had ever written to anyone. It was her first to him, and in it she poured her heart.

She had given it to Showkat along with her other letters. Not wanting it to stand out from the rest, she never mentioned its special importance, and there was no urgency for it to be mailed right away. Showkat had put them all in his coat pocket and smiled indulgently at his homesick, letter-scribbling bride. Rina knew that, for him, her unguarded sighs during a jovial day of playing house, or her quiet sobbing in the night to which he sometimes awoke after drifting from easy passion to contented sleep, was troubling. She tried to school herself and make amends to this gentle person who would do anything to claim the invisible portion of herself she kept from him.

Once she knew the letter was on the way, she remembers sitting back and trying to imagine Abba reading it, moved perhaps, to turning his face away to the wall, refusing to speak to Ma. She imagined Ma's letter: "He keeps reading your letter, won't let me touch it. He seems so changed ...." Often Showkat would catch her smiling and, misunderstanding, would beam back: "I'm happy too." Exactly ten days later, they received the shattering news: Abba had died.

Everything comes back to Rina now. After the initial shock, the one thought that had kept her going was that she had not delayed sending the letter to Abba. Oh! God, how often she had mentioned this to Showkat: "Thank God I sent the letter. You *did* mail it? It must have reached him, *na*?" Poor Showkat. He had held her tightly, in reassurance, she had thought then; his face averted in what she had misinterpreted as transferred grief. Once, when she had calculated aloud the number of days it normally took for US mail to reach Dhaka, she had caught him biting his lips to stop his eyes from brimming, and she had been so touched. Now she understood. Poor man.

Was Ma in on it too? And now she goes over Ma's vague responses: "Well, yes, the driver did bring some letters to the hospital ... darling, I was so exhausted then, running back and forth from home, getting your father's soup ... he hated the hospital food ... but I'm sure he got it .... "

Rina lifts her head from her desk and looks at the unsent, unread, stillborn letter into which she had invested so much life: the power to redeem the past and requite her thwarted love. For years, she had used its fragile wings to reach her dead father's cold heart, when all along it had been right here, a broken carrier pigeon dead before its flight. This failed and festering piece of her past needed a decent burial.

She gets up with an impulse to tear it up and throw it into the wastebasket. Instead she takes it to the kitchen and leaves it along with the other mail for Showkat to discover it: his secret burden of years. Then she makes herself a cup of tea. She isn't angry, she isn't sad, but her husband's kindness, protecting her all these years from the brutal knowledge of the undelivered letter, feels almost like a betrayal.

For a long time she looks out of the window to the backyard where Tanya and Showkat are puttering around. Their laughter drifts to her, and their closeness, for the first time, no longer makes her envious. She feels empty, free, and gets up to return to her study. She thinks she knows the story she will write.

In this version, the letter would get delivered; the father would not die but recover; the letter would never be mentioned; Ma and Abba would visit them; Abba would disdain everything American and rail against the world; Showkat and he would argue, grow formal and then silent; Tanya would roll her eyes behind her grandfather's back and complain to her aunt on weekends: "Nana is such a bore"; and they would all live happily ever after.

On the way, she picks up the envelope from the pile of mail, goes down to the basement and returns it to the bottom drawer.

It's the Heart that Matters*

Towheed Feroze

It was rumoured that Rahim Bux was working for the collaborators. He did not have a good reputation to precede him so when he invited the local Razakars to his home one day, people in the village knew where Bux's allegiance lay.

Before the war began, Bux was the local moneylender. Many farmers took money from him at a high interest and, failing to return the loan, had to forget about their collateral. It was also heard that Bux secretly supplied information about Mukti Bahini movements to his new boss. Anyway, when almost all the villagers were secretly cursing him, Bux was in terrific spirits. "Oi, who is around to get me a *paan*!" bellowed the man as he took out a cigarette. Everyone was saying that the war had brought misery for the good but profit for the likes of Rahim Bux. Bux knew that he was being compared to Satan, but he didn't care, "I know what I am pursuing and my conscience tells me to keep on going," thought Rahim.

"Here is your *paan*," said his wife, entering the room. "The whole country is suffering. People with a minimum sense of patriotism have either gone to war or are trying to help the cause, but all you are concerned about is making money. Don't you have a moral duty towards the country?"

Bux smiled and said, "Those who want to fight can go and fight. But I don't want to fight. Do you want to spend the rest of your life as a widow, desperately trying to make ends meet? I sure hope not. And money? My dear wife, where would a person be without it?"

"But, you have enough money already. Why do you crave for more?" she asked.

Bux laughed heartily and replied, "More? Can anyone have enough? Money is what makes the world go around."

She realised that it was futile talking to him and left, muttering something under her breath.

---

*Published in *Weekend Independent*, March 28, 2003.

Bux took the *paan,* relished the pungent taste, took a long relaxing puff from his cigarette and slipped into his imaginary world of accounts.

"No, we cannot let this man go on aiding the Razakars," declared Rouf Master with conviction. He was talking to a few local people.

"Have you heard that Rahim Mahajan plans to supply information about Mukti Bahini camps to the enemy?" asked one of the men.

"I hear that for information on Mukti forces, Bux will get paid handsomely," said another.

"We all know what he is up to, but we cannot do anything because the Razakar force is still very strong here and our boys are not equipped enough to come in and occupy the village," cut in Rouf Master. "But, we must try our best to hinder this rascal's malicious efforts."

"Bux is our man. He is scheming, he is greedy, he is slimy and he will even sell his wife for money. He will supply us with the right information," said Abu Hamid, the local top man of the group of Razakars.

"But, what if he betrays us?" asked someone.

"Bux? No, he will not betray us." Hamid was confident. "The lure of financial gain — getting money — is an overwhelming need for him. Let's say for him money is like oxygen. It makes him live."

"Bux has already told us that tonight at midnight, a group of Muktis will come to the house of Keramat Mian to get some supplies. Our men are ready. We will have the place surrounded and when they come, their hopes of liberty will be grenaded to bits," commented Salekhin, Hamid's deputy.

After a refreshing cup of tea, Bux prepared to go out.

"Where are you going?" asked his wife.

"Going to find out something," came the curt reply.

"Please!" she implored, "for Allah's sake don't go against your country and your villagers."

Bux dismissed her with a non-committal wave and strolled out. "Women! Always asking questions and making a scene!" he said aloud.

He was waiting on the outskirts of the village. With an unshaven face, unkempt hair and worn-out clothes, no one would give him a second glance.

Resting against the mango tree, he counted the minutes. His informant was supposed to be here any minute. At a distance he could see him and he just couldn't control a snigger. "What was he doing, dressed like a woman?"

The elderly "woman" crossed him, ignoring him totally. But while passing, "she" dropped a small piece of paper.

The night was dark and Keramat Mian's house showed no signs of activity. Hamid and his group had been hiding for about two hours, but so far the only adversary had been the brigade of unyielding mosquitoes. The ferocity with which they were attacking made Hamid think that they had joined hands with the Muktis. In fear of making noise they could not kill the mosquitoes, so the only thing to do was to sit back helplessly and let them carry on their blood-sucking mission.

"But, it is way past midnight. Where are the Muktis?" Hamid's whispered query was lost in the pitch-black darkness.

In the house under strong vigilance, two people tucked in bed were talking in hushed tones. "Who gave you the tip-off that the Razakars would be waiting?" asked the wife.

"I don't know. A man came with a shawl covered over his head and face. He told me to inform the Muktis and I did accordingly."

"But whoever it was, he took an awful risk," observed the wife but Keramat didn't reply as he was already lost in deep sleep.

"This is the second time this has happened. Someone is informing the Muktis," roared Hamid. The mosquito bites from the previous night had given him a swollen face and for one second he actually looked like a healthy pig. But Bux could not say that.

"Saar," Bux said, with all the subservience and sycophancy that he could muster, "I have no idea about who did this, but let me assure you that my information was not baseless."

Hamid did not doubt Bux but he was sure that someone was leaking out information.

"May I suggest that all of us get together at my house and talk this matter over. I will also ask Rouf Master to come over. It appears that there is a small group in the village actively working for the Muktis. If we give them some serious threat then it might work," Bux suggested.

Hamid liked the idea and it was decided that next afternoon all of them would gather at Bux's house.

"Have you heard that someone tipped the Muktis that Keramat Mian's house would be surrounded?" a villager, glowing with suppressed excitement, told the small gathering at Rouf Master's.

"Yes, we have and the worst thing is that as a result of that tipping, the situation in the village is not very congenial. The Razakars have asked me to be at Rahim Bux's house this afternoon. Who knows what they are planning. The village is under the vigilant guard of Abu Hamid's goons, so no one can go out to inform our boys. Let's hope someone gets the word through to the Mukti Bahini," came the rather concerned observation of Rouf Master.

At Bux's house, the kitchen was operating in full gear. After all, the bosses were coming today. "What a man my husband is! He goes against the people of the country, makes money from it and invites our enemies to lunch when our boys are fighting on empty stomachs," fumed Bux's wife angrily.

Overhearing his wife from the adjacent room, Bux laughed out loud with devilish delight, "My dear wife, why do you hate me so? Maybe I am not as bad as you think. After all, I am taking care of you and our children. What I am doing is for our good."

Rahim Bux's main room was filled with people. All the main collaborators were seated waiting for some dessert after a heavy appetising lunch. Rouf Master was in one corner, trying desperately to appear calm, but inside he felt that "today something will go wrong."

At frequent intervals, Hamid gave fiery looks at the Master. "Today you will be taught a good lesson."

The hookah came and all of the collaborators took puffs in turn. Hamid looked at Bux and said, "I have asked my men to bring the villagers. In front of them you will beat up Rouf Master and set an example. From now on anyone conspiring against us will be dealt with severely. The beating will act as a warning — next time we will not be so lenient."

A greasy smile hovered on Bux's lips and Rouf looked at him with marked disgust, but what Bux said took Master totally off guard. "No, my dear Hamid, we will not beat Rouf Master. I have a better plan — we will tie you and your disciples up and hand you to the Muktis. They will know what to do."

For one second, Hamid thought that Bux was joking, but his instincts told him that he was not. He and his followers tried to get up but they could not move.

"What is this?" he shouted in panic. Somehow their bodies had become paralysed.

"It is a small but very potent powder that I mixed with your tobacco. You see, my dear Hamid, it was I who was passing out the information, and don't expect your men, they have been neutralised by our boys."

"But how can you be one of them? You are a man who loves money, you are a traitor, a double-dealer, a loan shark," blurted out the leader of the collaborators.

"Yes, I am all that and perhaps more, but I am, at heart, a Bangladeshi," said Bux, taking out the carbine from behind the bamboo closet. Rouf Master's eyes became moist in pride as, pushing the door, the Mukti Bahini commander entered.

Story of a Night's Journey*

Shabnam Nadiya

njona first noticed the girl as she was moving toward the door of the bus. It was one o'clock in the morning. They were on their way to Cox's Bazar. The bus had stopped for the passengers to have a cup of tea, a bite to eat, a moment to stretch their legs. After hours of sitting scrunched up motionless in her seat, Anjona needed it. It was a big bus and comfortable, but, with her daughter's head resting delicately in the crook of her neck, she had been careful not to move too much. Her daughter was skinny little girl and needed her rest. With the excitement of the long awaited trip to the seaside, who knows how much sleep the child would get in the coming days? It would be a terrible thing if they returned to Dhaka just to have the girl fall ill with something — her sister-in-law kept insinuating anyway that Anjona wasn't a good enough mother.

As she was preparing to get off the bus, her husband said, "Where's your purse?"

"On my seat," she replied.

"Well, don't just leave it there, go and get it! Do I have to tell you everything? Women!" Her husband grumbled. As he looked away, Anjona stuck her tongue out at him playfully, making the children giggle.

Anjona turned around to return to her seat. She wouldn't have noticed the girl at all (she didn't notice people or her surroundings much these days), except that the sudden jerking movement in one of the seats caught the corner of her eye. The inside of the bus was half dark. Anjona looked and saw a figure huddled in the seat with the face twisted away. It was a female figure, a man sitting beside it. The man was laughing and saying something bent over the girl. In that single glance she noted that the two were holding hands. The sound of happy laughter touched her. Newly weds? Anjona passed them and went for

---

*Published in *Star Magazine*, August 22 and 29, 2003.

her bag. Maybe they were on their honeymoon, she idly thought, holding hands like that. She had never had a honeymoon. In fact, this was the first time she was going anywhere with her husband. On her way back she thought of turning again to have a better look at the girl, just to see her face, nothing more, but her husband called out, "Have you found it?"

"Yes," she said and hurried towards him. The children were waiting impatiently just by the steps of the bus.

"Hurry up, Ammu!" her children called, "You always make us late!"

Their father smiled at her, "Let's get something to eat."

Her son and daughter were chattering away excitedly between themselves. It was all such an adventure to them. Spending the whole night on a bus, dozing their way to the sea, walking into a brightly lit restaurant at one in the morning. Anjona took her daughter to the bathroom and instructed her husband to take their seven-year-old son. This was the only chance they would have of relieving themselves for the rest of the night.

"Ammu, you stand here while I go?" her daughter asked. Her eyes looked swollen with sleep and her long lashes blinked rather slowly as if unsure whether they were supposed to be awake at this time of night or not. Anjona felt a deep swirling inside her heart as she watched the frail frame of her child walk into the toilet. She recalled how disappointed her in-laws had been at the birth of this child. Everyone had been expecting a son. All the signs had said that the child was to be a boy. The shape of her distended belly, her morning sickness, the way she walked, the dreams she used to have — it was all there. And yet when the time came .... Anjona remembered cringing inside when she had woken up after her period of difficult labour to find out that she had given birth to a girl. Not that anyone had neglected the child. No, she was the first grandchild her grandmother had had and had been treated like a princess. It was just the way ... anyway, that had probably more to do with Anjona herself then the child.

Her daughter came out. Anjona handed her the bag, "You hold this while I go, okay?"

Her daughter nodded with a serious face. "Ammu, the flush doesn't work."

Anjona held her breath as she went in.

Her father had died when she was a child. Among the other deprivations that this fact entitled her to, Anjona had learnt when her family began looking for a groom for her, it also made her less saleable as a bride. She was refused a number of times because, according to the groom families, she had grown up without proper guidance. When she finally did manage to snag a husband, it was because of her complexion more than anything else. Well, at least she had managed to pass her fair skin on to her daughter — that would be a good thing when the time came to marry her off.

Anjona came out of the toilet and stood at the basin to wash her hands.

"Have you washed your hands?" she asked her daughter.

"No," her daughter said guiltily and stepped forward.

A moment's silence, then her daughter said, "Ammu, is Dadi very angry because we came to Cox's Bazar?"

Anjona's hands stopped moving under the flowing water, "Why do you ask?"

"I think she is."

Anjona rinsed her hands and slowly shook the water off them. She watched the water as it trickled endlessly out of the tap.

"Did she say anything to you?"

"She said … well, she said that if you had had better care and came from a better family then you wouldn't go dancing off to places the first chance you got."

Anjona handed her daughter a tissue, trying fast to think of something to say to her daughter without denigrating her mother-in-law too much.

"She said that to you?"

"No, she was talking to Asma Bua. I was playing in her room."

"Well! Anjona thought. That woman! Saying something like that to the maid … and then getting angry because servants these days didn't show proper respect. Her daughter was looking at her expecting some response. Anjona opened her mouth to tell her that her grandmother was old, that old people sometimes behaved strangely … she began telling her the things that a good daughter-in-law should. And then suddenly she didn't want to. She wanted to be bad and bitchy, and tell her daughter that her grandmother was an old hag and always had been an old hag and that the last thing she wanted her daughter to do was to emulate her grandmother in anything she did.

But she didn't. Instead of saying any of these things, Anjona pulled her daughter close and said, "Here, let me comb your hair. It's an absolute mess."

"Ammu!" agonised her daughter as she twisted away. "Not now. I want a coke!"

And so Anjona followed her daughter out of the toilet, envying the slickness with which childhood could keep unpleasant thoughts and memories out of sight and out of mind indefinitely. It was such a long time since she had been a child.

How dare she say something like that? She was the mother of two children now! And after twelve years of marriage the fact that she had lacked the stern rigour of a father's discipline and that one of her female cousins had eloped still made her a girl from a family with loose morals. Still made her less of everything that her husband's family was. Her mother-in-law had made a career out of making Anjona feel less. Less nice, less moneyed, less pretty, less decent, less respectable, less religious — why on earth she had deigned to let Anjona enter her family at all was a mystery.

Anjona sat at the table her husband and son had been holding for them and tried not to think. She watched her family as they talked, joked and laughed while they ate and sipped slowly at the cup of tea she had ordered. She was going to the seaside with her family — this was a good thing. For a few days she would not think of her mother-in-law or her sister-in-law or about the "women trouble" (as her husband called her in-law problems whenever she attempted to discuss them with him). For a few days she would be glad just to be alive. For a few days she would feel what it was like to be alive.

But how could she have said something like that in front of the maid, in front of her granddaughter? Anjona couldn't decide which was worse.

Everybody was done eating and drinking. "Are you sure you don't want anything to eat?" Her husband asked her. When she shook her head without saying anything he called to the waiter for the bill.

The bus assistant came to their table with a smile and said, "Aren't you Blue Bird passengers? The bus will be leaving in fifteen minutes."

Her husband nodded and said, "We'll be out in ten minutes."

The assistant left. Her son began an argument with his sister about changing their seats. He wanted to sit with Ammu this time. Her daughter said no and stuck her tongue out at him. Her husband interrupted their argument, "No fighting — that was the deal, remember?" And all through this, while all this was going on around her, Anjona sat there with a slight smile fixed to her lips and saw and heard nothing. All through this, all she could think of was after all these years, after all these years making a home for her husband, being a good little wife, after the pain and pleasure of having two children, what was she? No matter how nice she was, no matter how "good" she tried to be, no matter what care she took of her mother-in-law, Anjona was still the girl whose mother had not taught her properly how to sew because she had once sewed uneven pleats in her mother-in-law's blouse. She would forever be the fatherless girl whose sisters eloped and whose relatives made bad marriages, the girl whose family was not quite up to the mark in terms of character and morals. "Nothing really changes in life," she thought to herself sardonically. "We just grow heavier and more wrinkled."

Anjona left the shiny roadside restaurant with her family and boarded the bus. The honeymooners whose happiness she had wanted to steal a glance at were nowhere in her mind at the moment. Yet, when she climbed into the bus, the man's seat was empty and the girl was standing half in the aisle trying to put a bag in the overhead compartment. Her head was covered with a red, heavily embroidered *orna* effectively hiding her face. Anjona would have passed her by unnoticed this time except for something familiar in the way the girl's slim body moved. As Anjona moved forward, the girl slid into the darkness of her seat and could be seen no longer except as an obscure shadow, the contours of which merged with that of the bus window and the seat.

Puzzled, Anjona followed her husband and children to their own seats, wondering why the girl felt familiar. This time — their disagreement resolved by their father — the son came to sit with the mother with a triumphant smile at his sister. Anjona took a scarf out of her bag and handed it to her husband to wrap around their daughter's throat. Her son chattered to her excitedly about all the things he expected the sea to be, and the crabs he was going to catch and the shells he was going to collect, the bus and the journey, the food he had just eaten as the bus once again resumed its journey. Unlike the daughter who was older, in his intense excitement the son did not require too deep a response to any of his talk, and judicious interjections of "hmm" and "really?" from his mother were enough to keep him happy. Soon he began dozing, his head occasionally bumping against his mother's shoulder. Someone snorted in their sleep somewhere at the back. Anjona sat and thought throughout the night.

Dawn arrived, peeking through the ragtag curtains spread over the bus windows. An hour at most and they would be there. People were stirring throughout the bus, waking up to the unaccustomed — to early light. Anjona watched a shard of sunlight scraping her son's cheek as he slept. His immature face seemed to bear a queer imprint of his father's face. He was a good man, the children's father. But that didn't make much difference to her life. Anjona had decided to have a "talk" with her mother-in-law once she got back home. It was about time. For once she would behave with them the way they behaved towards her. For once she would attempt to be someone.

Her husband stretched and looked at her, "Haven't you slept at all?"

"No," she replied briefly.

"I've had a grand sleep," he yawned, "but I'm still sleepy."

Anjona moved the curtain and looked out of the window without answering. Her daughter rubbed her eyes and sat up straight. "Ammu, are we there yet?"

Anjona didn't answer.

Someone at the front called out to the bus assistant, "Bhai, how long till we get there?"

The assistant walked down the aisle holding on to the backs of the seats, "Half an hour at the most."

"That was fast," said Anjona's husband.

"Yes, Sir, the roads were clear and our drivers are very good." The assistant moved to the front of the bus again.

"Are we early?" asked Anjona.

"Oh, yes, we're only supposed to be at Chittagong by now. We're almost an hour and a half ahead." He reached across and shook their son awake. "Come on, sleepy head. Don't you want to see the sea?"

The child sat up and blinked then smiled eagerly at his parents. "Where is it? Are we there?"

"Of course not, stupid, we'll be there in half an hour," his sister replied with a wise air.

Their father laughed.

"Abbu, can I sit with Apu now?" asked the son.

"Okay ... but no fighting!" Anjona's husband climbed out of his seat to let brother and sister sit together.

She moved to the window seat; he sat down beside her. He dozed off again almost immediately.

After a while, he asked, "Aren't you hungry? You didn't have anything to eat in the night."

"Didn't feel like it," she replied shortly.

"Is there anything wrong?" he asked.

"What do you mean — wrong?"

"Well, you sound ..."

"I sound what?" she didn't even let him finish.

He turned and looked at her. "Look," he began, "If I have...."

"Your mother told my maid that because of my family background I go dancing off the first chance I get."

He didn't say anything. Just looked at her.

"She said it to the maid," Anjona repeated. "In front of our daughter."

Her husband exhaled slowly. "If Amma said...."

"Yes, yes, I know, you're not to be bothered with women trouble, it's not your problem. It never is." Anjona moved her body slightly away and looked out the window.

Soon they had reached Cox's Bazar, and they were even treated to a glimpse of the sea like a trailer of coming attractions for a forthcoming film. Her son was bouncing up and down on his seat in excitement, while her daughter tried to retain her composure in keeping with her elder sister status. But her excitement at the sight of the waves billowing onto the sandy beach was betrayed by the sheer exuberance of her smile.

"Ammu, did you see, did you see?" they clamoured. Although this was the first time for Anjona too, somehow she didn't feel as excited as she had thought she would be.

The bus stopped and people began tickling towards the exit, still half-wrapped comfortably in sleep. Anjona checked the seat pockets a last time and followed her children off the bus. She climbed down onto the road and stood a bit to the side with the children, while her husband went to the side of the bus to see about their luggage. The people who had got off before them had already got their bags and were beginning to drift away — some looking this way and that for rickshaws, some moving purposefully ahead to their destinations on foot. It was then that it happened.

Her husband turned and beckoned to her to come and help him with their bags. Anjona told the children to wait there while she went and helped, their father. As she walked towards him, the couple she had thought of as honeymooners were walking towards her, carrying a bag each. The girl still had the red *orna* covering her head. As they walked toward her, for the first time, Anjona saw the girl's face. She stopped in mid stride. It was Sheila. Her mother-in-law's niece. That was why even in the darkness of the interior of the bus, Anjona had felt that the girl was familiar, for Anjona had known the girl for the whole twelve years of her marriage. Sheila, who was studying history at the university. Sheila, whose mother had complained that marrying their boy to Anjona had not been such a good idea. Sheila, who was not walking with her hand lightly but intimately resting on the man's arm. Sheila who was not married.

Anjona felt a peculiar sense of satisfaction, bordering on cruel exultation. Well, well, well. Now where would the good name of the family be? This family whose daughters danced off with men the first chance they got? So this was how Sheila spent the time she was supposedly staying in the university hall studying with friends. Now what would Sheila's mother and aunt have to say about this, she wondered? Particularly to the undisciplined, misguided, coming-from-a-bad-family daughter-in-law.

Thoughts raced through Anjona's head in seconds, vindictive, cold, satisfied thoughts. Then their eyes met and she looked at Sheila's face. For a second there was recognition in the eyes that were glowing with happiness — and then there was just heartstopping fear. Ashen white, the girl's face twisted in fear, as if the future had come and suddenly stood right in front of her. Her male companion (he was a boy really, Anjona now saw), not understanding, was looking at her with concern and was asking what was wrong. In about two seconds he would follow her stricken gaze and look at Anjona.

And at that moment Anjona felt as if she could never ever look into her daughter's eyes again with a clear conscience. She felt that forever after when she laughed with her daughter in shared happiness, or asked to be let in on a secret that only children were supposed to know, there would always be a small place where that sunshine could not enter. And that small piece of darkness she would carry around in her heart for as long as she lived, perhaps longer.

Anjona smiled at Sheila's stricken face. There was so much that she wanted to say in that one smile — so much disappointment and joy and love and laughter was stuffed inside her that it was like a fire in her belly that reached and seared the inside of her throat. Anjona said nothing — for there were no words that could say the things that needed to be said.

Anjona walked past Sheila as she walked past the other people from the bus. She smiled at her husband, a smile as clear and happy as her daughter's, a smile that could swallow misery and turn it into something so preciously close to joy, and said, "Come on, hurry up, slow coach, the children are waiting."

Detached Belonging

Dilruba Z. Ara

She stared at him. She could not make out whether he had impaired hearing, or if it was that he really couldn't understand her Swedish. Each time she opened her mouth to say something, he put his right hand behind his ear, cupped it and leant towards her. The gesture embarrassed her, surprised her, infuriated her. But during her seven years in this country, she had learned to cope with such non-verbal assaults on herself. Whenever she encountered attitudes of this kind, she invariably alienated her mind from herself by diving deep down into her past, by going back to her childhood, by reaching out for her forgotten ego. That journey always provided her with a unique sensation of being superior to her environment. At this moment too, it happened. It happened in her head. All of a sudden Dr. K appeared as a person extraordinarily limited by his professional outfit. The white coat! She watched. But she listened no longer to him, for she heard her own voice in her head. For sure, you're a first-rate doctor, but would anyone recognise you without your coat? Even if I come from a poor country, my individual history is richer than yours. My progenitors are held in esteem by all my fellow countrymen. Ah! You are probably thinking that like many other fortune seekers I came to your country to taste your riches. No, Sir, you're absolutely wrong. I came here because of love. Only for love. Had I been admitted in a hospital at home now, everyone would have known me. They would have understood me .... At least I think they would .... Suddenly she felt exhausted and her thoughts took a different route. And so what? What does that matter? I might not survive this illness. In any case, I'm condemned to a life of anonymity. That's how it is .... She could no longer ignore Dr. K. The fragments of his extensive lecture on the high standard of Swedish hospitals floated now freely into her ears. But all this she knew even before she had fallen ill. She also knew that the hospital midwife was responsible for her present condition, and that, holding this eulogy on Swedish medication, Dr. K. was actually trying to minimise the midwife's professional incompetence. A Swedish midwife. A genuine Swedish midwife. Blonde with pale eyes behind a pair of blue glasses .... She hid a large yawn behind her hand. The tablets. Yes, the tranquillisers were getting hold of her. She dozed off for a minute.

Dr. K. rose. "Don't worry! We'll take good care of you. As I said, Swedish hospitals have a good reputation."

He turned and left.

She yawned again, stretched out for the remote control, pressed a button. It was news on the telly. She switched it off. With a tremendous effort she turned herself on the bed. Took the book that was lying there. It was a book about her creed. Islam.

Later that day a strange young man made his appearance. He came in as if he were an old acquaintance of hers, and settled down by the top of her bed. He introduced himself as an ex-orderly of the clinic. Then he fell into an abrupt silence. His fingers combed through her long black hair, bringing back the memories of her father's fingers on her head during her childhood. She sank into a luxuriant feeling of being cared for, at the same time as she struggled with herself to tell him that he shouldn't be touching her hair.

She was about to tell him that, when he suddenly said: "I'm so sorry! What's happening to you is gruesome. It's terrible ... terrible!"

She looked up at his face. He had aquatic blue eyes and a mass of curly golden hair. Like a cherub's. He seemed so concerned. For a moment she forgot her own tragedy and smiled. During her four days at the hospital, she had had several unexpected visitors. She was well aware that her case was not even one in a million in Dr. K.'s words. Her ailment had given all these hospital people an opportunity for a new experience, as much as it had rendered her a new identity. It was amusing, undeniably. She was no longer just any foreign woman, but a particular foreign woman with a rare disease. A phenomenon for a case study. An object of attention. A curious sense of delight pervaded her mind at the thought, which she with another part of her mind tried to reject. She knew that it was an ignoble feeling. But, despite all her efforts, she failed to keep the feeling at a distance. The smile clung to her face for a while. She was, after all, a human being of flesh and blood.

She was also carrying a human of flesh and blood. In other words, she was expecting. The foetus in her womb had already reached an age

of twenty-five weeks. She had been feeling below the weather for a
long time, and had already been at hospital in the beginning of her
pregnancy for nausea and weight loss. She was discharged after two
weeks. Since then she had been seeing only the hospital-midwife once
a week. But the midwife staunchly disregarded her ever-increasing
complaints. Her last visit to the maternity hospital had ended in the
following manner five days earlier.

Having measured the curve of her belly, the midwife declared,
"This is a curvature for twins. Your belly has really become big."

"You know that there's protein in my urine. I've gained six kilos in
two weeks in spite of the fact that I can't keep any food down. What's
wrong with me?"

The midwife, who was a robust woman, straightened herself,
pushed back her blue spectacles on the bridge of her protruding nose.
"There is nothing wrong with you. Either you're going to have twins, or
one large baby."

The sick woman closed her eyes in exasperation. She didn't wish to
be an imperfect patient, but intuitively she knew that she needed
professional help. Back at home she could have changed clinics, but
here she had no option. She belonged to this district and this was the
only hospital in the vicinity. She had already travelled thirty kilometres
to come here.

She breathed deeply for a while and then screwing up her courage
pleaded: "But, I can hardly recognise any symptoms from my first
pregnancy. My nose bleeds. I've terrible bouts of headache. I see
flashes of lighting. My blood pressure has gone up, and now I'm
swelling like a balloon. There must be something wrong. All this seems
to me to be the pure signs of toxaemia. I've read a lot of literature, and
if you don't mind I would like to see my doctor. Could you please
arrange for me to see him?"

The midwife put the yellow measuring tape around her neck and
took a step backwards, thrust both her hands in the pockets of her
white coat and made a face as though her professional pride was being
harassed. A deep frown appeared on her forehead, and her eyes
narrowed behind her thick glasses. How would this woman from a
third world country know what was good for her? It was she herself
who had all the knowledge about all mothers and all deliveries. She
was not just any midwife, she was a Swedish midwife. Swedish
midwives were highly acclaimed all over the world. Naturally the body

belonged to the woman and the baby was in her womb, but how would she know what was good for her? Only the midwife could decide whether she needed to a see a doctor or not. And that she certainly did not.

"You read too much," the midwife said, putting on a grave face. "Doctors are for ailing people. Pregnancy is not an ailment. Go home and take rest."

The pregnant woman felt her blood boiling in her veins, but she had already tired herself by trying to be persuasive. She was not equal to one more attempt. An ill-defined feeling of revolt sizzled and dissolved within her. Seven years of practised muteness was not easy to overcome. It would need a lot of practising. She repeated to herself that it would be beneath her dignity to argue with an ordinary midwife. Had she been at home, she would have taken different measures. Yes, she would certainly have. She would have put the midwife in her place. She would have made herself heard. Her parents, her relatives, her siblings would have seen to that. But here she was alone in spite of the fact that her husband was Swedish. Really Swedish. Just like the midwife. He was there in the room, but he made no protest either. Slowly she sat up in bed. A terrible pain stabbed through her rib cage just under her right breast. Her heart palpitated so loudly that she thought the sound would upset the tranquillity of the room. She gasped for a moment before raising herself. Her legs buckled under her. But her mind set them to work. It took her whole two minutes before she could shuffle out of the room.

Her husband said anxiously: "Can you manage?"

"I must go to a doctor. Perhaps we can ask the almoner at the maternity clinic to help us. I know her."

"You do?"

"Yes, I got to know her, last time I was hospitalised."

"Well, in that case, we can give it a try."

A couple of hours later, thanks to the almoner, she was checked by Dr. K. He himself did the ultrasound scan on her, and told her that the foetus in her womb was dying. The disease had a strange name. It was called *idiopathic hydrop fetalis*. An incurable disease. And the woman herself was seriously ill. But there was still time to set things right. Meetings were held behind closed doors. She was sent from one hospital to another, one doctor to another. Investigations after investigations. But everywhere she was given the same answer. The foetus would most probably die in the belly, but could she continue carrying a dying child? To abort a foetus of twenty-five weeks was against the law. One had to apply for permission from the National Board of Health and Welfare. But what if they got permission? Would she be able to cope with the trauma if they removed the live child and then let it die? Would she? Would she be able to go through such an ordeal in her present condition? She was seriously ill herself. Shouldn't they at least try to save one life? These were the questions that worried the doctors of the maternity clinic.

She had to make a real effort to adjust to the situation. A cabin was fixed up for her in the maternity clinic. She was helped into hospital clothes and tucked up in bed. Her life was now in the hands of the doctors. She tried to think of her parents, of her son, but she couldn't keep one thought separate from the other. Too many things were happening at the same time. Every hour. On the following day permission for abortion was granted. But she was in a quandary. How was she to let them take her live child away and then let it die? The child was still alive. She could still hear the sounds of its heartbeat. But her condition was getting worse. Her body itched and hurt all over. Her stomach distended grotesquely. Each limb was swelling up. Her legs were becoming elephantine, her fingers becoming like bulbous sausages. Her accumulating weight kept her confined to bed. From a distance one could hear water gurgling within her. Medical teams trickled into her room ceaselessly. Everyone was extra sympathetic. Someone wondered whether she had any relatives nearby who could come to visit her, someone wondered whether she longed for any special meal. Someone else suggested shrimp-filled crepes.

She shook her head. Her family was at home. A long way off. On the other side of the globe. She longed for her home. She longed for her parents. She longed for mashed potatoes with mustard oil, for a refreshing bowl of *dal*. How could they ever fulfil her wishes? How could they ever understand that a seriously ill person doesn't long for foreign cuisine?

That morning Dr. K made his appearance in her room much earlier than usual. He had a few people with him. All identically dressed in the white coats of their noble profession. They encircled her. One presented himself as a doctor of anaesthesia, one as an X-ray expert, and one as a midwife, and so on. It was the fifth day. A Sunday. On Sundays doctors never performed operations, but they were all there.

All ready to cut her up. Take her child away from her belly. She held her breath.

"We'll have to take you now," Dr.K said.

"Your life is hanging by a thread," one lady doctor added.

"We don't need your approval any more. We must try to save you."

"You can't fight any more. Every second is valuable."

"I'm not a murderess," she answered.

"You're going to murder yourself."

"No, no, no ...."

She woke up to find herself in a different room. For a moment she was surprised. Confused. She saw that her feet, hands, arms, nose and finger tops were attached to diverse tubes. The room was equipped with several computer screens. Quite a few bags of blood and other substances hung from a holder by her head She couldn't tell what time of the day it was. The curtain was drawn across the only window. She was vaguely aware that two people in white coats were moving about in the semi-darkened room. They seemed weightless. Like people on the moon. It took her a while to realise that she was in an ICU cabin. But why? Why had they moved her here? She would have liked to return to her old room. She made an effort to speak, but her tongue fell back in her mouth. It was as dry as a desert and coarse like a cactus leaf. Her neck was hurting. Her eyes were dry. Her stomach scooped out. Empty. It was not at all difficult to lie on her back. She thought of the child. They had taken the child way. She was not very sad. But she should be sad. Ashamed of her lack of maternal feelings, she looked up at the white ceiling. The child was gone. Gone from her womb. But her breasts were leaking. Her shirt was soaking in milk. The child was gone. But the food was still there. Life continued as usual. Even if she had died, life would have continued. What was then the meaning of living?

But the child was not yet totally gone from the world. Her tiny corpse was still in the hospital morgue. And it took ten whole days, before the woman regained some of her lost strength. On the eleventh say she sat up on the bed and declared, "I want to see my child."

"It's just a chunk of meat. Not a very pretty sight. Why do you want to see her?" wondered Dr. K.

Her eyes widened a little, but she was neither angered, nor saddened. Just a tiny bit surprised. Her first child too had been born in the same hospital. Dr. K had taken care of him as well. That child had

had cheeks like apricots, and his hair had been a riot of black curls. Passersby used to stop by his cot to admire his unusual beauty. Now Dr. K said that the second issue from the same uterus was an aberration which would shock even the mother.

She sighed, "Wouldn't you like to see it, if it were yours?"

"Naturally I would. I'm a doctor. I'm used to nature's vagaries. By the way, have you ever seen a corpse?"

She gaped. This time genuinely surprised. Who hadn't seen corpses in her native country? There one lived together with death. What a peculiar question! God almighty! But she hid her thoughts well, and answered, "I've seen children being killed in front of my eyes."

A scene shot through her mind. Nineteen seventy-one. In the old town of Dhaka. A man snatches an infant from a young mother's arms and throws it like a ball on the sun-heated asphalt. The skull crushes. Brain and blood blend with the dust and dirt. The mother wails. But just for a moment. There is the sound of a machine gun. Her body falls next to her child's. They lie there together. Mother and child. Dead.

"Is that true?" The colour had drained from Dr. K's face.

She had to blink to chase the scene away as she smiled and nodded embarrassingly. She understood that her past had made her more experienced than this middle-aged doctor. Experiences made one wise. That meant, she was wiser than Dr. K. Now she didn't have to reach out for her forgotten ego to feel good about herself. This awareness both gladdened and troubled her. She looked at Dr. K. and nodded abstractedly.

Dr. K. stood up. "I think you'll be able to handle it. But, she has undergone a post-mortem, mind you."

"Yes, I know."

"You're welcome."

When she reached the high door of the morgue, the janitor of the morgue came forward. He whispered, "She doesn't look that bad."

It was not difficult for her to understand that with these words the kind man was trying to save her from an unexpected shock. She gave him a glance of gratitude. And took one step into the room, and took it in. It was a big room. High in the ceiling. Rectangular. White. Lavishly lighted. The glass-paned tall window in one of the smaller walls was closed. A drape hung over it. A row of high-backed chairs stood along each longer wall. In accordance with her wishes, Dr, K had wrapped the child in a towel and had laid it down on the narrow bed, which was set horizontally on the floor. At the top of the bed burned two candles with a fat red book in between. The Bible! The woman suddenly froze at the realisation and swallowed a mouthful of saliva. Her dead child had the Bible by its head. She didn't know what was the most shocking: the empty chairs, the dead child, or the Bible. There was an explosion in her mind. She wanted to cry out. But, instead, she closed her eyes, reciting verses from the Quran silently. It took her a while before she could gain her bearing to take one step towards the bed. Her child. Her daughter was lying there. An extremely small human being in an extremely large bed. The whole scene reminded her of Swift's description of Gulliver in the land of the giants. Tiny feet and tiny hands. Ten toes and ten fingers. Delicate feet. Like a baby doll's. But these were made of flesh and blood. Not of plastic. The face was swollen. Like a puffed-up pita bread. One could hardly see what was what. She leant over the body to lift it up. Suddenly the towel slipped away, revealing the rough thread and the hasty stitches from the dissection. She felt her energy being sapped away. One more unexpected thing would break her down completely. She must keep her feelings at bay. Whoever did it obviously didn't think that the baby would be on display. She must not blame anyone. In Sweden many people chose not to see their dead relatives. Death belonged to hospitals, morgues, churches and graveyards. Not to living souls. She held the child hard against her bosom and sat down on a chair. Two drops of tears coursed down her cheeks. The child should be put to rest in peace immediately. Following Islamic rituals. But where was she to find an Islamic burial ground? There had to be at least one in this country. A few minutes passed. The candles burnt. Dr. K remained seated quietly in one corner, while her husband sat next to her. As quietly. The janitor had left them to themselves. She glanced across the room. The empty chairs reminded her once more of her isolation. Had she been at home now, her relatives, neighbours and friends would have been sitting there. They would have lightened the burden. They would have completed all the necessary rituals to bury the child.

Strength!

She needed strength.

She kissed the infant, raised herself and put it carefully down on the bed. She must start investigation at once. The dead don't like to wait .... She must find a solution.

As she walked through the empty subterranean corridor of the hospital, she said, "Dr. K, I would like to go home. Please release me."

"Why? You're not completely well, yet. Your blood pressure is still too high."

"I must go home. You don't understand. I've a lot to do."

"You must be under constant care at least one more week."

"I must go home. I must."

"I'm responsible for your health."

Suddenly she halted. Then turning, she faced Dr. K, and grabbed his hand in hers. "Thank you. Thank you for everything you've done for me. I shall never forget your kindness. But, please do let me go home."

Dr. K stared at her for a while, and then said, "Well, I'll have to consult my colleagues."

"Thank you ever so much!"

They moved on. Out of the corners of her eyes she looked at her husband. He was so trustworthy, but so blind about her private needs. Could he understand what was going through her mind, what feelings were surging through her? Would he ever be able to understand what she had given up to be with him? She had married out of her circle, but had been fighting as though possessed to retain her identity. The result of that struggle was this loneliness. She could no longer rescue herself from this loneliness. She couldn't even express herself. She had not only left her country, she had also left her language. During her seven years she hadn't tasted loneliness in this manner. She had never been aware of such perfect desolation. Her child lay there, sewn up like a jute sack with the Bible by its head. What else could have happened to underline the extent of her losses? Her heart shuddered. She lowered her head and walked on. The corridor was infinitely long. Cold. Barren. Like a lost route in a no-man's-land.

Tick-Tock

Munize M. Khasru

enu sat at her dressing table and sighed. Gave her hair a few
desultory swipes with the comb, then set it down listlessly. She
looked at herself in the mirror and wondered how things could
have possibly gotten this bad. The mirror reflection showed her
husband Bijoy sleeping. The worst part of it was the way she was
beginning to take the negative situations into her stride. Maybe the
day was near when she too would sleep without fretting.

The first time this year she had heard about a bomb blast in a
public area, she was appalled. Seven people were killed and more than
fifty others injured in twin bomb blasts at a CPB rally at Paltan
Maidan and at Bangabandhu Avenue on January 20th. Later she read
that the investigators arrested eleven suspects but had the confession
of only one man. Her initial horror changed into a state of indignation
as she realised that all the criminals behind this act would probably
never be brought to justice.

A few months later, Renu and her family were at the cultural event
at Ramna Batamul, celebrating the Bengali New Year. She felt elated
with a sense of optimism as different singing groups welcomed the
New Year in. People from all walks of life thronged together, enjoying
the fresh morning air when, suddenly, there was a terrifying blast. Ten
people died and twenty others were injured that morning, in what she
later learnt was a bomb explosion.

Personally traumatised, Renu spent the following days tormented
with situations of "what if." What if they had been closer to the
Chayanaut stage? What if the suicide bomber had been standing next
to her eight-year-old son? What if the second bomb near the Ramna
entrance had exploded just as they were rushing through it to safety?

Her anguish diminished when newspapers finally reported the
confession of the Vice-Principal of Madani Madrassah. Explaining his
actions, the mastermind behind the bomb attack said he and some
others had decided to attack the cultural function to "put the government

in a bind as the government attacks devotees with beards and caps."
Renu gulped at this explanation. How did killing innocent people put
the government in a "bind"? Didn't this just make the people turn to
the government more for justice and security? Besides, last she knew,
political debates and arguments were meant to be sorted out in a
parliament. Not under large trees. When she asked her journalist
husband this, he had no answer for her.

In such times, when Renu found no answer or meaning in the life
around her, she would turn to the House of God. Her community
church had always been her place of sanctuary. Even if Father John
could not quell her anxiety, simply sitting in the quiet, age-old place
renewed her inner strength. She would look around the empty pews
and visualise all the thousands of people before her lifetime that had
found direction here. And she could imagine all the thousands more
who would come after her lifetime, for the same purpose. There was
peace in knowing the cycle of life always went on.

"Sometimes, Renu," the priest told her once, "you should not try to
understand God and His actions. Sometimes you need to keep faith not
because of something, but *despite* something."

So Renu stayed her course and kept her faith. Till June 3rd when
ten people were killed and twenty-six injured in an explosion during
Sunday Mass at a Catholic Church in Baniarchar. Some speculated
that it was due to religious friction between the Christian, Hindu and
Muslim communities. Others suspected a long-drawn inter-church
rivalry between parish leaders. Renu found both theories questionable
and hoped the investigators would be able to find the truth. But days
passed and no news gave her a sense of closure.

Lost, with no place to go. That's how Renu felt. No cultural event
could be enjoyed in peace. No place of worship could be safe. It didn't
matter what faith you believed in. It didn't matter if you were a
devotee with beard and cap or a man of God with a white collar. It
didn't matter which political party you supported. It *especially* didn't
matter if you were a common civilian. Everyone was spiralling down
the same violent sinkhole.

In June alone, Renu counted four major bomb-related incidents.
The worst was on June 16th when twenty-two were killed and over 100
others wounded in a bomb explosion at Narayanganj Awami League
Office. She watched the local news in silence as the camera panned
over blood, body parts and wailing people. She did not allow herself to

indulge in any hopes of understanding why. Later, when she read about the arrest of a suspect, Renu remained unmoved. Apparently the suspect had distributed sweetmeats after hearing news of a rival's death in the explosion. Her eyes scanned over the news item but her heart didn't register even a slight off-beat tremor.

On June 18th, Renu counted three different news items involving explosives. A bomb was removed from Ahsanullah Science and Technology University at Tejturi Bazar. There was a bomb scare in the Chittagong court building that turned out to be a hoax. And a bomb threat that halted an exam at British Council. All day long Renu remained troubled about the news. Finally, at night when she and Bijoy were getting ready to retire for the night, she burst: "This has become a free-for-all activity."

"What?" asked Bijoy.

"It seems anyone can make a bomb. And anyone can hold the public for ransom, without fear of punishment. The bomb threat at British Council was in demand for Taka ten lakhs. Although no transaction of money or bloodshed transpired from it, it just goes to show how easy it is to participate in such deadly activities," Renu concluded gloomily.

"Well, it takes two hands to clap," her husband replied. "On the one hand we have these terrorists. But on the other hand we have the investigators who are, deliberately or not, failing miserably to catch the criminals. In most cases the responsible agencies tell us of their initial progress but then they slow down as time passes. Sometimes, if the media doesn't pursue them, they halt investigations totally."

"So why don't you journalists keep at the investigators?" Renu asked him.

"Oh we do, we do. But the only answer we get is 'the criminals will be nabbed soon' or 'we're close to the fact'. The real culprits of the bomb attacks always seem to be beyond the arm of justice. They arrest innocent people that obviously lead nowhere. Some sources blame the leading political parties for pointing fingers and hindering investigation. An investigator of one bomb blast told me in confidence that he was asked to frame charges against a particular group. At any rate, with all these smoke-screens, the public gets confused and tired, and slowly the news is no longer news."

"Will this kind of violence continue unchecked? What is one to do?" she asked in frustration.

"Go live with your uncle in his cantonment house or appeal to your local MP to push for a Common Civilian Family Members Security

Act." Bijoy answered sarcastically. With that, Bijoy turned over in bed and went to sleep.

But Renu couldn't sleep. She got up and went to her dressing table. And there she sat, looking at her reflection, looking for an answer.

Suddenly, she stirred from her state of reverie. What was THAT she heard?

"Tick-tock, tick-tock."

She paced her room in agitation to find the source of the sound. Had all this disorder violated even the sanctuary of her own bedroom? WHAT was that she heard?

"Tick-tock, tick-tock."

Was that the sound of yet another bomb about to blast away the innocent residents of this quiet area for some illogical reason? Or was it the sound of her beloved country, counting down the last precious moments till it collapsed into doomsday?

The Wait*

Rubaiyat Khan

ear lay bunched up on the prayer mat. Amma tried counting her rosary beads, but her eyes flickered across the cool cement floor and outwards. Beyond the balcony lay rainsoaked trees and telephone poles, jutting upwards to catch a shred of blue sky. A pale, iridescent sun drifted in and out of thick, cumulous clouds, and she wondered why it still chose to play hide and seek — the rain had stopped hours ago.

Beside the bed stood half-empty bookshelves, and Amma noticed the cobwebs for the first time, bulging with the weight of trapped, dead bluebottles and dust particles. Flies and dust had randomly met the same fate, and now they pooled together into the sticky mess of intricately woven threads. Spears of delicate green pushed through the dampness of the walls on the eastside, near the balcony. The moss had taken to life, untamed, so much so that it now appeared to bulge and sag with the damp of many monsoons.

The bed was still unmade, the way it was the morning he left.

The crumpled up shirts on the edge of the bed, the tottering piles of manuscripts on the wooden mahogany desk (the one they had been given as a wedding gift), and crumpled up papers overflowing the bin. The cigarette stubs and ash strewn all over the bedside table, the ash-tray, upright, on the floor, the mouldy tea cup not altogether empty, that he had drunk out of, the morning he left — and never came back. They were all there, as they should be. Even his smell lingered between the folds of his shirts, when she opened his cupboard. She couldn't allow herself the luxury any more. She wouldn't allow herself to clutch them to her bosom and inhale deeply of them. Not because she loved him a little less everyday — God forbid! — but because she was afraid she would use up that smell. What would she possibly have left to hold on to after that? Amma closed her eyes. Best to meditate.

---

*Published in *Star Magazine*, November 2001.

She didn't want God to be displeased with her. After all, God would be
the one to bring him back. Some day. Some evening, even if it was the
day before she was buried in her village home. He would come back
one evening, wearing those same worn-out rubber sandals that he had
refused to throw away because they were so comfortable, and his good
silver watch that always caressed his left wrist. He would be back in
the house, shoving off his sandals, and requesting his hot cup of tea.
He would call out to her. Amina? Amina! Amina …. Where are you?
I'm home ….

Now she shut her eyes and counted the green beads between her
fingers — they clicked dully against each other, fitting together like
stacks of spoons. Fifty-five, fifty-six, fifty-seven, fifty-eight, fifty-nine,
sixty … . God loved her in measures.

The low, piercing wail of a child brought her back. A series of dry
coughing ensued and her mother-in-law called out to her thickly, in
between short gasps of breath. Her asthma was working up again. She
could almost hear the dull scraping sound from deep within the old
woman's lungs as she sucked air in and exhaled. She stood still for a
moment, contemplating, letting her eyes travel to parts of the room.

His room.

When the baby was fed and fast asleep on the crib, and Anila – who
was more like its mother than an older sister – was in her room, and
the old woman lay content in bed after her seven o'clock tea, she would
slip into the past, into this room, and try walking in his footsteps. She
would stare outwards, her jaw and her heart motionless, as she stood
on the balcony for what seemed like endless hours. Her vision and
hearing blurred with the dim streetlights and the absurd, hollow
clanging of the rickshaws, swarming like confused moths on the road.
The bus ride. She would never forget the bus ride back home that
night. The streetlights. She remembered how they stood in indifferent
columns. Smug, gigantic. Black, licorice sticks. Stiff, lolling tongues,
streaming urine light on her in mockery as she had staggered along
the narrow stone streets, alone, making her way to the house. She had
noticed even then how the walls bordering the neighbouring houses
were choked with damp moss.

How could she tell them of her visit to the police station? She had
swallowed her pride as she'd filed the missing report. She had nearly
fainted with shame when she was later informed that night of her

husband's voluntary departure. He had left voluntarily. Disbelief still sat on her like a heavy cloak.

Amma drifted back into consciousness. The low, piercing wail of the baby grew more insistent and the old woman's voice trembled with hunger and agitation.

She stepped out of the room, and closed it shut behind her.

Branded

Nuzhat Amin Mannan

Wherever Ruma went, she ended up talking about her marriage. The unwed mother at Ruma's son's pre-school in Richmond had gazed at her in dismay. The twinkly-eyed pensioner on her way to Marks and Spencer had patted Ruma's shapely hands unaccountably. Ladies sipping coffee and chewing hazelnut cake at a Connecticut home shifted uneasily on chintz-covered sofas and the Silverman brood sitting around a Thanksgiving dinner table enjoying kosher turkey tried not to look mortified. In Damascus, senior wife and new wife stared and exchanged glances between themselves as a Sudanese female interpreter delivered the questions. A male Singaporean who had graduated from Berkeley had asked if she was all right with the fact that her husband could have if he wished three more wives. And even down in Dum Dum Airport the immigration came up with a goosed-up rule requiring her to tell them when she had become engaged and if she remembered the date of the wedding!

"Talk for five minutes and I can be goaded to talk about my marriage," Ruma quipped. "I am getting quite good at sharing things with people I have never seen in my life and will never see again."

Her story's focus changed from week to week based on who her audience was. If she was planning to beguile a male audience, she highlighted the drama of the nuptial. For a female audience, she spun a heart-wrenching tale about how she quickly had to learn to put her husband's family's wishes first. An eastern audience she rivetted with tales of jewels that her mother had started saving the day she was born. To a western audience she described the shock of meeting someone for the first time seated on a bed which was like a blind date in reverse, first consummation and then progressing very very swiftly towards other protocols! To some she talked about dowry and to others she talked about ceremonies. When she pleased she discoursed on the matchmaker's role; when she was in another kind of mood, she claimed that she was destined to marry Tahmid — she was made out of a bone taken of his ribs. To sceptics she said that there was no such thing as a 100% perfect marriage (love or arranged); to believers she exclaimed that arranged marriages could not be anything short of a miracle.

Ruma Dastagir was seventeen when she was engaged. To a "Customs and Excise official," her father had said with an authoritative treble that would have put Old Agamemnon to shame. Who the Customs and Excise official was and what he exactly did, she didn't have the foggiest clue. The things that she would have liked to know such as his height, his complexion, the quality of his breath, if he had the habit of using hair oil with deadly repercussions ... her family was able to tell her precious little. They couldn't agree among themselves, whether it would be right to say that he might be taller than a certain uncle (who was generally thought to be short). They were quite agreed that he was a little on the plump side like a late grandfather (who was quite obese). The Customs official, Ruma gathered, was somewhere amorphously between "pale shades of dark" and "dirty shades of fair." She sighed a huge sigh of relief when the engagement fell through as the Customs official was placed on suspension for committing an obscure "financial irregularity." Ruma could not imagine what custom her fiancé could have broken to merit the suspension. To herself she said that she was only seventeen so she could dream on for a proposal .... Let him be fantastically rich or drop-dead gorgeous or an immigrant to USA, she pleaded inwardly.

Little had she imagined that the engagement broken at eleven o' clock in the morning had become ancient history and by four o'clock the same afternoon standing in front of a hair salon in scorching June heat she was asked to make up her mind. "About whom? The man sitting on the motor-bike?", she had asked out of polite concern. "No, that's the uncle, silly. The other one who just sneezed right now," her sister-in-law remonstrated. By eleven o'clock the next day, Ruma had a ring on her finger. Her fiancé was a fleeting image in her mind, someone sneezing violently, puckering up his face against the force exhaling out of his nostrils. She hadn't been able to make out if he was sweet or cunning, temperamental or placid, an angel or a demon. To boot she didn't know what he did either this time. Out of goodness of one's heart someone had kindly appended 'Dr.' before his name on the invitation card. Ruma guessed he was a physician. A week before the marriage was to be solemnised, someone had blurted that he was a Doctor of Philosophy. In Economics! An Economist at an International

Organisation. That is when it occurred to her that she couldn't afford
to be a frog in the well anymore! She was on the verge of being a
married woman. Ruma had better, she thought, gather her wits about
her, FAST.

It isn't very complicated, her unmarried cousin about sixteen years
of age had assured her. Do as he tells you to. Blush if you must but
don't scream too hard. Sound advice, but doesn't prepare a witless
seventeen-year-old all that much. Ruma's husband had had enough of
endless wedding customs officiated by throngs of doting women. Once
he was alone with his wife, he put his best foot forward. Trying to
regain himself — be once again natural, original and composed, he had
to unwind first, and so he told Ruma leisurely the story of Cain and
Abel. It was a roller-coaster for Ruma. Two weeks ago, he was a stranger
with a sneeze-puckered face whose features she couldn't satisfactorily
recall. Five hours ago she was sitting biting her nails ... the man might
be a pervert for all she knew! One and a half hour ago he was someone
reeking of liberally applied Brut *pour homme* talking about the house
of Abel and Cain and lo and behold there he was kissing in a courtly
fashion every centimetre of her vertebrae.

One mustn't assume that there is something disturbing about this
sort of passion eking an existence for itself out of nowhere. The foreign-
ness of falling in love is chillying not the carefree commitment such
marriages impose. Falling in love is the risky, unknown part. Figuring
out how to fall asleep in each other's arms before one has had a chance
to properly get acquainted requires surprisingly little dexterity. The
physical proximity felt like something one encounters on a camp.
Awkwardness was the adversity that was magically bonding them
together. She had felt so relieved that his breath smelt like fresh
crushed ice when he stared into her eyes and made her turn into a
wifey smooth jelly. When Tahmid fell asleep, Ruma stole a glimpse of
his face. It was flushed and appealing. In fact her husband looked
almost smugly surrendered to forces beyond him. He had a new-found
respect for Bangalee women. If these women could haul him down to
an atrocious, flower-decked stage, force him to grin while they dabbed
turmeric paste all over his forehead and cheeks, there was no knowing
what else they were capable of. That Ruma was seventeen and an
under-grad was quite beside the point. That he was twenty-seven and
was being taken seriously as a competent analyst of soft loan
environment in LDCs was quite beside the point. If Adam and Eve
pulled it through, perhaps so could they.

For two months, it was madness. Like love. Or methodical. Like love-making. Doors and windows were not opened if it could be helped. They looked too sick to eat, too listless to care that they looked as crumpled as the sheets they came up from, too disengaged from the rest of the world to know Monday morning from Saturday evening. She told him how her school years were a nightmare because of her distressing maths phobia as she kissed his lobes. He narrated how he had gone on a study tour and had nearly drowned in the Kushiara River as he with one free hand expertly undid her hair.

Cemented together, in the most ingenious and mysterious way possible, two months later they were back being themselves again. Tahmid missed a preliminary report deadline and came back to his senses. Ruma missed her period and came back to hers. The lurid chapter of groping, feeling, touching and loving a semi-stranger unceremoniously closed.

Arranged marriages were so neatly programmed, there wasn't the tiniest room for going beyond the drawing board. Adventure, mystery, drama, horror — everything was in-built and kept in tidily-designated corners. No way could Ruma manoeuvre beyond them, had she even tried. Sometimes she cleaned the kitchen till it gleamed because she loved doing so (and did not expect to be thanked for) explained why arranged marriages worked. Sometimes the yawning boredom she felt watching *The Bold and Beautiful* during lunch and helping her children each night with their schoolwork explained what an arranged marriage was all about. It was learning how to manage. To do without un-arranged vagaries, surprises or climaxes. And Tahmid. She did know him like her own skin. Even though he had a quiet vexing power to be absent even when he was present ... he had imparted to their arranged marriage a poignantly settled quality. It was indubitably "arranged." The attachment "arranged," the absences "arranged," its meaning "arranged" and its strangeness "arranged."

Feeling often like a small boat scudding all by herself on a vast ocean, Ruma felt saved when she quite by accident discovered the fact that her arranged marriage had the most exotic twang to it. Single-handedly, she reinvented her space and her species: that of "the arranged-marriage wife."

The wife walked conspicuously some seven inches behind her husband, the distance delicately there to show how she had come from the other part of the world where women didn't expect husbands to offer them their arms or open doors or pull chairs for them. They walked like vivid coolies trailing behind a master — apart, unacknowledged, frequently getting eyes rolled at them for not walking any faster.

Ruma got tingles from being the only woman in the room wearing a saree, the only one to refuse the alcoholic drinks when offered. Setting off everyone in a flutter to get her an orange juice, she waited with an "oriental" poise for the questions that would flit her way sometimes for the entire course of an evening. "Cradle snatcher," Madeline King had chided Tahmid who had introduced his wife and then had drifted away to some other corner of the room. Ruma chewed the radish on a flaky morsel of beef *hors d'oeuvre* she had taken and told Madeline King that she wasn't quite in a cradle, she had turned seventeen two weeks before her engagement. She told King that it didn't occur to her that she wouldn't like living with a husband chosen for her by her father. "Do you like it with him?" Fredrick Moss asked, lightly coating the tempura with a little garlic and soy-sauce dip. "How would she know, he is the only one she has been with, right?" Madeline King handed her used plate to the waiter. Ruma swallowed the implied insult and said energetically. "Actually, there is more to a marriage than liking or not liking each other." "And what would that be?" Moss and King echoed together. Ruma knew she had landed in a waffle but went on heroically, "Well, like understanding and compassion because," and she threw in a mysteriously sad pause, "because we have different expectations than people in love marriages." She had become a rage; it was quite dull to not have Ruma Hassan at parties and coffee mornings. Not only did she wear the most exotic colours — peacock blue, tangerine, papaya green, neon pink, mustard yellow and coral reds — she carried adorable feminine accessories — beaded purses, Burmese ruby strings belonging to her great-aunt who was born in Mekong, opal ear-studs, and open-toed stilettos. "So what would have happened if you wanted to marry someone else? Or not marry at all?" Ruma shook her pretty head of hair and said. "Arranged marriages are a necessary institution. If we didn't have that, there would have to be sex education in the class rooms ... we don't want that, not if we can help it." She was wearing turquoise with a light fawn-coloured chiffon that stole everyone's breath away, but they couldn't help listening to what she also said about necessity and sex.

"But what if you had wanted to wait ... until somebody you thought was just right for you came along. Would your family have respected your right to do that?" a Korean married to a Norwegian corporate manager asked in subdued tones as she bought raffle tickets at the Arab Women's League Bazaar in Kempenski Hotel. "I suppose," Ruma replied, fetching out her purse, "But Song, why bother about buts and ifs? I wasn't compelled to do anything. I chose to follow my mother's footsteps." "What if it hadn't worked?" Nenad Serjevicz asked. "Arranged marriages are more resilient. Love marriages are like dinosaurs. First hint of trouble they wilt and die. Arranged marriages are like amoebae, the fiercest survivor there can be."

Their twentieth anniversary was quietly observed. Tahmid had taken his wife to St. Lucia for the occasion but that is all that he had time for. The LDC Summit on the lush island was proving to be gruelling work. Tahmid snatched two hours of sleep if he could a day. The plenary sessions were rife with arguments and dissents over every single word, every single punctuation mark. Ruma strolled, watched scuba divers, wrote postcards and bought a pair of fake Gucci sunglasses.

"You look like you could do with some company," Henry Bouvais said, standing by her as Ruma waited to inch nearer the buffet table at La Mer. "Are you here for the Summit?" she asked even though she thought he looked far too much like Sidney Poitier to be at a LDC Summit. Bouvais was taken by her soft voice. "Where are you from? India?" he hazarded a guess. Picking up some cold salmon, she told him she was from Bangladesh. "Are you married?" he asked as if he wished she wasn't, picking up some mussel salad. "Oh, yes, twenty years!" she replied, feeling her eyes mist suddenly. "Lucky man," he replied in an obliquely flirty tone. "He's working, the LDC Summit, you know," Ruma ventured towards the French windows with pale lemony curtains. "Arranged marriage?" Bouvais asked, inviting himself to her table and getting her chair out for her. "No, love," Ruma replied and looked straight into his eyes and smiled at the lavender-coloured man.

Forty Steps[*]

Kazi Anis Ahmed

Mr. Shikdar, having died the previous evening, was now lying six feet below ground. He was not sure of his death, but those who had buried him were absolutely certain of it. As he lay there swathed in a white shroud there was little left for him to do except wait for the angels Munkar and Nakir.

He recalled having set out for Molla's, but his memories of the time and incidents after that were unclear. And though he could not remember his burial this was the progression he imagined for the events leading to his current predicament: When he lost consciousness he was standing on a mud aisle in the middle of the rice fields (but this picture could have been retained in his mind from one of his many earlier visits to Molla). Whoever found him — a harried clerk returning home for the weekend or maybe a band of *pan*-chewing farmers on their way to see the village opera — must have thought he was dead. Evidently they hadn't bothered to consult a doctor, otherwise would he be lying here now?

The rituals of the last ablutions and special prayers were performed under the careful ministrations of Molla. They dug a hole with rusty shovels, while he lay there exuding the sweetly nauseating smell of camphor. Some of them sized bamboo branches to the width of the hole, while others prepared to lower him. Had his eyes been open, he would have seen the rectangular slice of sky overhead blocked off bit by bit by the bamboo branches that were placed across the opening of his grave to slowly form a slanting roof. Had his eyes been open, he would have been able to prevent this terrible mistake. He wasn't entirely sure if his interment had happened prematurely. Was this a dream perhaps? Maybe his wife would wake him up any minute and tell him that he was having a nightmare. Did one have such vividness of sensation or lucidity of thought in one's dreams?

---

[*] *Forty Steps* was first published in the *Minnesota Review*.

If he had actually died, there was only one way of verifying it now — by counting the steps. Forty steps. Or so he had been told by Yaqub Molla, who had read seven translations of the Qu'ran. He had also read all the Hadiths and even some of the less respectable religious literature. Contradictory information garnered from his readings had convinced Yaqub Molla of the following fact: All Muslims are visited in their grave by the two interrogating angels Munkar and Nakir. One chronicles all the good deeds that the deceased might have performed. And the other all the bad ones.

Yaqub Molla had also discovered, mostly from evidence culled from medieval texts, that Munkar and Nakir arrived as soon as the last of the mourners went as far as forty steps from the grave. Mr. Shikdar had been much intrigued by the alleged behaviour of the angels. Why was the number forty so significant? Didn't the arrival of the angels ever coincide with the thirty-ninth step? How could they manage to be so precise with so many people dying all the time?

From the muted collision of rubber soles against damp earth, Mr. Shikdar could tell that his mourners were walking away from his grave. The reverberation caused by a procession of rubber-soled feet was followed by the clattering of a solitary pair of *khadams*. Mr. Shikdar concentrated on that lonesome pair of wooden footwear for it presumably belonged to the last of his mourners. He counted the steps taken by the *khadams:* nine, ten, eleven ....

On the day he died Mr. Shikdar was awakened by a fluttering in his chest. These days waking up was not necessarily a pleasant experience for him. He rubbed his chest with the side of his palm in steady circular motions. He did not sit up until he was able to breathe regularly.

He shaved standing in front of his bedroom window. It overlooked the Bararasta, which was the only concrete road in Jamshedpur. The rest were gravel or mud paths. It was a Tuesday. and on Tuesdays the grocers were permitted to open shop on the Bararasta, rather than in the bazaar at the periphery of the town. The spot of Bararasta right in front of Mr. Shikdar's house was monopolised by the fishsellers. Warm haggling voices and the rank smell of dead fish floated in through Mr. Shikdar's window.

"First hilsa of the season, take it for your son-in-law," yelled Abdullah, the fishmonger.

"How much for the hilsa?"

"Five hundred."

"Pah, for five hundred I could buy the whole river; this is just a hilsa."

"Yes, but try cooking the river and try cooking my hilsa," said Abdullah, who was usually more interested in the bargaining than in the selling. People would stand around and quibble with him endlessly, even if they had no intention of buying fish.

Towards one end of the Bararasta sat the meatsellers. Headless, skinned goats were tied by the ankles and hung upside down from iron hooks. Closer to Mr. Shikdar's residence, the neutral area between the fish and meatsellers, was occupied by the poultry, vegetable and fruit stalls. Mr. Shikdar noticed Yaqub Molla, standing next to a cart piled high with ripe, red mangoes. Molla, wearing a long green *kurta* that reached down to his knees, was waving his arms violently. He was evidently outraged by the price of mangoes. Watching the crowded, hustling street took Mr. Shikdar's mind off his ailment and he felt lighter.

The monsoons are late this year, thought Mr. Shikdar. For the past few weeks, tattered white clouds had been racing across the sky without stopping over Jamshedpur. Mr. Shikdar looked at the clouds gathering in the northwest corner of the sky. The laziness with which they piled on top of each other promised the first shower of the season.

Mr. Shikdar erased the white lather on his face with the meticulous application of his razor. He used a folding razor with a black-ivory handle; it had belonged to his father. He stropped it every morning with swift strokes against a black leather belt, which was hung on the wall next to his window. The belt too he had inherited from his father.

He was so well practised in this early morning ritual that he did not need to look into a mirror; instead he looked out of the window. He brought to his shaving the same precision and diligence with which he practiced his art: obstetrics. And an art it must be called, since Mr. Shikdar had no formal training in the scientific methods of delivery. He had become an obstetrician by default, for that was never his ambition.

In his youth Mr. Shikdar had been to the City with explicit instructions from his father to learn something practical. He had enrolled himself in the medical college with the intention of becoming a dentist. The people of Jamshedpur had such bad teeth that as the only dentist of the town he imagined he should be able to have a thriving practice. He spent all day learning not only the basics of modern medicine but also the principles of ayurvedic treatment. His own studies did not, however, attract him as much as the occupations of his peers in the neighbouring art college. He was befriended by one of the art students, an English boy named Dawson, who had once come in for first aid. Shikdar started spending his evenings with Dawson in the hostel room that Dawson had turned into a studio, because he didn't live there. Dawson's father, a retired civil servant, hadn't left the country even after it became independent. Dawson lived with his parents, but spent most of his time with his friends in the art college. He had, according to his friends as well as himself, "gone native." And his complexion was so exceptionally tanned that were it not for his blonde hair even in appearance he could have easily passed for a "native."

Shikdar was always amazed at Dawson's capacity to replicate some real object or person on his canvas. Dawson did not always rely on direct observation for his art; sometimes he would draw from memory or imagination. Often his drawings and paintings appeared to have little correspondence to any real object or setting; these he called "abstract." Not all the abstracts were incomprehensible; from a jumble of colours the shape of a broken table, a sliced watermelon or a naked torso could sometimes be identified. At first Shikdar did not particularly care for these abstract paintings, but he was nevertheless intrigued by them. It was not only the art works themselves that mystified him, but even the very nature of this profession aroused his curiosity. To think that a bright young man his age could actually take drawing or painting — considered to be amusements for children back in Jamshedpur — to be not only a matter of serious concern but also a career possibility was vaguely disconcerting. He did not, however, hold the student artists in contempt. If anything he regarded them with a mixture of awe and wariness. Slowly as Dawson gained his trust as a friend Shikdar learned to relax in the company of these artists; he was new to the City and knew no one else. Dawson and he drank tea late into the nights while Dawson worked and the floor of the dingy room became spattered with paint drops.

Dawson was not only a friend to Shikdar but also his mentor. There were at least two things that Dawson took upon himself to teach Shikdar: the City and the arts. Shikdar accompanied Dawson on his outdoor trips. They stood on street corners, while Dawson hurriedly sketched obese ladies being tugged in rickshaws. He rendered portraits, usually in red pencil, of old men sitting on their haunches in tea-stalls. But these city-drawings did not have the same attraction for

Shikdar as did Dawson's landscapes. The country was small enough
that the natural scenery did not change much from one part to another.
Dawson's landscapes reminded him of Jamshedpur. Landscapes of the
summer: cracked earth in burnt sienna and cloudless blue skies. The
winter: dense grey fogs pierced by yellow lantern lights. And the various
stages of monsoon: dark clouds gathering in the distance, sheets of
rain blurring the view, naked children huddling in the mango grove,
bamboo bushes bending under cyclonic winds, and in the end, broken
branches, unripe fruits and dead crows lying in puddles of mud-water.
Anything on Dawson's canvas that even remotely resembled Shikdar's
memories of Jamshedpur made him nostalgic.

Dawson not only showed Shikdar his own paintings and those of
his friends but also taught him to appreciate the works of the Great
Masters. The works of the Masters were unfortunately not directly
accessible, because they were by Westerners, mostly dead, and the
works themselves were preserved in museums and galleries in very
distant lands. They had to content themselves with reproductions in
whatever form they became available. Dawson had by a lucky stroke
managed to buy up the book collection of a compatriot art afficionado
when the man was leaving the country and had come in possession of
several large volumes that had names such as Titian and Constable,
Goya and Gauguin printed on the covers. At first Shikdar felt very
uncomfortable about the way women were depicted in these books. He
thought it inappropriate and even unnecessary. Once he told Dawson,
"I know this is great art, but this art is not for us. Also, you must know
that portraits are prohibited in Islam." Dawson replied gently,"I'm glad
then that I am not a Muslim." His religious misgivings notwithstanding,
Shikdar did not lose interest in art. He would often go to galleries and
eagerly try to understand why the woman's hair was blue or why the
the faces were featureless. Dawson, who never failed to be amused by
his friend's earnestness, would always agree with whatever meaning
Shikdar made of a particular piece and, to leave no doubt about the
soundness of Shikdar's judgment, would say things like, "Also notice
how the red is so richly textured here."

Mr. Shikdar was not able to entertain his bohemian dalliances for
too long for the same reason that prevented him from finishing his
medical studies. His father's sudden death brought him back to
Jamshedpur. He minded the dispensary his father used to keep and in
his memory the days of his student life gradually came to acquire a

luminous quality. Although he had been rather critical about the ways people had in the city, once he had left the place those very ways and manners came to seem glamourous, even natural. He would tell people about boys who smoked in public and drank, though this they did in private. And he told them about girls from respectable families who joined the boys in these activities. Some of the Hindu girls danced on the stage; classical though the dances might have been, it was still dancing. He told the envious or disapproving Jamshedpuris about boys and girls who went together to the Botanical Garden on Sundays and how nobody cared. It was understood that the peripatetic affairs of these young couples were not restricted to walking in the Botanical Garden. The more his audience seemed to be shocked by his stories, the more colourful they became. He even insinuated his participation in some of these urban social customs, adding "When in Rome ...," but left the nature of his involvements unspecified. He regretted the lack of culture in Jamshedpur, but gradually fell into the routines of the locality.

"Salam Shikdar Sahib, I brought a hilsa for you," said Abdullah, standing on the street outside Mr. Shikdar's window. This was his way of selling things to Mr. Shikdar. He would appear unbeckoned with the catch of the day (if he had failed to find a customer for it) and wave it in front of Mr. Shikdar's window. The sun gleamed on the silvery scales of the hilsa. "Salam, Abdul, take the fish to Begum Sahib," said Mr. Shikdar. His wife's name was Noor Jahan, but, like all married women of a somewhat advanced age, she was referred to as Begum Sahib. Abdullah walked away, nodding happily.

By the time Mr. Shikdar went to his dispensary, the waiting line had already spilled out of his verandah onto the street. Mr. Shikdar lived in a one-storeyed L-shaped house. Only one leg of the L had existed during his father's time. But over the years Mr. Shikdar had made little additions. He had paved the whole courtyard with concrete except for a rectangular patch of green in the middle where he had planted a few palm trees. He had also erected a boundary wall around the house to protect his personal territory from the encroachments of his less affluent neighbours. These little signs of prosperity could not, however, be explained by the income from Mr. Shikdar's dispensary alone. But the impoverished residents of Jamshedpur were so awestruck by Mr. Shikdar's relative affluence that it had never occurred to them that Mr. Shikdar might be enjoying some secret source of income.

Jamshedpur had supposedly not always been so impoverished. Legendary tales describing the once prosperous condition of

Jamshedpur were still told by the old men of the village. Not all the stories were untrue. Jamshedpur had actually been a splendid town even before the Mughal era and had started declining only during the British period. The situation of Jamshedpur did not improve even after the British left the country. But the British never left the country completely. There were always some who wanted to help and some who wanted to study, and yet others who claimed they were trying to promote understanding. Six of these British gentlemen came specifically to study Jamshedpur. Layers of civilisation, they believed, were waiting to be exhumed. All of them, but one, the youngest member of the group, were archaeologists. Mr. Shikdar was delighted to discover that the young companion of these archaeologists was none other than his friend Dawson. After leaving art college Dawson had had a hard time of it in the city. The local critics berated him for being too European, and the galleries did not exhibit his work as prominently as they did those of his peers. Dawson had gone off to England, where he had been met with just as much hostility. But there he was able to get a job with these archaeologists, who were only too happy to find in him not only an artist but also a compatriot capable of performing the duties of a local guide. Dawson had already toured many parts of the country with the archaeologists and said that he was hoping to gain an intimate knowledge of the country through his travels. He hoped that a deeper acquaintance with the country would help him mitigate the much criticised European element of his art.

The archaeologists went around in a gray Land Rover to various parts of Jamshedpur. They dug in places that corresponded to the black crosses on their maps. After their initial survey was over, they fixed the sites for the principal excavation and started employing a good number of local people. When Mr. Shikdar asked them what they expected to find they said anything was possible. They claimed to have unearthed the ruins of an ancient public bathhouse and the remnants of a sewage system in the neighbouring district of Vijaynagar. Both the discoveries were dated to the time of Emperor Aurangzeb.

Mr. Shikdar was very excited about the prospect of a major archaeological discovery in Jamshedpur. But before any major discovery could be made, a minor one created such a havoc that the possibilty of any great exploration seemed to be precluded permanently. On a holiday, with the special permission of Molla, the archaeologists went to visit the mosque situated on one end of the Bararasta (not the end where meatsellers sat on Tuesdays). True to their inquisitive profession, they were unable to content themselves with admiring, as most people did, the imposing white dome of the mosque, adorned with stars and crescents engraved in deep blue lapis lazuli. Their gaze refused to remain stuck in that upward direction. They scrutinised the beautiful edifice more closely, even if surreptitiously, than anybody had dared or felt compelled to ever before. When their visit was over, they went back to their camp, muttering among themselves that the mosque must have been a Hindu temple at one time. The bottom of the five oldest pillars in the western section of the mosque had fallen further into disrepair than was the case with the rest of that holy mansion. The archaeologists had noticed, from the corner of their eyes, the fragments of dancing figurines carved on the red sandstone of the pillars. This evidence, though not gathered through the formal application of the methods and tools of their profession, was sufficient to bolster their casual speculations. They had little doubt that the mosque had once been a temple.

They decided to keep this discovery to themselves, but word got out. It caused tremendous uproar in the local community. Two low-caste Hindus were killed in Jamshedpur in the ensuing riots. Their beheaded bodies, tied upside down from bamboo poles, were paraded on the Bararasta. Moti, the Muslim shoemaker, was killed by retaliating Hindus from the neighbouring district of Vijaynagar. Similar incidents began to occur in other parts of the country. Several Muslim girls were allegedly raped in a Hindu village. The next day a Hindu holy man was forced to eat beef by a gang of young Muslim boys in another village. The more widespread the news of such atrocities became, the longer they helped sustain the anger of the indignant masses. The excavators abandoned their project and fled in their Land Rover. Dawson, however, was unable to leave because he was suffering from a severe case of diarrhoea. So his compatriots left him behind, promising to come back later with a British doctor from the capital. This promise was not fulfiled, probably because foreigners were not allowed to go to the riot-stricken area of Jamshedpur. However, even after the affair of the mosque had subsided, Dawson's colleagues did not reappear. Mr. Shikdar, in the meanwhile, took Dawson under his care.

Dawson never left Jamshedpur. He opened a furniture shop on the Bararasta and gave up the practice of art in favour of craft. On Tuesdays, merchants from the city would come in their engine-cars to take the delicately carved wooden lamps that Dawson made. He endeared himself with the townsfolk by wearing the local costume, knee-length *kurtas*. He even started wearing the wooden clogs, a local specialty, that the Jamshedpuris themselves had abandoned in favour of imported rubber shoes.

When Mr. Shikdar had first returned to Jamshedpur, he did nothing more than offer first aid and contraceptives, though the poverty-hardened Jamshedpuris had little interest in such services. But then the only doctor of Jamshedpur died, and patients started coming to Mr. Shikdar. At first Mr. Shikdar refused to offer treatments he was not qualified to administer. But the desperation and the persistence of his patients forced him to address some emergencies: pulling out teeth, lancing festering boils, adjusting displaced bones. He also rigorously studied the medical books Dawson had given him by way of acknowledging his friend's hospitality. One of them, *Gray's Anatomy*, he had learned by heart. Late nights when he used to pace, muttering passages of the book to himself, his wife would ask, "Do you have to memorise the whole book? Why are you doing this?"

"I am doing this because I can," was his reply.

Armed with his newly acquired knowledge and gradually increasing experience, Mr. Shikdar soon had the confidence to treat all ailments, even ones that were seemingly unknown to the medical profession. And then when the octogenerian midwife of Jamshedpur became blind, her patients too turned to Mr. Shikdar. He stopped promoting the use of contraceptives soon after he assumed the responsibilities of the midwife. In his first few deliveries he was assisted by a chaste manual in the vernacular that had the requisite instructions but no diagrams.

Mr. Shikdar, slender and timid in his youth, had by then become a balding, beefy man of some authority. Now in his fifty-ninth year, he was completely bald and had a white moustache. His appearance could be considered grandfatherly, though he did not have any legitimate claims even to the position of a father. Mr. Shikdar, dressed in all white, sauntered down the veranda towards his chamber. His clients stood up one by one as he passed them and touched their foreheads with the right hand to show their respect. Mr. Shikdar held his chin up with the deliberation of a man who knew his worth.

"I have that pain again, Shikdar Sahib," said Yaqub Molla pressing his abdomen with both hands.

"Do you want me to forge the property deeds for the seven acres next to the pond?" asked Mr. Shikdar. He did not take Molla's complaint seriously. He knew that whenever Molla wanted to collaborate with him on some new scheme, he usually came in pretending to be in the throes of colic. Such displays were meant for the other patients waiting outside, so that they would suspect nothing. But Molla, totally taken up with this play-acting, often carried it into the privacy of Mr. Shikdar's chamber.

Molla had drawn Mr. Shikdar into his schemes out of very particular reasons. To begin with, there were few literate people in Jamshedpur and Molla needed someone who was conversant in the vernacular for his purposes. Yaqub Molla himself, like a true Muslim, had never deigned to learn anything but Arabic; if he conversed in the vernacular at all it was simply out of necessity. Mr. Shikdar also had the added advantage of enjoying immense popularity with the townspeople. Because to them he was not only a healer of pain but also someone they could call on for any purpose even remotely literary: reading the paper; writing letters, affidavits, or money orders; deciphering legal notices, public announcements; copying Qu'ranic verses for wedding invitations and tombstones; fabricating genealogies, and under the influence of Molla, forging documents. Mr. Shikdar had initially resisted the idea of tampering with legal papers, but Molla argued that the two of them would be able to take better care of the lands than the actual proprietors. Moreover, they needed the forgery only to get started; after that it would be legal business and Molla promised that he would take care of it all. Eventually, Mr. Shikdar relented. Besides, his patients did not pay him enough for his services. Fewer and fewer people came to Mr. Shikdar nowadays for the various literary services that he once used to dispense, because mass education had infiltrated even the dark recesses of Jamshedpur. Electricity, some said, would also come to Jamshedpur very soon. But the early association that he had formed with Molla had not waned over the years.

"No, Shikdar Sahib, I am really in pain. I am not here to talk any business today."

"So you don't want the seven acres?"

Molla shook his head vehemently and spoke through groans, "Please relieve me of my pain first and then talk business."

Mr. Shikdar asked Molla to lie down on the bed in the corner of the room and pressed various parts of his torso with a pensive frown on his face. He relied on the touch of his fingers to diagnose most ills and even to cure some of them. Mr. Shikdar realised that Molla's pain was not the usual stomach ache he suffered or feigned. So he gave Molla one of his more potent pain relievers. Molla sat on the edge of the bed gasping, his hollowed cheeks puffing out every time he breathed out.

"What did you have last night, Molla?"

"Nothing, Shikdar Sahib, it's not my fault I tell you. There's something in the air. I will come and talk to you tonight, if I feel better."

After Molla, came the other patients and most of them with uncommon complaints. Mr. Shikdar was kept unusually busy in his chamber all morning. He had to enter repeatedly the windowless room adjacent to his chamber that had "laboratory" painted in red on its white door. He came back from that room with small glass vials, labelled and corked, with blue, red or golden liquids inside. The mixes were colour-coded according to the strength of the concentration. The blue bottles were the cheapest. They were for the poorest of his clients. They contained distilled water and artificial colouring. The more expensive brands contained some aspirin. Today the condition of the patients compelled Mr. Shikdar to offer the aspirin doses even to those who had money enough only for the distilled water.

Mr. Shikdar usually left his dispensary at one o'clock for lunch. But the deluge of patients detained him till two-thirty today. When he walked towards the interior of his house, many were still waiting in the verandah.

When Mr. Shikdar entered the dining room, his wife was still sitting at the table.

"Really, Begum, why do you wait for me when I am late? You should go ahead and have your lunch," said Mr. Shikdar.

. "I did. I am just sitting here," said Begum Shikdar.

She removed the cane covers that kept the flies from sitting on the food. His favourite preparations of hilsa were served for lunch: hilsa with mustard seed and hilsa in coconut milk. There was also *khichri*, a delectable mix of rice and lentils, with fried onions sprinkled on top. The *khichri*, Mr. Shikdar guessed, had been prepared in anticipation of the season's first rain.

"This looks really delicious. I could smell something in the kitchen this morning. Terrific."

Begum Shikdar seemed untouched by the compliment. She was ten years younger than her husband, but looked younger than that. Her hair was still all black and her skin taut. In fact, nothing but an incipient double chin and slightly creased forehead indicated her true age. In her youth she had been the most ravishing beauty of Jamshedpur. Her father was not a local, but he came from the north; that made her all the more attractive to the Jamshedpuris. Her father, Mr. Zahir, had taught English in a girls' school in a nearby city. He had moved to the obscure town of Jamshedpur because people in the city had been spreading malicious lies about his daughter. True, he was a liberal man, who allowed his daughter to mix freely, without the pain of a chaperone, with the boys in her college and even in the neighbourhoods. She went with them to the museum or ice-cream parlours, the park or the movies, or wherever it was that young people went. Perhaps Noor Jahan was a flirt — weren't most girls her age? — but the things they said about his daughter! And probably all because she didn't have time for any odd boy who wanted to become her friend. It pained him that people could be so jealous, so mean-minded. When the situation got too nasty for his taste — obscene and threatening letters were sent to his house and many of the neighbourhood doors were closed to his daughter — he decided to leave. Once he came to Jamshedpur, Mr. Zahir decided to play it safe. He tutored Noor Jahan at home, forbade her to go out and allowed her to receive only female visitors.

Mr. Shikdar had ingratiated himself with his future father-in-law by participating in informed discourses on English literature. Under the tutelage of Dawson, Mr. Shikdar had had some lessons in literature too when he was in the capital. "I never thought I'd find someone in Jamshedpur who wanted to discuss literature," Mr. Zahir had said to Mr. Shikdar the first time they had met. He was genuinely interested in the subject. But Mr. Shikdar's enthusiasm was induced in not a small part by his interest in the enchanting Miss Noor Jahan. The women talked endlessly about the beauty of Noor Jahan. She had such enchanting manners, they said. Mr. Shikdar hoped that he would be able to glimpse that much talked about beauty if he could become a regular guest in that house.

Mr. Zahir decorated his drawing room with inauthentic pieces of European furniture. Shabby rattan chairs were displayed in the garden, where the two men sometimes took tea. They discussed Gibbon. They also listened to Beethoven on a broken gramophone that Mr. Zahir had received from the English principal of his last school. The sessions with Mr. Zahir were extremely edifying, but they did not serve their intended purpose for Mr. Shikdar, because Noor Jahan was always conspicuously absent. This puzzled him at first, for he didn't think that the daughter of a progressive thinker like Mr. Zahir would

be observing *purdah* — Mr. Shikdar had imagined that Noor Jahan
would be somehow like the girls he had known in the capital, if the
distance from which he had known them could be called "knowing." Mr.
Shikdar's visits started decreasing in frequency and his enthusiasm for
literature too would have been severely diminished had it not been for
the annual fair.

The fair took place on the Bararasta and everyone, even the legendary
beauty Noor Jahan, came to it. All of Bararasta was decorated with
bright red banners for the fair, and blue and yellow festoons were tied
to the stall gates. Vendors and craftsmen came from Jamshedpur and
all the neighbouring districts. Earthenware and brassware captured
the attention of housewives. Young boys tugged at their mothers' sarees
to lead them to where the bamboo and clay toys were being sold. One
year the toy-seller from Vijaynagar came to the fair with plastic dolls,
which blinked both eyes when tilted at a certain angle; they blinked
only one eye after the first week. And another year a man in a red
tailcoat sold mouth organs. No one had seen them before, but they
became an instant hit with the children. Molla did not trust their
cacophonic tunes and confiscated them, saying, "These toys aren't
proper for Muslim boys!" The same man appeared the following year
with an accordion, which too was confiscated even though he played
harmoniously. The red tail-coated man was never seen again, but the
fair was never lacking in attractions. There were snake-charmers,
monkey-trainers and fortune-tellers, who excelled in their familiar
tricks. Remnants of a once prosperous circus were also a regular feature
of the fair: acrobats somersaulted and children rode a rib-showing
horse. But every year, invariably, the biggest attraction turned out to
be the makeshift Ferris wheel.

Four box chairs were mounted on a wooden structure of uncertain
footing. The whole thing was painted red, although the paint had
chipped in many places. It was manually rotated by two strong-armed
men; one pushing the chairs away from himself while the other, standing
opposite him, pushed the chairs upwards. A third man who collected
money screamed hoarsely, "Come, ride the Ferris wheel, boys and
girls, we'll spin you to the moon." The youngsters who waited in line
shrieked as loudly as those who were being spun around.

Mr. Shikdar saw Noor Jahan, for the first time, at the annual fair.
He could not see her very well, because she was riding on the Ferris
wheel. Moreover, he was standing forty feet away, a distance often
accepted by suitors for seeing the girl. Her hair had come loose from

the bun and flowed behind her as she kept rotating in the same circular path. There were many pairs of bedazzled eyes, forty feet in every direction from Noor Jahan, that followed the figure in a blue silk dress. All the young men who gazed at the gyrating beauty from the prescribed distance were smitten with love. The sight of Noor Jahan redoubled Mr. Shikdar's enthusiasm for Gibbon.

Suitors began to throng the Zahir household soon after the annual fair. There were prodigal sons of wealthy land barons and old merchants who wanted a second wife, there were bearded religious men who promised salvation in the afterlife, and idiots from the cities who had to find their wives in the provinces. Most of the admirers managed to horrify the father no less than the daughter. Mr. Zahir, unsure of the young Shikdar's feelings for his daughter, started making suggestive yet cautious remarks in his presence. Mr. Shikdar facilitated matters for Mr. Zahir by introducing the anxious father to a distant uncle of his. The two elder men came to the decision that Mr. Shikdar and Noor Jahan would make a perfect match. Mr. Zahir had some reservations because Mr. Shikdar was not at the time quite as affluent as many of the other suitors. "But," he reasoned, "that boy has culture." Mr. Shikdar, by virtue of being a cultured man, had the good fortune of marrying Noor Jahan the following spring.

On their wedding night Mr. Shikdar was very nervous. He had never talked extensively with a girl who was not related to him and definitely never at such close quarters. He had also never been alone in a room with a girl. He was keenly aware of the significance of this moment and the urge to say something appropriate made him tongue-tied. After many minutes of embarrassing silence, he lifted her red veil and asked her gravely, "Have you heard of Beethoven?"

Yes. She nodded her head.

"And Gauguin? Have you heard of Gauguin?"

No. She shook her head sideways.

"That's all right," said Mr. Shikdar. "I'll tell you about Gauguin."

He told her about Gauguin and also about Gibbon. He mentioned the Governor General, who had once come to their college. Did she know how fond he was of painting? When he was in the capital, he had spent so much of his time in the company of painters. They always appreciated his comments and suggestions. He drowned himself in a blissful nuptial garrulity, while his young bride fell asleep.

In a week's time they kissed for the first time and made love soon after. And it was in bed that Noor Jahan turned out to be not the shy and docile sixteen-year-old that Mr. Shikdar thought he had married. Some of her nocturnal movements took Mr. Shikdar by surprise. He recalled having seen an English copy of the *Kamasutra* in her father's bookshelf.

"Can you read English?" asked Mr. Shikdar one night.

"With a dictionary I can get the gist of things," said Noor Jahan.

"Would you like me to teach you English?"

"Yes. Why not?"

But Mr. Shikdar never had to take the trouble of teaching his wife English. The task was taken out of his hands by Dawson. The controversy surrounding the mosque had erupted soon after Mr. Shikdar's wedding. He had brought a critically ill Dawson into his house for treatment. Dawson was not the only one suffering from this diarrhoeal disease. It had become an epidemic and, when the first of Mr. Shikdar's patients died after a night of violent retching and vomiting, he became afraid that his distilled water might not do the trick this time. He decided to go to the city to consult the big doctors and bring back medicine that would be more potent than the things available in his stock.

When Mr. Shikdar was leaving for the city, Dawson clutched his hand and asked, "Shikdar, am I going to die?"

"Sure," said Mr. Shikdar, "but I couldn't tell you exactly when." He placed a reassuring hand on Dawson's fevered forehead and told him that his temperature was already going down. He told the languishing Dawson, "Don't worry, by the time I come back from the city, you will probably have recovered."

Noor Jahan was left on her own to take care of Dawson. At first she felt piqued at her husband's thoughtlessness. She called in the blind midwife to help her with the nursing. Her decision was partly influenced by an inclination to preempt possible innuendoes. She couldn't very well be left alone in a house for a week with an Angrez; the Shikdars had no servants at the time.

Dawson's pale white complexion had turned greenish-yellow in his sickness. But at times when he felt slightly better he was at his humourous best. He did not lecture Noor Jahan on Gauguin or the Governor General. Instead he told her about himself: childhood in the capital, Oriental Studies at the university, expulsion after a year for unruliness, entry into art college, civilising Shikdar, a tour of England and now in Jamshedpur. He asked Noor Jahan about herself: why had they moved from the city — when had her mother died — was there any truth to the scandals — did she really want to learn English — what did she think of Shikdar — did he really snore so loudly — and was she happy?

They taught each other the languages they knew best. But very quickly the language lessons became subsidiary to their amorous exchanges. By the time Mr. Shikdar came back with the remedy for the diarrhoeal disease, Noor Jahan's vocabulary of unutterable English words already far exceeded that of her husband's. Dawson did not leave even after he was cured of his illness; he stayed on at the Shikdars'. Initially, Mr. Shikdar was quite happy with his house guest, with whom he could talk endlessly about the glorious times they had had in the city. Noor Jahan would sit in on these sessions at times and listen smilingly.

Mr. Shikdar was also pleased to see his wife making real progress with her English. But eventually he couldn't help noticing that the teacher and the pupil looked at each other a little too tenderly. Mr. Shikdar, of course, could not ask Dawson to leave; the man was his friend. And what if his suspicions turned out to be false? Also now that he was getting to know his wife better, he realised that she was not the purdah type. She had had a different upbringing in the city. And what with his progressive ideas, was he going to get jealous about the first man who spoke to his wife? No, it would not do to ask Dawson to leave abruptly, it might even suggest scandal when there was perhaps none. Maybe he should observe them more closely, maybe sudden visits to the house from the dispensary. He started leaving his stethoscope behind. When Noor Jahan asked him why he was being so forgetful lately, he stared at her silently.

Dawson was finally removed by Yaqub Molla, who appeared suddenly one morning with the declaration that he had found a house and a manservant for Dawson. So Dawson no longer needed to suffer the inconveniences of living at somebody else's house. "Dawson Sahib, follow me kindly, if you please," said Molla and walked out with Dawson's belongings. Mr. Shikdar was most grateful to Molla for his diplomatic, and, he hoped, timely intervention. So when a week later Molla turned up with some documents that he said needed minor adjustments, Mr. Shikdar could not refuse his services. He agreed to Molla's suggestions, and asked only that he be allowed to retain a vestige of moral propriety. They had lengthy conversations about the ineptitude of the people to use their land properly. Shouldn't the rice fields really be turned into brick factories? And they talked about the good things they would do with the proceeds from their ventures.

Mr. Shikdar prospered in a manner that did not seem to be in keeping with the earnings from his tiny dispensary. But his contentment was incomplete because his wife did not forget Molla's speedy removal of Dawson. "What kind of a man gets an outsider to remove his guest?" she would say not directly to him.

"I didn't ask Molla to do anything. He took Dawson away on his own."

"Did it on his own? And who let him? Shame, what shame!"

"As if there wasn't any shame in staying alone with the Angrez."

"We weren't alone, the midwife was here."

"Blind midwife, fine chaperone you have there."

"Don't taunt me. You are the one who asked the stupid Angrez to stay with us in the first place!"

"But I didn't ask him to push you on the swings, did I?"

"You are so jealous; you can't even tolerate me having some innocent fun, can you?"

"Have all the fun you want, but please see to it that things are done in good form."

"Good form? And who decides what's in good form? I suppose shooing your guest out was in good form."

"Dawson had to go. We could not have him stay on with us forever."

"Of course not. But you gave him such a goodbye, he doesn't even come to visit anymore. And what will people say when they hear about this?"

"Yes, what will people say?"

Mr. Shikdar could not match his wife's diatribe. Although he felt that Dawson's removal had become necessary, he could not find the right words to convince his wife of this fact. When she realised that she was pregnant, she dropped the subject completely. The two of them conspired towards a reconciliation; they would not carry the bitterness of the first months to cloud the happiest occasion of their life. Mr. Shikdar decided to celebrate the news by inviting Dawson, Molla, and the few other venerable members of their small society. The party was held in his courtyard, which he had recently paved with concrete. There was a fenced-in area of green and four palm trees in the middle of the courtyard. Mr. Shikdar and his guests sat under the palm trees. A table was laid out and covered with a red and white checkered cloth. Mr. Shikdar brought out his father-in-law's gramophone which he had received as part of his dowry. Dawson had brought over some records that had been popular in their college days. Everybody had tea and Dawson got up and demonstrated some European dances. He taught Mr. Shikdar the jitterbug. They danced together while the other men clapped. Dawson's clogs clattered on the pavement.

Begum Shikdar refused to come out of her kitchen, but she served the most delicious *samosas*, *chatpati*, *luchi*, and *halwa* that her guests had ever tasted. Later in the evening, when the guests had left, she still stayed in her kitchen. Mr. Shikdar could not persuade her to learn the jitterbug. From then on Begum Shikdar's preference for the kitchen over the veranda gradually became more pronounced.

In the later stages of his wife's pregnancy, Mr. Shikdar started spending more and more time with her, and in the last one month he did not make any night calls. He was worried by his wife's persistent gloom and did everything in his capacity to cheer her up. His endeavours were unrewarded, and he feared for the health of both mother and child. When the birth became imminent, the blind midwife moved into the Shikdar household of her own accord. Even though Mr. Shikdar had taken up her job, she did not stop visiting the houses where a child was expected.

Normally neighbourhood women and close female relatives were present on such occasions. But it was already well into the monsoon season. Those who lived close by were prevented by rain, and those who lived far away by the flood from coming to attend on Begum Shikdar. Besides, Mr. Shikdar, being the only person of his gender in obstetrics, did not have the usual array of assistants that the midwife used to have. He was usually attended by only one or two of the closest female relatives of the patient. On the night that his wife went into labour, there was no one besides himself and the blind midwife to facilitate the arrival of his child. After several agonising hours in labour, very early in the morning, Mrs. Shikdar delivered a blonde baby girl.

The next morning contradictory reports were circulating in Jamshedpur. The men talked under their breath in the bazaar, "Have you heard?"

"Yes, so sad, she is such a nice woman and he is so generous. That such a thing should happen to them!"

"They don't deserve such misfortunes."

"No, surely not."

"So was the baby stillborn? Or did it die after birth?"

"How could it be stillborn? The midwife says that she heard a baby crying."

"What baby crying? She probably heard the mother crying."

"You think she can't tell a baby crying when she hears it! She's been delivering them for sixty years."

"The old hag's already lost her sight and now she must be losing her hearing as well."

"And, what about the baby's grave? Haven't you seen the little mound of earth under the palm trees, in their courtyard?"

"Sure, they could have buried the child, but the question is did they bury it before or after it died?"

"Don't even think of such horrible things. Why would they want to do such a thing?"

"Why, do you think? Remember exactly how long ago the diahorrea epidemic was and remember where Dawson was at the time?"

"Yes, now that you say so. I also wonder why they were in such a hurry to bury the child. Besides, everyone went to pay their condolences, but Dawson wasn't there."

"I went to his house, he wasn't there either." The men quarrelled and speculated, but no one was able to establish a satisfactory story about what had happened.

Most stories in Jamshedpur had two versions. Those carried by mouth and those carried by the chimney fumes. By late morning the chimneys of Jamshedpur started belching essential details and embellishments to the story that had been reported by mouth. Women who worked in the kitchen were aware of facts that eluded their otherwise knowledgeable husbands. Whispers, innuendoes, speculations, as well as slander and vituperation, and in some kitchens, even gallows humour were added to the usual ingredients that went into the pots simmering on the earthen stoves. The fumes, usually grey, were a sickly green today; or perhaps the monsoon clouds were refracting the daylight into the strangest colours. The fumes did not seem to rise to the sky; instead, they hung low over the houses and mingled with fumes from other chimneys before insinuating themselves into some other kitchen.

Chimney-fume reports: Yes, the midwife had heard a baby cry. She was blind but not deaf. Dead babies don't cry. Who could tell if there really was something under that mound of earth? Was the grave just a distraction? A cover-up, so that no one would ever again ask anything about the Shikdar baby? And what business did Dawson have in the city? He never needed to go to the city ever before for his wood carvings.

And didn't someone see him going with a small bundle in his arms? Why were Shikdar and Molla in such a hurry to bury the child? In Jamshedpur, everybody could be called on at all hours if a misfortune were to befall any family. Why then did Molla and Shikdar not call anyone else for help? Why the hush-hush?

By mouth it was reported that Begum Shikdar had gone into labour the previous night. It was also reported that a child had been born, but it was dead at birth. Before dawn Mr. Shikdar had reportedly buried the child with Molla's assistance. They thought the longer it was kept in the house, the worse the mother would feel. No, they hadn't had the time to inform many people before the burial. It was after all quite late at night. Dawson had been informed; he had paid his condolences but he had had to go off to the city on urgent business.

In a few years time everyone in Jamshedpur would come to know that Dawson had had a child by a woman he kept in the city. Men would sit around the Bararasta on the bazar days and see Dawson taking the engine-car to the city, evidently to visit his putative offspring.

"Leave it to an Angrez to do something like that."

"I tell you, city women have no morals."

"Thank God, there aren't any women like that in Jamshedpur."

"Dawson isn't a bad sort after all," some would say. "He provides well for the woman and the child."

Dawson's frequent city visits had resulted in an expansion of his business and he always claimed that it was his business that took him to the city. Those who had been to the city would agree unanimously that Dawson had a beautiful daughter.

The chilling of the relationship between Mr. Shikdar and his Begum would be widely ascribed to their childlessness. Marriages, fat-elbowed women would claim, are bound to go sour if you don't have children. That Mr. and Begum Shikdar slept in different rooms became common knowledge because of gossiping servants. And the chimney fumes would add that Mr. Shikdar refused to share his room with his wife because she had given birth to a stillborn baby.

The Shikdars, however, like all affluent couples, managed to keep up appearances. They greeted each other in the mornings, and asked about each other's health. They confessed to each other new signs of advancing age and suggested remedies. Whenever there was a wedding, they went together and they never quarrelled in front of guests. He gave her new sarees on her birthdays. She wove him a pair of sandals for their last marriage anniversary (thirty-third). They even remained on cordial terms with Dawson; otherwise people might suspect something. Dawson did not visit them anymore, but there was no sign of overt hostility. They fell into the conventional routines of town life. Mr. Shikdar kept himself busy in the dispensary. But also he invested a lot of time at the religious school that Molla and he had jointly established. Mr. Shikdar was widely recognised for his various charitable efforts. Begum Shikdar took to the kitchen and waited for her husband at meals.

"How many patients did you see today?"

"Everybody's sick. They complain of stomach aches."

"I hope it's not another epidemic."

"I don't know. It very well might be. I haven't been feeling very well myself. I can't fall sick at a time like this."

"Yes, you do look tired. Take a nap after lunch." Begum Shikdar ladled some more *khichri* on her husband's plate. It was one of his favourite dishes. They wondered if it would rain today. The clouds had moved closer to Jamshedpur. And Begum thought she could smell the earthy vapours that always came before a storm. They said rain was badly needed for the crops. The drought last year had hit the farmers very hard. Poor fellows possibly couldn't survive two consecutive years of drought.

Begum Shikdar rambled absent-mindedly, but Mr. Shikdar seemed not to notice. He was feeling very drowsy. He no longer had the energy of his youth. After lunch naps had become a necessity for him. The thought of the people waiting in the verandah made him feel guilty about napping. He promised himself, as he lay down on the bed, that he would nap for only an hour.

The patients waited in the veranda. They gave Shikdar Sahib an hour for lunch. When he didn't show up after lunch, they gave him another hour for the nap. When he still didn't return to his dispensary, they asked the servant to see if Mr. Shikdar would be coming out to his dispensary again. The servant went and called his master timidly from the door. After a few calls, when Mr. Shikdar still did not awaken, the servant went and told Begum Shikdar about the poor patients and about Mr. Shikdar's sleep. Begum Shikdar told the servant to take a cup of tea to Mr. Shikdar and nudge him gently. The cup of tea turned cold on Mr. Shikdar's bedside table. It rested on a leather-bound copy of the verses of Omar Khayaam, which his grandfather had given him as a wedding present. He did not stir to the servant's intrepid nudgings.

The dejected patients left one by one, when Mr. Shikdar didn't wake up even after three hours. The servant, feeling guilty on his master's behalf, served tea to the few persistent patients who still lingered on the veranda. They finished their tea, while second, third and fourth cups turned cold on Mr. Shikdar's bedside table. Begum Shikdar had to come in herself to her husband's room, which she hardly ever did nowadays. She shook her husband violently by the shoulders, "How much longer are you going to sleep? The poor patients are still sitting on the veranda. Are you really feeling ill?"

All the commotion finally woke up Mr. Shikdar. He looked at his wife with glazed eyes. Begum Shikdar had to slap some water on his face, before he came to his senses. He sat on the edge of his bed looking glum. He told his servant, "Tell the patients I am not feeling well. I'll sit in the dispensary early tomorrow. Tell them to come then." The fluttering in his chest had started again. When his breathing regularised, he drank a cup of tea.

He looked out of the window. It was already almost dusk and a faint rosy shaft of light illuminated a side of the wall. He stared at the light on the wall as it slowly receded into a corner and vanished. He felt very removed from his surroundings. Waking up so late in the afternoon always did this to him. It ushered strange, sad, silly thoughts into his head. It reminded him of things and places that had become irretrievably distant. He remembered the girl whom he had once wanted to draw; he had even taken a few lessons in drawing from Dawson at the time. He remembered the first time he had seen her white foot, looking whiter because it was encased in a black leather shoe, stepping out of a car. He had not looked at her. He did not remember what she had looked like that day or what she had been wearing. He was no longer even sure if he had seen her outside the girl's college or if it was outside the tea shop that all the students went to in those days.

But he remembered the white foot that had gently stepped out of a car. Why should he remember that foot or that shoe or that girl? He remembered, looking at the foot, he had thought at the time, if the owner of that foot were to walk through a desert, not a speck of dust would cling to her heels. Silly, silly, can you really remember a foot for so long, when you have forgotten more important things (he did not remember the name of the boy with whom he had shared a room for a year; it was probably an 'A' name: Asgar, Asmat ... ?). But he remembered the foot with such vividness that it made him want to cry.

He had spoken to the girl only once. They happened to be sitting at the same table because of common friends. When they were introduced he had smiled, thinking how shocked she might be if he were to say, "I have already made a careful note of your left foot. Have you ever walked through a desert?" But that wouldn't do at all. "Do you really draw? Will you do a portrait of me?" she had asked animatedly. "I've always wanted to have a picture of me, drawn not photographed," she had said. He had thought she was serious. He had imagined all the different angles from which her head could be immortalised on paper. He had finally settled on 'the side of the face looking from behind' angle for drawing her. But he no longer recalled what the side-of-the-face looked like from the chosen angle. And even if he did, could he actually have drawn it? He had immortalised nothing on paper. Only a silly foot stuck in his head. There was so much he was incapable of doing. What had happened to the owner of that foot? Had she married? Had she ever had her portrait done?

The only way he could shake off the urgent sentimentality of his nostalgia was by grasping something immediate: a thought (Molla and his seven acres), a real physical feeling (the aching in his chest), an object (the open pages of the *Rubayiaat*) or a person (his wife sitting in the cane chair). He turned his eye from the corner of the wall, which was warmed even a little while ago by a faint pink light, to his wife. The servant came in with an oil lamp and placed it on Mr. Shikdar's side-table. Begum Shikdar's shadow loomed large behind her on the wall. The gentlest breeze disturbed the lamp-light and the shadow wavered ever so slightly. Mr. Shikdar suddenly felt glad that the woman who was sitting on that nearby cane chair was his wife and that she had been nearby for thirty-three years. He said, "Have all the patients gone already?"

Yes, she nodded her head. "How are you feeling now? Is it that chest pain again?"

"Much better. I think I'll go out for some fresh air."

Mr. Shikdar stepped out on the Bararasta. He walked down the street, leaving the mosque behind him. Two consecutive left turns brought him to a gravel path on one side of which was a large red brick building: Dawson's house. The house was dark. Dawson wasn't home. Mr. Shikdar remembered that today was Tuesday; today the engine-car went to the city. Dawson, he guessed, must have gone to visit the girl. Mr. Shikdar decided to go to Molla's instead. They had the seven acres to talk about anyway. In the evenings Molla often sat on the patio of the mosque reciting the Qu'ran. But today he wasn't there. Mr. Shikdar remembered that Molla hadn't been well today. Molla's house was a little far. He would actually have to get off the mud paths and walk through one of those narrow aisles through the paddy fields to reach Molla's house.

Walking through the rice fields, Mr. Shikdar wished he had brought a lantern with him. He also wished he had brought an umbrella, as a warm and large drop of water fell on his shoulder. He remembered that white foot again, and he laughed now thinking of how sorrowful it had made him feel just a little while ago. Sure he couldn't draw, but there was so much else he had done. He had, in fact, done more for Jamshedpur than any other single person. The people of Jamshedpur revered him. He had made something of his life, in spite of some of the terrible unpleasantness of it. But those were very faraway, forgotten issues. He had surely amounted to more than Dawson, who, for all his talent and erudition, had been nothing more than a furniture-maker. This thought seemed to satisfy him. There was suddenly a void in his stomach and the faint smile of satisfaction turned into an expression of first bewilderment and then pain. He felt wild thumpings against his rib-cage. He sat down on the muddy ridge dividing the land, looking around to see if anybody saw him. His white *kurta* became smeared with mud, and he started to sweat profusely. Molla's servant found him the next morning lying on the mud aisle, his mouth slightly parted.

It had rained all night in Jamshedpur, and the whole village had kept vigil at the Shikdar household. In the morning, when the sky had cleared, they took Mr. Shikdar's body to the graveyard. Dawson had returned just that morning from the city. As soon as he heard the news, he rushed to Mr. Shikdar's house. But the mourning procession had already left for the graveyard. Begum Shikdar was in her room, surrounded by the village women, some of whom had stayed the night with her. Dawson paid his respects from the door. It would not have been proper for a man, if he weren't related to the bereaved, to enter the widow's room. He said in English, "You can never tell when some things will happen." Begum Shikdar didn't say anything; she nodded in agreement.

When Dawson reached the cemetery, they were already lowering Mr. Shikdar's body into the grave. He saw the body of his friend wrapped in an unstitched white piece of cloth, a tuft of white hair showing on his chest, where the cloth had been ruffled out of place. Cotton balls had been stuffed into his nostrils to prevent any bleeding, but they too had become slightly displaced. For a second Dawson thought he saw the fluffy strands of cotton flutter as though Mr. Shikdar were breathing. But he knew that those who are close to the deceased will see the most impossible things; it was probably the breeze. They can see their dear one's chest rising and falling many hours after death. Mr. Shikdar's mouth was found open at death and had to be closed shut with a white ribbon that went under his jaw and ended in a bow on the pate of his head. His eyes too had been found open at death, but Molla had shut them himself.

But what if Mr. Shikdar's eyes were still open? Wouldn't they then have realised that he had only fallen into a deep, but not the deepest, slumber? The townsfolk, whom Mr. Shikdar had treated so diligently for so many years, had learned nothing from him. They could not correctly diagnose any illness with the touch of their fingers. A comatose Shikdar had been buried by his heavy-hearted, reverent fellow Jamshedpuris. Their mistake would never be known to them. But Mr. Shikdar, coming back to consciousness, for a few seconds, would suspect that a terrible error had been committed.

He had serious doubts that the angels would show up. The only thing he could know with certainty was the number of steps taken by the wooden clogs. He could hear the sound of the clogs slowly receding into the distance, but that didn't prevent him from keeping count: thirty-six, thirty-seven ....

The Other Side of the Mirror

Tulip Chowdhury

"Life holds up different pictures at the various stages of life. But poverty has the same picture, a huge void, an ugly monster crying out, 'Wants, wants and wants ... !' It never seems to end ... ." Shanti, the mother of two children was telling herself. She often reminded herself of this truth. It was just a part of her never-ending chain of poverty. Living as the wife a farmer, she had been through happier days when they had good crops and the year used to run on their own harvest. But for the last five years, the monsoon rains had been either too long or they had had long dry spells. Either way their harvest was at stake and that meant they had to buy their food round the year.

High up on the tree a yellow bird was calling out loudly. Yellow birds are believed•to call when there is to be a wedding. Shanti wondered whose wedding it was bringing. She smiled secretly as she thought of how one day her six-year-old daughter Sumi would grow up into a young lady and would have to be married off. She could well imagine how days would fly and her daughter would reach out to life. Girls were married around twelve or fourteen in the villages. Shanti had watched television programmes in the landlord's house about the evil effects of early marriages but it was quite impossible to avoid this village rule because no one would marry a girl who was too old according to the villagers.

"Maybe our neighbourhood Lakhi is getting married! And if that is so, it means a little feast ahead!" Shanti thought wistfully.

As she went on wondering what lay ahead, two black crows started calling out ominously. The spark of light that had been touched by the yellow bird seemed to dissolve in darkness at the hidden evil in the crows cawing.

A gust of cool air blew in reminding her that winter was not far away. And it brought in more foreboding thoughts. Although the sky was brilliant with the late autumn sunshine, she could imagine the coming bleak, cold winter days. It meant hard days without sufficient warm clothes. God, why did the cold days have to come? It only brought more troubles for her,

Shanti had been resting under the shade of the mango tree before getting started on the day's cooking. She remembered that there was no rice at home. That meant borrowing again! She called out to her daughter, "Sumi. Sumi … go and get some rice from the Boro Bari."

Boro Bari was the village leader's house and they were kind enough to lend some rice once in while.

Sumi, sitting in the veranda of their house, asked, "Will they allow us to borrow? We didn't return the last rice."

Shanti sat still momentarily, reflecting on the possibility of not having any meals. She could picture her two children sitting down with empty plates. Tears moistened her eyes and she had an idea.

"Tell your Boroma that your father has gone to the next village for some work and when he returns we will be sure to return the rice." Boroma was the leader's wife who was rather kind towards Shanti. After all, rice cakes in winter days were not made without her help.

It was difficult to think up excuses every time she failed to keep her word and return the things she had taken from her neighbours. At times she felt angry at her husband for not being able to provide them with adequate food and clothing. But then she told herself that at least she had a good man, a man who had not married for the second time, a man who did not beat her and, most important of all, had not been unfaithful to her. Shanti knew that if her husband had ever been to any of the places where unfaithful men went she would have heard the rumours. The villagers, though a small community, were certainly very fast in catching up on the latest gossip.

Shanti sighed. Despite her sorrows about life's unfairness, she felt proud to be the only wife of a good man. Her clothes might be worn out and her larder might be empty, at least she could hold her head high when it came to family matters. Here at least her vicious cycle of poverty had not yet reached its gnawing teeth. Just then Manik, Shanti's four-year-old son, came running to ask for some sweets.

"Where can I get sweets all of a sudden?" she asked her son as she lovingly hugged his frail little body. He had been in better health when she had been breast-feeding him. But now with the little food she managed to put in his plate, he had grown much thinner.

Manik looked at his mother for a while and then asked, "Where did Ruku get his sweet? I just saw him eating it." Ruku was the son of

Hiram Khan, the owner of a local store. They were quite well off with the store running well.

"They bought it from the sweet shop but I don't have the money to buy it for you." Looking at her son's crestfallen face she added, "Maybe when your Baba comes, he will get it for you."

"Why don't you have money? Ruku's mother gave the sweets to him!"

Shanti wished that she had an answer for her son's question. And indeed why didn't they have money? Wasn't what she had or did not have the Lord's will? Did she have any other consolation? Maybe she could hold on to a ray of hope, hope that makes people endure the most bleak days of their life. Maybe some day things would change and maybe she would have enough to eat and have good clothes to wear.

Hearing footsteps on the dry leaves, Shanti looked up to find her husband Kutubuddin walking towards her. She was surprised, for he was due to be back the next day. He looked sort of happy. Maybe he had got some money! Shanti's hopes spread wings, filling her heart with happiness. Her husband!s smiling face touched her with its radiance and she smiled back.

"Why, you are back early. Have you got some good luck?" she asked, taking her husband's shirt from his hand.

"Wait, let me rest and then I have something to tell you," he said, settling down on a low broken bench that served as a sitting place for the whole house.

"There is village nearby called the Shaina. I went to do some work there for a rich farmer. The farmer has sons in Saudia Arabia who send him money and they are so rich!" He was looking intently at his wife as he began talking. Shanti listened with anticipation, getting more hopeful every moment. She knew about that look on her husband's face; this rare light was there when there was some real good news.

In the meantime Sumi came back with the rice. Kutubuddin stopped until his daughter moved away. He then continued, "It seems that the farmer knew our local leader and had been told about me. Evidently the leader spoke very well about me. It happens that the farmer has a widowed daughter whom he wants to marry off again to a good man."

Here Kutubuddin stopped. He looked for a long while at the open, honest face of his wife. His own hard, honest features took on a grim look. He sighed as he continued, "The farmer wants me to marry his daughter and in return he will send me to Saudia Arabia. Imagine how much money I could earn once in the country of the Saudis. It's all money. You should have seen the farmer's grand house filled with expensive furniture. And the food they eat! They live like kings! I think I should accept the offer. Don't you think so, too?"

Shanti could hardly grasp what he was talking about at first. Voices seem to be shouting out to her. She heard voices telling her that this marriage would bring money into her home. Yet another seemed to cry out that she would be losing the dignity of being the only wife of her husband. Why had she been strutting like a proud peacock all these days? Wasn't it because of her husband? Yet, at the back of her mind she thought of the poverty, thought of all that they needed and didn't have. Indeed, were they not floating aimlessly in a sea of wants? Had they finally got a boat to take them ashore? She gave a short laugh and yet her eyes filled with tears. Marrying into a rich family of course would bring them some relief—even if it meant her own husband!

"Is the rich man's daughter beautiful?" she asked through tear-filled eyes. All of a sudden she seemed to see her husband in a new light. She still wanted to believe in his goodness and wanted to believe that what he was about to do was for their own good, for their children's sake. She continued to look at her husband, still feeling proud that she had a father for her children. Kutubuddin went on talking about how rich his prospective in-laws were and how well off Shanti and the children would be if only he could enter that rich house!

Shanti sat there listening to her husband, trying to picture happier days, days when her children would have their plates full. She felt glad, as if some heavy weight had been lifted from her shoulders, and yet there was an unbearable pain in her heart. Somewhere deep down in her soul she felt a soft tremble, as if somebody was stealing something. She thought of the call of the yellow bird. Indeed news of some wedding had come and she could also hear the ominous call of the crows. A puzzled expression settled on her eyes. Indeed life could be perplexing! How poverty played its vicious games!

Wet Sandals[*]

Maithilee Mitra

A renaissance artist painted a picture of a reflection. Centuries later it was discovered that the museum had hung the picture upside down. All this time had gone by, generations of people had stood before the painting, not knowing they were looking at it the wrong way.

Sometimes you think you know a person. You sleep with him, you dream of him, you memorise what he likes and dislikes. Then suddenly one day you realise that you had it all wrong. You feel like an idiot. In embarrassment you want to kick your brain for not seeing the obvious. You feel helpless because there is nothing you can do to correct the past; revisiting it doesn't help. But relief overcomes you because now you stand corrected. No more mistakes. No more guessing. No more chances. Only the truth. Only the truth, and yes, the bruising pain.

Parvin woke up really groggy. It was still raining outside. She pulled back the curtains and peeked at the sky, only to find the dark clouds screaming endless rain. The incessant dull rain always made her melancholy and reminded her of all the depressing things in life — poverty, wars, wet sandals. She didn't understand how this kind of weather could inspire Bengalis to imagine, romanticise or smile, let alone write long essays or complex poetry.

Parvin thought about all the inconveniences the rain would cause today — damp clothes, frizzy hair, slow traffic, white mould and, yes, most annoyingly, slippery, wet sandals. She got out of bed and tried to shake off her pessimistic lethargy by stretching her arms and attempting a yawn. She was not looking forward to her work day. Last night she had stayed up reading. Faizur had gone to a business dinner. Parvin had chosen to stay home. Boredom was easier to handle alone.

When Faizur had walked into their room last night, Parvin had been almost asleep. He had kissed her hair gently when he came to

---

[*]This story won first prize in the *New Age*, Rains Literary Contest, 2004.

bed. Smiling inwardly, she had basked in the warmth of his touch but she lay still, too tired to talk or reciprocate.

Parvin dragged herself out of the shower and started getting ready for work. Faizur was still asleep. She made as little noise as possible as she put on her makeup. She didn't want to wake him up. Hoping the rain wouldn't dampen her clothes the way it dampened her spirit, she put on a freshly laundered *salwar-kameez* and looked at herself in the mirror for a brief second before grabbing her keys and leaving the room.

Despite the rain and flooded streets, her commute by bus was not too slow. And thanks to Abdul, the guard with the umbrella, her clothes weren't too shabby either. But, yes, her sandals did get wet — aargh. Now her feet would be cold and damp all day. In the office, Parvin made a cup of tea and took it to her desk. She sipped on the warm beverage and felt its warmth in her chest while she turned on her computer.

As she checked her e-mail, Parvin glanced at Faizur's picture that sat on her desk and wondered why he hadn't called yet. He usually called her by 9, when he reached his office. It was 9:25 already. Must be the traffic, she thought, and decided to give him a couple more minutes before calling him.

Parvin replied to a few of her e-mails. She looked at her files and checked if she had any meetings today. She looked at her watch again and picked up her cell phone to dial Faizur's number. But before she hit the "call" button, her phone rang. She looked at the phone monitor to see who was calling but didn't recognise the number.

"Hello," said a female voice on the other end. "Are you Parvin?"

"Yes," she said, angrily thinking about her parents who were always in the habit of giving out phone numbers of their children. "Who is this?"

Silence. Parvin first covered her free ear with one hand and listened closely to see if she had gotten disconnected. No. Her heart started beating a little faster. "Who is this? Hello. What's up?"

"It's about your husband," replied the voice. "He — ," again silence followed.

Parvin felt a tightening in her chest and stomach. "Is he all right?" Her voice quivered as it got louder. "Has anything happened to him? Who are you?" The phone felt hot against her sweaty palm.

The voice calmly said, "Well, I have called to tell you something. Your husband is having an affair with my sister. And I want you to know so I can stop my sister from ruining her life with this jerk."

Parvin couldn't believe her ears. She pushed against the ground with her feet. *No, it's not a dream,* she thought. *This must be a prank call.*

"Don't bother me like — ," Parvin began to say sternly before the lady interrupted her.

"If you go home right now you'll find them, right at your house," the voice said confidently. "I didn't want to tell you this, but there was no other way."

This ridiculous prank needs to stop, thought Parvin angrily. She could feel her ears getting hot from anger. She looked around to see if there was anybody nearby before she yelled into the phone, "What kind of nonsense is this? Where did you even get this number?"

As calmly as before, the voice answered, "My sister left her cell phone at home by mistake today. I looked up your husband's number in her phone and called him. I asked him for your number, saying that I was an old friend of yours."

Parvin didn't know what to say. She hung up the phone. She felt a little dizzy and nauseated. *This must be a mistake,* she thought, *but then why do I feel so anxious?* Parvin put down her phone on her desk. She tried picturing Faizur with someone else but it seemed impossible. She thought of the conversation with the woman again and took a deep breath. She picked up her purse and walked out of her office. Abdul tried to hold his umbrella over her head but she brushed him aside and rushed to the street.

Fifteen minutes later, Parvin was in the back of a taxi, her hands clutching onto her purse. She looked out of the moving taxi at the people on the street. She felt removed from everything around. On other days, she noticed every little sound, every little dot on the streets. But today seemed like a dream. Her surroundings were blending into a blur of motion, a long, colourful sari of motion. She blinked and looked at her nails, as if hoping they would reassure her that all was well. She couldn't see her nails, instead she saw the ugly pink and brown skin on her hand. She thought, *Here I am in a taxi, going to see if Faizur, my husband, is with someone else, someone who I don't know, someone who isn't me.*

Four years ago she married her old high school classmate, Faizur. He was crazy about her in school, but at that time she was busy being crazy about someone else. Once she graduated from university and was still single, her parents started seriously bothering her to get married, so she turned to him for a partner.

When they had got married, Faizur was ecstatic. To a lesser extent, Parvin, too, was happy to be marrying someone sweet and sensitive. He had a very carefree attitude towards life. He didn't mind her sense of privacy and he wasn't stingy about money. She could come and go as she pleased — he never asked any questions.

Faizur was expressive about his love for her. Like the time he sent her a dozen roses at work — all the other women were so envious. Or the time he took her on a surprise river cruise for her birthday — she couldn't believe how much work he had done to make her happy.

Parvin sat in the taxi and raked her memories to see if anything in their relationship was amiss. Like any married couple, they fought sometimes but she gave in most of the time. After working all day she really didn't have the energy or desire to have arguments at home. Parvin started to ponder if she had noticed any signs of unhappiness or strangeness in Faizur's behaviour but she couldn't.

Parvin thought about any neglect in her behaviour towards her husband. Was she too cold towards him? Once in a while Parvin would read a romance novel and wonder why she couldn't be head-over-heels about her husband like the heroines of those novels. When she said that to her older sister, Shilpi, she had laughed and said, "That's normal in semi-arranged marriages. It takes a few years for the heart to fall in love."

"In a purely arranged marriage the bride is caught in such a web of *nouveau* romance that she doesn't realise anything until a year after the wedding," Shilpi had said. "By the time that honeymoon phase has ended, enough has happened to make the couple fall in or out of love. In a pure love marriage, the wedding causes a kind of disillusionment but, again, you have enough memories and familiarity to keep you together. The worst case is the semi-arranged marriage. You know a person enough to not have an intense romantic cyclone in your heart but you don't know him well enough to read his thoughts — it's quite stressful. Don't believe those bimbos who tell you otherwise." Parvin had laughed.

Parvin wondered about the phone call. *What if the lady is right?* thought Parvin. *If she is right what will I do? I can't be with someone who has betrayed me. How can I be with someone who loves someone else?* All of this seemed so baffling. Parvin wanted to shake off her discomfort but something inside her felt strange, something dark and depressing. She felt her cold damp sandals and shuddered.

If Parvin thought about it, she knew that she liked and loved Faizur. He was pleasant and cute; Parvin noticed other women eyeing him at parties. She liked his sense of humour and missed him when he was not around. She liked being the only one to know that he always slept with his head covered by a *kantha* and she liked being the only one he came to when he was distressed. She enjoyed their little home. She liked telling him boring petty things that she was embarrassed to tell anyone else. She liked knowing that whatever happened, he'd always be there for her.

Before Parvin knew it the taxi was in her lane. "Right here," she said to the taxi driver when they were in front of her house. She paid him and, without taking the change, she walked towards the house. She frowned when she saw Faizur's car parked in the driveway. *Maybe he's not feeling well,* she thought.

The house looked bigger than ever. Suddenly she was aware of every little thing around her. It was as if she had been catapulted from the universe of blurriness into that of minuteness; a blurry image that just became sharper and crisper. She noticed every little detail of the structure that was their house. The windows, the grains of concrete on the stairs, the wood on the door.

In the slow drizzle, the house looked ominous, scary and suspicious. Parvin climbed up the wet stairs to the main door. She turned the knob and opened the door. She nervously looked around. She felt like an intruder in her own house, an intruder walking into the privacy of her own life.

Parvin listened carefully for any sound. At first she didn't hear anything. She wondered where the servants were — she couldn't hear any of them. Then she started hearing noises upstairs — people shuffling, muffled voices. *Faizur is probably on the phone with someone,* she thought. She hesitated for a second before she walked towards the stairs. She didn't want to go upstairs and face Faizur. *What if I have it all wrong,* she thought.*What will I tell Faizur?* It would be so awkward. A part of her just wanted to run back to the office and forget about the whole thing. Maybe later she could ask Faizur and live with whatever answer he gave. But something else was eclipsing her thoughts, something that she couldn't name, something that was blowing out the candle of her soul. Her mind started to go numb again and she felt the sweatbeads on her face — she plopped down on a chair in the living room.

After a few seconds, Parvin mustered up whatever will power she had and called out, "Faizur!"

The shuffling upstairs stopped. Parvin called out again, "Faizur! Are you upstairs?"

Parvin heard footsteps, Faizur's footsteps coming down the stairs. She hadn't even realised that she herself was halfway up the stairs before she saw him. And her.

For a second, both of them were looking at Parvin. A long second. Parvin slowly turned around and went downstairs. She saw a shadow walk past the living room and out the main door. Click — the door shut.

Faizur entered the living room and sat on a chair with his elbows propped on his knees. Parvin sat with her face in her hands. She could hear the raindrops hitting the glass window next to her. Her whole world was trembling. This world that she used to find so cozy, so solid, was starting to melt under her feet. She looked at the rain. She felt like the rain was washing away all that was familiar to her. She didn't even know this man who was sitting in front of her, this stranger who knew her so intimately. She looked up at Faizur, he looked distant.

"Parvin," said Faizur. "I've been meaning to tell you for a while — "

"Tell me what?" asked Parvin. "What is there to say, Faizur?" Her questions travelled from some dull distant land. She felt like walking away from all of this but she couldn't move a single limb. *Maybe it's all a misunderstanding*, she thought, but she knew it wasn't. And if she walked away she, never know the truth — *why someone else?*

"Why, Faizur?" asked Parvin, staring into the rain. She bit her lower lip to prepare herself for the answer.

Faizur didn't answer her. He stood with his head lowered. She looked at him and imagined herself in bed with him. In her imagination, she saw the shadow in the room, a shadow that wouldn't go away. She got up from the chair, picked up her purse and walked out of the main door. She heard her name being called as she walked out into the rain. Her face felt like a desert; she looked at the clouds and let the rain touch her face. The rain met her tears and washed her face as she walked along the street, dipping her sandal-clad feet in every single puddle she passed by.

A Small Sacrifice
Farah Ghuznavi

When I woke up that morning, it seemed like any other day. If I had known, perhaps I would have done things a little differently. Perhaps I would have spent less effort on trying to scrub the blackened grease off the cooking pots, and snatched a few more moments looking out of the *jali* (wire-mesh) in the veranda, hoping to catch a glimpse of the parrots that sometimes played in the mango trees at the back of the compound.

But I didn't. So when the *begumshaheb*, the mistress of the house, nudged me awake with her foot, I scrambled to get up quickly. I had been dreaming of my mother — it was *Eid*, and she had made *shemai* for Shawon, Shyamal, Shiraj and me. We didn't have *shemai* very often, but we were all convinced that Ma's cooking was the best in our *para*. Sometimes the women from other houses asked her for advice on how to cook something, because Ma's father had been a well-known *baburchi* in Dhaka. We had never met our *Nana*, and the glory days of his time in Dhaka were long past by the time I was born. By then, Ma was just a pretty girl, from a family which had seen better days, chosen by my *Dada* as a bride for his second son.

Even so, the early years of my childhood were happy ones. I was the first child — and the first grandchild — in the family, so it didn't matter so much that I was a girl. Indeed, my name, *Shahazadi* (Princess) was given to me by my Dada; though everyone called me by my *daknam*, which was Onu. I had other names too, pet-names given by my father: *shonamoni, janer tukra*. When my father came home at the end of the day, he would call out, "Where is Onu? *Amar shonamoni koi re?*" My father and my grandparents loved me so much, that my mother often told me that I was spoilt. But I knew she didn't mean it. She was happy in those days, too.

Besides, I knew that my situation was unusual. My friend Rekha's family were very poor. She had eight brothers and sisters, and when the ninth child was born, they named her "China." The foreigners who came to visit one of the local NGO offices were very impressed. They thought that she had been named after the country China, which we call "Cheen." Actually, her name means "unwanted."

By the time my third brother, Shiraj, was born, things had changed a lot for our family. My grandparents were both dead, their sons had fallen out with each other, and two of my father's brothers, Shahed and Jabbar, had successfully cheated him and his other brother out of any claims to my grandfather's property. My father was a proud man; he said he had his *manshonman* (his honour), so he refused to go on fighting them, or to beg for his share. He had asked the village *matbars*, the community leaders, to intervene in the matter. But my uncle Shahed was married to Selim Matbar's daughter, so they all sided with him.

Our family moved out of the compound into a small shack on another relative's land, but my parents found it increasingly difficult to feed their growing family. When my *Dada* was alive, he had ruled the family with an iron hand, and my mother often lamented to our female neighbours that he had not allowed any of his daughters-in-law to use *jonmoniyontron* (contraception). At the time of my grandfather's death, my third brother was already on the way, and none of us could have imagined how our financial circumstances would change.

Within three years, my father could no longer afford to send us to school, and my brother Shawon and I, as the eldest children, were expected to help our parents in any way we could. My brother started to work at the village tea stand, serving the locals as well as the truck drivers who regularly passed through. I helped my mother with the household work, and looking after our cow and chickens. But things just kept getting worse.

My father worked as a day labourer for one of the landowners nearby, but we could not manage on what he earned, and the humiliation he felt at doing this work changed him. My mother said it had made him bitter — "*Bhalo manushtarey noshto koira disey.* It has ruined a good man." It was mostly she who suffered the brunt of his anger, although he never hit any of us, the children. Sometimes I felt as though he just looked for reasons to become angry with my mother, and despite the regular beatings, my mother seemed to accept this as her fate. In all the hours I spent bathing her bruises with cold water, she never said a word against my father.

I remained my father's favourite, however, his *janer tukra*. So it was a shock to me, when one day one of my *khalas* suggested that my parents send me to work for a family in Dhaka. My aunt actually raised the issue with my mother, pointing out that it would mean one less mouth to feed at home, and that whatever payment my parents received for my work could help meet the family's expenses.

"I know it will be hard for you to manage without her, but think about the benefits. It is just a small sacrifice! And you will have her back for the *Eid* festivals, anyway. It will mean that you can look after your boys better — they are the ones who will take care of you in your old age." My mother did not respond to what my *khala* said, but her comment about the boys being more important made me feel bad, even though I knew it was true.

I need not have worried too much about that, though. My father was enraged when my mother raised the subject with him. "Do you think I'm a beggar?" he shouted, "that I have to send my only daughter to another man's house to work as a servant?" It's true that I didn't want to go to Dhaka either, but I felt bad that night; I knew my mother had received a beating because of me.

A few months after that, after my *khala* had repeatedly promised him that I would be sent to a good family, that they would feed and clothe me well, and that they had promised to send me to a local school, my father finally gave in. I knew he didn't want me to go – nor did my mother — but somehow this had become something we could not avoid.

I think that in the beginning I *had* hoped that the family in Dhaka would be kind. It was not long after I arrived there, that I realised that all the promises that my *khala* had made to my parents were lies. I don't know whether she knew the truth herself. I certainly don't believe my parents knew it. But perhaps I would have had to come to Dhaka anyway. We just couldn't manage at home anymore.

I consoled myself with the thought that I would be home for *Eid*. But *Rojar Eid* came and went six months later, and the *begumshaheb* insisted that she needed my help preparing for the festivities. They had promised that I could go home for *Korbanir Eid*, but I couldn't help wondering how she would manage without my help at that time. Still, I didn't want to think about the implications of that too deeply, so I clung to the hope that this time, they would keep their promise. And surely my father would not let them keep me away from him for so long ....

The family I lived with had two children — Ronnie, a few years older than me, and Shoma, who was younger. But their lives were very different from mine. Ronnie was a skinny boy, who loved to play all kinds of sports, and the *begumshaheb* worried constantly that he didn't eat enough. She spent a lot of time preparing good food to tempt his appetite. Both the children had nice clothes, and Shoma had many dresses. The *begumshaheb* liked her to look pretty.

At home, only Shawon and I got new clothes, and that was usually a couple of times a year. Our two younger brothers mostly made do with Shawon's old clothes. Shoma had one dress that I particularly liked. It was red, with puffy sleeves, and was edged with white lace. I didn't tell anyone, but I secretly hoped that someday, when Shoma grew out of the dress, they would give it to me. Shoma was tall for her age, so it would definitely fit me.

They both went to school, and sometimes it reminded me of the time when my brother and I were still studying. I had enjoyed lessons, especially in the early years of school. Even after it became difficult to manage the cost of uniforms and books, I was able to manage all right. Most of the teachers liked me, because I worked hard, and I found many of the things we studied interesting. The only subject I had difficulty with was English. No one at home could help me with that! Still, after Afshin master allowed me to sit at the back of his tutorial classes, I improved in that too. And I was really happy the day that I came third in the annual exam, in my last year at school.

Now, I helped the *begumshaheb* to make breakfast each morning, and ironed the children's clothes, and got their schoolbags ready. I woke up in the morning long before they did, and usually went to bed after them too. Once in a while, I would stand in the corner and watch television when they did. Ronnie never said anything to me, he was too busy with his own things, but Shoma used to make me fetch her things and get me to scratch her back or braid her hair. She would also complain to her mother if she ever saw me watching television. I couldn't understand why she hated me so much. She was like her mother, that one.

And while they were at school, I did the household work as the *begumshaheb* instructed me to. The work never seemed to finish, and she was rarely happy with me. "What kind of donkey from the village are you? Do I have to show you everything? Can't you do anything right?" she would often scream at me. She had already told me to call her *begumshaheb (madam)* instead of *khalamma* (auntie), and to call her husband *shaheb*. I tried to do things the way she wanted, but often, she changed her mind. And somehow, I never seemed to get it right however hard I tried; it was almost as if I became more accident-prone when she was around.

In the beginning, she didn't hit me that often. But after she started, it got worse and worse. One time, when I was cleaning the fish, she slapped me so hard that I cut my hand on the *boti* (curved kitchen knife). That time she was scared that the *shaheb* would find out, so she told me to lie and tell him that my hand had slipped. He didn't like it when she shouted at the children, or slapped me, so she never did it in front of him. It wasn't that the *shaheb* was particularly kind, but he liked peace and quiet in the house. He became irritated at any type of noise or commotion. But he was usually at work, so he didn't know how often I got beaten.

The *begumshaheb* was a strange woman. She had many friends, and sometimes they would come over for tea in the mid-morning or late afternoon, before *shaheb* came home from work. Sometimes one of her friends would compliment her how well I did my work, which usually pleased her. She would say, "I have taught her everything she knows. When she came here, she was such a *khat* — just an ignorant peasant!" I always felt bad when she said that. But at those times, she seemed happy, and they would all laugh and gossip about their neighbours. Yet when the *shaheb* was home, she was much quieter, and often sullen. She even snapped at Ronnie and Shoma.

I couldn't understand why the *begumshaheb* sometimes got so angry. She had everything she could want. I thought about how excited my family would be to see all the things that these people had. Their flat was large and had lots of fancy things; they had a fridge, a VCR, a big TV, even a car that the *shaheb* used each day to get to his office. When I first came to Dhaka, I was amazed to see that they had a beautiful *paka* bathroom — I had never used an indoor toilet before. In the village, some people had sanitary latrines — a porcelain basin at ground-level with a footrest on either side — but there were no "chair" toilets.

Sometimes, when *begumshaheb* was resting in the afternoon, I would sit on the verandah by myself and think about home — imagining what my parents and my brothers were. I would daydream about how we used to play *ekka-dokka* and *chhi-buri*, splash about in the cool water of the village pond as the sun blazed overhead (my mother was always worried that I would become, *kalo!*) sneak about trying to identify the trees from which we could steal a few *kacha aam*, to devour as *bharta* with chilli powder and salt — nothing ever tasted as good as those stolen green mangoes!

Sometimes a whole afternoon would go by while I was daydreaming, and the *begumshaheb* was sleeping. But once the children came back from school at three o'clock, things got really busy. And it was at that time, and before the *shaheb* came home at six-thirty, that I was most likely to be on the receiving end of the *begumshaheb's* wrath. Things were never done quickly enough for her, and I always worried about dropping one of the heavy pots in the kitchen, or spilling something, which really made her angry.

This morning, things started badly because the children awoke late, and the *begumshaheb* and I were rushing around, trying to get them ready in time to leave with the *shaheb*, as he set off for work. In the hurry, I dropped one of the teacups, and it smashed on the ground, scattering the dregs of the tea. The *begumshaheb* dealt me a stinging blow to my cheek — so hard, that my ears started ringing, and tears sprang to my eyes.

"It is only a teacup, for heaven's sake! You don't have to hit her for it!" the *shaheb* rebuked her sharply.

"What do you know? She never does anything properly! It's all right for you. You don't have to deal with her stupidity all the time!" the *begumshaheb* shouted back.

To my amazement, the *shaheb's* hand flew out and delivered a sharp blow to her cheek. "Don't you ever raise your voice to me like that again!" he thundered, before stalking out of the room.

As she lifted her face to look at me, her reddened cheek clearly marked by the force of his slap, I saw the hatred in her eyes, and I knew that I would pay for this; both for being the cause of her injury, and, more importantly, for being a witness to it.

The door slammed as the *shaheb* and the children left. I didn't dare look at the *begumshaheb*. There was a moment of utter silence, and then it was as if a *kalbaisakhi* storm came down on my head. A hail of blows landed all over my body, and, although I lifted my arms in a futile gesture to shield myself, it was useless. She seemed crazed by her rage, and I knew that there was nothing I could do to stop her. I had a sudden fleeting hope, that if she beat me very badly perhaps they would have to send me home. It would be a small sacrifice, and well worth it to see my family again after so long.

But then I had no time to think anymore. Somehow, I stumbled into the kitchen, followed by the *begumshaheb*, hurling shrill abuse at me, "*Haramjadi*, bastard, I'll show you! I'll teach you a lesson you'll never forget!" I looked up in horror, to see that she had picked up the heavy wooden *belon*, and was coming at me with it. The first blow landed on my leg, and I heard a sickening crack, and felt an indescribable burning pain shoot through my leg. Another blow landed on my back. As I screamed in agony, I saw her raise the rolling pin again, and I closed my eyes in anticipation of the blow.

As the *belon* landed against my ear, a red haze seemed to flood through my head. When I opened my eyes again, my vision was blurred. I could see the *begumshaheb's* mouth moving, but I couldn't hear what she was saying. I wondered—with a surge of terror — whether the blow on my head had made me deaf.

And that was my last thought before, mercifully, everything faded away, and I felt myself falling into a deep, soft darkness ....

Contributors

Kazi Anis Ahmed completed high school in Dhaka. Afterwards he received his Bachelor's, Master's and Ph.D., respectively, from Brown, Washington and New York Universities in Comparative Literature and Creative Writing. He has been involved in writing in both Bangla and English and has been published in Bangladesh as well as in America. "Forty Steps" was first published in the *Minnesota Review* and nominated for a Pushcart Prize in 2003. Ahmed now lives in Dhaka where he is the Director of Academic Affairs at the University of Liberal Arts Bangladesh.

Syed Badrul Ahsan went to school in Quetta, Pakistan, before completing his Higher Secondary at Notre Dame College, Dhaka. Subsequently, he finished his Bachelor of Arts (Honours) and Master's in English Literature from the University of Dhaka. He started teaching in the late 1970s, but then switched to journalism in the early 1980s. From 1997 to 2000, he served as Minister Press at the Bangladesh High Commission in London. At present, he is deputy editor of the *New Age*, an English language daily in Bangladesh. Ahsan writes poetry, daydreams and loves walking in the rain. He has been a columnist for the weekly *Dhaka Courier* since the early 1990s and is a frequent contributor to *Asian Affairs*, the quarterly journal of the Royal Society for Asian Affairs, London.

Mohammad Badrul Ahsan is a banker by profession. He is also a columnist for the *Daily Star*. A selection of his columns have been published in *A Good Man in the Woods and Other Essays*. He has also written *In Search of a Nation*, a book on the philosophy of history. He has co-authored *A Strategic Model for Multinational Corporations*.

Shahid Alam completed his Honours and MA in Political Science and Public Administration respectively from the University of Dhaka before joining the Foreign Service. He studied at the Fletcher School of Law and Diplomacy and later completed his doctoral studies at Boston University. Resigning from the Foreign Service, Dr Alam turned to acting, studying at the Royal Academy of Dramatic Art. He has acted in plays and directed both stage plays and movies. He has published a number of short stories and his novel, *Green Fire*, has been accepted by a US publisher. He is at present a columnist for the *New Nation*.

Raza Ali completed his Honours and Master's in English from the University of Dhaka, which forms the background of his story "The Debt." Ali left Dhaka in 1969 to complete his doctoral studies at Syracuse University. He is now settled in Toronto, Canada, where he teaches in a high school. Teaching keeps him very busy, but he does occasionally contribute articles and book reviews to the *New Age*.

Dilruba Z. Ara was an Honours student at the Department of English, University of Dhaka, but then left for Sweden. She enrolled at the University of Gothenburg, Sweden, getting her degree in English Language and Literature, Linguistics, and Classical Arabic. Later she took a degree in Swedish and obtained her teaching degree in English and Swedish from Lund University. At present she teaches both Swedish and English in a high school in Malmö. She has been writing since childhood, her first story being published when she was in grade three. She has written a novel which is awaiting publication. She has also translated part of *Pippi Longstockings* by Astrid Lindgren into Bangla. In her free time she also paints and has had a solo art exhibition in Sweden. At present she is preparing a volume of Shahed Ali's selected works in English translation.

Tulip Chowdhury is the pen-name of Nur Asghar Chowdhury. She teaches at an international English school in Dhaka and writes features and stories for newspapers. She also has a poetry collection, *Rain Drops*.

Towheed Feroze studied History at the University of Dhaka and Journalism in London. A worshipper of freedom, he is a journalist working for the *New Age*. He loves to think of himself as Simon Templar aka The Saint and says it is odd that being such a restless person he should enjoy writing. But, as he says, this is a strange world with a lot of strange people.

Farah Ghuznavi is a development professional, who has worked, among others, for Grameen Bank, the United Nations Development Programme and Christian Aid, both in Bangladesh and in the UK. Her particular areas of interest include microfinance, gender equality, human rights and HIV/AIDS. She writes a regular column for the *Star Weekly Magazine* entitled "Food for Thought.". She is a political animal with strong opinions and a passion for social justice. Her interest in current affairs has made her a self-confessed "news junkie" who needs at least one hour of BBC World a day to remain functional!

Roquiah Sakhawat Hossein (1880-1932) was a writer, educationist and social activist, perhaps best known for setting up a school for Muslim girls, Sakhawat Memorial Girls' School. While R S Hossein, as she generally signed her articles, wrote mostly in Bangla, *Sultana's Dream* was written in English. First published in 1905 in a Madras based English periodical, *The Indian Ladies Magazine*, it was published by S. K. Lahiri & Co., Calcutta, in 1908 as a book. She later translated her story into Bangla as *Sultanar Swapna*. Her other writings include *Abarodh Bashini* and *Motichur*. Most of Roquiah Sakhawat Hossein's writing was a passionate critique of the social mores and customs that prevented women from achieving their potential. She was also a poet.

Khademul Islam was born in Karachi, Pakistan, taught at the University of Dhaka and lived in San Francisco, USA. He is currently the literary editor of the *Daily Star*, Dhaka, Bangladesh. He is also a literary critic, short story writer and translator.

Syed Manzural Islam teaches at the University of Manchester. Apart from *The Mapmakers of Spitalfields* – from which his story of the same title has been taken – Islam has also written a novel, *Burrow* (under the name Manzu Islam), which describes in greater detail the lives of Bangladeshi immigrants in East London. He is also the author of *The Ethics of Travel: From Marco Polo to Kafka*.

Razia Khan was professor at the Department of English, University of Dhaka till her retirement. At present she is professor and head of the Department of English, University of Liberal Arts. She writes fluently in both Bangla and English. She made her name with her novel *Battalar Upanyash* (1958), published shortly after she finished her M. A. Her other novels include *Anulkalpa, Pratichitra, Chitrakabya, Draupadi,* and *Padatik*. She has two volumes of poetry in English, *Argus Under Anaesthesia* and *Cruel April*, as well as a volume of Bangla poems, *Sonali Ghasher Desh*. She has also written plays, including *Abarta* and *Tinti Ekangkika*. She has won several awards, among them, the Bangla Academy Award and the Ekushey Padak.

Razia Sultana Khan taught for several years at the Department of English, North-South University, before taking leave to study Creative Writing in the United States. She writes both poems and short stories, some of which have been published.

Rubaiyat Khan completed her early schooling in Dhaka before leaving to study in the States. She completed her Bachelor's in English Literature from Knox College, Illinois, where she also completed a Post-Baccalaureate in Creative Writing. At present she is working as a senior staff writer at *New Age*.

Munize M. Khasru completed her Bachelor's and Master's in the US. Apart from writing short stories, which have been published in local dailies, she has also written a book for children.

Nuzhat Amin Mannan teaches at the Department of English, University of Dhaka. She is also a translator, poet and short story writer. Many of her short stories have been published in newspapers and journals, at home and abroad. She has also published a volume of poetry: *Rhododendron Lane*.

Maithilee Mitra is a translator and short story writer. "Wet Sandals" won first prize in the *New Age* Rains Literary Contest, 2004. She has written three bilingual books for children. Recently, her children's story "Billy Boy" was accepted for publication in *Ladybug Magazine*, a leading US children's magazine. Ms Mitra lives in the United States with her husband and two children.

Shabnam Nadiya completed her Bachelor of Arts (Honours) and Master's in English Literature from the University of Dhaka. She is a translator and short story writer. Her short stories have been selected for a number of local and international anthologies and magazines including *Galpa* (Saqi Books), *World View, Bonfire: An international conflagration, Texts' Bones,* and *The Beat.* Many of her translations have also been published in newspapers, magazines and anthologies such as *Different Perspectives, The Escape and Other Stories,* and *1971 and After* (all from 'The University Press Limited), *Galpa, Kali O Kalam* and *Words Without Borders*.

Farhana Haque Rahman began her career as a journalist in the early 70s. During this period, she was the principal anchorperson and commentator on Bangladesh Radio and Television and was honoured with the Bangladesh National Television Award for outstanding performance in the field. She later worked in Lesotho and Ethiopia before moving to Rome, where she took up freelance journalism and also served as a communications and information consultant for United Nations agencies. She is currently an international civil servant in Rome. Ms Rahman used to write regular columns in *Holiday* and *The Courier*, but her professional duties keep her too busy to do so at present. Her publications include a volume of translations, *Poems of Shamsur Rahman*, a book of her own poems, *Leaves of the Sun*, a compilation of satirical articles, *Stalking Serendipity and Other Pasquinades*, and a novel, *The Eye of the Heart*.

Aali A. Rehman has lived in Rajshahi for almost forty-five years. A graduate of Rajshahi University, he has been a teacher in the Department of English at the same university since 1976. He lives on campus with his wife, Lutfe Ara, and the younger of his two daughters, his elder daughter being away at engineering school. Professor Rehman likes to describe himself as a very occasional, but painstaking, writer.

Neeman Sobhan did her B A and M A in Comparative and English Literature from the University of Maryland. Since 1978, she has been living in Rome, from where she writes a column for *Star Weekend Magazine*. Some of her pieces have been anthologized in *The Abiding City: Ruminations from Rome*.

Syed Waliullah worked in the *Statesman* during 1945-1947. After the Partition, he moved to Pakistan, working initially in Radio Pakistan. From 1951 to 1960 he served as Press Attaché at various Pakistan missions before moving to Paris in 1961. He served as First Secretary at the Pakistan Embassy till 1967, when he joined UNESCO. One of the foremost Bangla novelists, with his first novel, *Lal Salu* (1948), being a classic, Syed Waliullah also wrote in English, both a number of short stories as well as a novel, *The Ugly Asian*, which is being published by the Bangla Academy. Waliullah received several literary awards, including the Ekushey Padak, posthumously.

Niaz Zaman is professor of English at the University of Dhaka. Apart from writing academic articles on literature and women's folk art, she also writes poetry and fiction. Her story "The Dance" won an *Asiaweek* Short Story Award and was later anthologized in *Prizewinning Asian*

Fiction. Her other writings include a novel, *The Crooked Neem Tree*; two anthologies of short stories, *The Dance and Other Stories* and *Didima's Necklace and Other Stories*; an anthology of poems, *No Lilacs Bloom: A Washington Journal*; and a one-act play, *A Celebration of Women*. She has recently started writers.ink to publish creative writing in English as well as academic books on literature.